Sarah Banks

Ethics and Values in Social Work

Fourth Edition

First edition 1995
Reprinted six times
Second edition 2001
Reprinted five times
Third edition 2006
Reprinted eight times
Fourth edition 2012

Published by
PALGRAVE MACMILLAN

Palgrave Macmillan in the UK is an imprint of Macmillan Publishers Limited, registered in England, company number 785998, of Houndmills, Basingstoke, Hampshire RG21 6XS

Palgrave Macmillan in the US is a division of St Martin's Press LLC, 175 Fifth Avenue, New York, NY 10010.

Palgrave Macmillan is the global academic imprint of the above companies and has companies and representatives throughout the world.

Palgrave® and Macmillan® are registered trademarks in the United States, the United Kingdom, Europe and other countries.

ISBN: 978–0–230–30017–0

This book is printed on paper suitable for recycling and made from fully managed and sustained forest sources. Logging, pulping and manufacturing processes are expected to conform to the environmental regulations of the country of origin.

A catalogue record for this book is available from the British Library.

A catalog record for this book is available from the Library of Congress.

10 9 8 7 6 5 4 3 2 1
21 20 19 18 17 16 15 14 13 12

Printed and bound by CPI Group (UK) Ltd, Croydon, CR0 4YY

To social workers around the world, as a small contribution towards your ethical struggles for individual and social justice

Brief contents

Contents

List of figures, lists and tables

Figures

Lists

Tables

List of practice focus boxes

Cases for discussion

Preface to the fourth edition

The Introduction to the first edition of this book, published in 1995, started with the statement: 'Social work is currently in a period of change.' I retained this statement in the second and third editions. In the Preface to the second edition, I noted the editorial comment in the magazine *Community Care* (1999/2000) that ushered in the new millennium with the headline 'A new century of uncertainty'. The article claimed that: 'Few professions have changed more than social work in a decade.' This comment related to Britain, but similar shifts in the organization and practice of social work were also occurring in many other countries, as the introduction of market principles, the mixed economy of welfare and the increasing concern with quality assurance and standards took hold. Those eagle-eyed readers who look to see how much has been revised in this new edition will notice that the statement: 'Social work is currently in a period of change' has been removed from page 1. It has been replaced by the sentence: 'Social work is the kind of occupation that is always in a state of change, as it is linked so closely to social welfare systems that shift with global economic trends and in response to government social and economic policies.' This is why new editions will always be required and why social work ethics is such a challenging and contested area of study.

At the time of writing, major changes are continuing in the field of social work, social care and social welfare services more generally in Britain. Having established regulatory bodies in England, Scotland, Wales and Northern Ireland in 2002 to register social care practitioners and oversee professional education, proposals are now being made to move the regulatory functions for England to a broader body that also registers health professions. Having developed complex electronic mechanisms for the surveillance and tracking of certain categories of social work service users, particularly children and young people, some of these systems have been abandoned or significantly revised as they have proved to be ineffective, unwieldy and too costly to maintain in a time of economic austerity. Calls for a greater focus on professional judgement and discretion, rather than procedures and bureaucracy, are beginning to be heeded, at least in the field of child protection. In England, a government-sponsored review of social work (Social Work Task Force, 2009) has recommended the establishment of a 'college of social work', with the aim of enhancing the status, credibility and expertise of the profession. At the same time as these trends towards the increasing 'professionalization' (or at least institutionalization) of social work, there has also been a growth in strength of the service user movement, leading to a greater service user voice in the policy process and in social work education and practice. There has also been a mobilization of social workers, alongside service users and academics, calling for a more radical social work, to challenge not just the increasing managerialism in social work, but also the trend towards market principles, consumerism and the large cuts in welfare services that are being implemented in response to the economic crisis that started in 2008.

Just as I was finalizing the book in summer 2011, a series of street disturbances involving a high proportion of young people took place over a few days in several major English cities. These disturbances were popularly referred to as 'riots' and involved theft from shops, violent clashes with police and the destruction of commercial and residential property. This sparked a great deal of political comment and controversy over the causes and contributory factors, and what should be the responses of government, courts and local communities. These riots were indicative of the fragility of our grossly unequal and consumer-oriented society, the impact of welfare cuts (particularly youth services) and high levels of unemployment (particularly among young people). They also raised the perennial ethical questions for social workers, youth workers and community workers about the role of welfare workers in the containment, control and preventive measures that will follow these disturbances, and how they can pursue a continuing quest for social justice and social transformation in times of economic austerity and neoliberal policies. These incidents in Britain, and some of the cases from countries around the world at the end of each chapter, are a clear reminder that 'the professional is political'. They are also a reminder that 'the political is ethical', as social workers make choices about whether and how to take action to control, make responsible and/or empower people and whether and how to challenge unjust systems, institutions and regimes.

The turn to ethics

The growth of interest in ethics as a topic noted in the second and third editions has continued apace. There is a marked growth of publications on ethics in public policy and the professions. This reflects a growing interest in ethics generally, as issues relating to climate change, global terrorism, new developments in medicine and the persistence of poverty and inequality worldwide raise new challenges about collective responsibility, individual choice and the interests of future generations. There is continuing concern with 'standards in public life' as high-profile cases of corruption, lying or malpractice come to light. Ethical issues in social work are no exception. The number of specialist textbooks on ethics and values in social work published in Europe and the English-speaking world is growing rapidly (for example, to list just a few published since I wrote the third edition of this book: Banks and Nøhr, 2012; Barnard et al., 2008; Beckett and Maynard, 2005; Bowles et al., 2006; Charleton, 2007; Congress et al., 2009; Dolgoff et al., 2009; Reamer, 2006; Zaviršek et al., 2010). Interest in social work ethics as a specialist topic is also growing in the global South (see, for example, Barroco, 2004; Joseph and Fernandes, 2006). Two specialist journals on social work ethics have been established, the *Journal of Social Work Values and Ethics* (a US-based electronic open access journal) and *Ethics and Social Welfare* (a British-based subscription journal). Book-length texts focusing on specific theories and approaches to social work ethics are also beginning to emerge, such as Clifford and Burke (2009) on anti-oppressive ethics and Banks and Gallagher (2009) on virtue ethics, and on specialist interdisciplinary areas such as mental health, information-sharing and decision-making (Barker, 2011; Clark and McGhee, 2008; Connolly and Ward 2008).

While the focus of professional ethics in the middle to latter part of the twentieth century tended to be on developing lists of principles and how to handle conflict between principles, say, between respecting the self-determination of service users and promoting their welfare, the interest noted in the second edition in what I have called character- and relationship-based ethics ('virtue ethics' and 'the ethics of care') is continuing to develop, as outlined in Chapter 3. The growing emphasis, particularly by feminist ethicists, on diversity and difference, context and relationships, narratives and discourses is highly relevant to social work and is increasingly being used by social work academics and practitioners.

Situating ethics

I have been increasingly exercised by the fact that the earlier editions of the book are being read in a number of different countries. This has heightened my awareness of the national and cultural specificity of some of the language, concepts and approaches used and has caused me to question how a book about ethics can be relevant across a range of different cultural, legal and practice contexts. In a desire to make such a text more relevant to different parts of the world, it is tempting to remove the contextual specificity and keep the discussion at a more general level – the level of universal and abstract principles. Yet the 'universal' ethical principles in the 1948 United Nations Universal Declaration of Human Rights, and included in the international statements on social work ethics, have themselves been criticized for taking a particular western perspective on ethics, based on the notion of individual rights, which does not reflect prevalent cultural norms and beliefs in many parts of the world. Indeed, one of the developing themes in the ethics literature is the importance of context – the richness of everyday life in which decisions and dilemmas are located. In the sociology and social work literature, the recognition of cultural diversity and the specificity of responses demanded are key features. So unless this book were to be turned into an international encyclopedia of social work ethics, with many more contributors, the complexity and diversity of social work practice cannot be adequately covered.

It is important, therefore, that I locate myself and my ideas (and hence this book) in my own context – writing as a British academic, schooled in western philosophy, with practice experience in social and community development work in England. Many of the case examples and references to laws, policies and trends relate to Britain. Some of these will have relevance across the world, others may not. However, as a way of broadening the scope of the book and encouraging readers to engage with the commonalities and differences in social work around the world, at the end of each chapter I have added international cases, followed by questions for discussion.

In the first edition of the book, the main focus was on what has been termed 'principle-based' ethics, with an emphasis on ethical decision-making as essentially about prioritizing and then acting upon ethical principles, such as respect for self-determination or the promotion of welfare. In the second edition, a new chapter was added covering 'character and relationship-based' approaches to ethics. This reflected the fact that these approaches might fit better with non-western cultures. It also took account of the recent revival of virtue ethics in western philosophy (based on qualities of character rather than principles of action) and feminist and other situated approaches to ethics, with a stress on the importance of care, responsibility and relationships between particular people. I argued that ethical being and acting could plausibly be regarded as based on a plurality of values of different kinds, including principles, qualities of character and particular commitments to people. I acknowledged that in real-life interactions, where the actual verbal and nonverbal communication can be heard and felt and emotions come into play, situated ethics is paramount. However, in a textbook and in the context of teaching, I suggested that it was easier to continue to analyse case examples of ethical problems and dilemmas in terms of principles. The process of analysis of cases, although artificial, does in itself play an important role in developing ethical awareness and reflection. However, in the third edition, I added further coverage of character and relationship-based approaches, attempting to weave these aspects into some of the discussion of cases, particularly in the final chapter.

If we accept the embeddedness of ethics in all aspects of life, and in particular in social practices, then it is important to study how certain ethical beliefs and qualities of character are constructed and performed during the course of everyday encounters in social work. Such ethnographic studies add to our practical understanding of social work ethics, although we do need to bear in mind that they originate within a different disciplinary and methodological framework compared with the more philosophically oriented approaches that have been common in the professional ethics literature (the relationship between philosophical and social scientific studies of ethics is discussed further in Banks, 2004a). The development, especially by feminist philosophers, of situated and contextualized ethics perhaps offers a bridge between the philosophical and ethnographic approaches to the study of ethics. This book does not aim to offer or give accounts of empirical studies of what social workers do in practice, but is based on a developing view of ethics as comprising abstract philosophical theorizing and as situated within policy and practice contexts. I have tended to use illustrative case studies based on real accounts given by practitioners in order to maintain a closeness to the practice experiences of social workers.

Changes in the fourth edition

All the chapters in this fourth edition have been updated and several new case examples have been added within the chapters – including cases about the experiences of a social worker implementing 'personalized' approaches to care, an asylum seeker being denied a 'normal life', a youth worker responding to local riots, a staff team reflecting on how to engage with young Muslim men, and a Christian social worker reflecting on how to respond to women seeking abortions.

In some places, material has been added to reflect new thinking in social work or moral philosophy. For example, a section on the ethics of proximity has been added to Chapter 3 on character and relationship-based ethics. The ethics of proximity is most strongly associated with Levinas, the French/Lithuanian philosopher, who focuses on the face-to-face meeting of two human beings as the origin of ethics. Although it is difficult to develop an ethics of proximity as an ethical theory for social work, the idea of the primacy of the pre-rational relationship with the other person is attractive as an antidote to depersonalized, managerial and market-driven approaches to social work. A new section outlining a 'situated ethics of social justice' has been added at the end of Chapter 3, which draws together elements from principle-based and character and relationship-based approaches into a preliminary framework for a progressive social work ethics.

Parts of Chapter 4 on professionalism and professional codes have been significantly revised, and account has been taken of some of the latest codes of ethics of national associations for social work in different countries. For this edition I did not do a large-scale systematic review of all the latest available codes of ethics, as in previous editions this had resulted in a rather descriptive and detailed analysis of form and content. Instead, some of the main features of codes of ethics are highlighted, along with some significant commonalities and differences between those from different countries. More attention is paid to the role of professional regulation and codes of practice, and a new section on the limitations and critiques of codes of ethics has been added.

In Chapter 5 on service users' rights, the role of service user movements and recent trends towards the 'personalization' of care are highlighted. The idea of service users as 'consumers' and 'customers' is further developed to reflect the growing trend towards market-type principles in adult social care in many countries in the global North. This theme extends to Chapter 6 on social workers' responsibilities, with the addition of a fourth model of social work in Table 6.1 – social work as a 'quasi-business'.

A new section 'Ethical decision-making and "ethics work"' has been placed in Chapter 7. Ethical judgements are presented as one component of decisions, and the making of judgements and decisions as just one aspect of ethical life. The concept of 'ethics work' is introduced as the work undertaken by practitioners in identifying ethically salient features of situations, exercising moral imagination and compassion, experiencing emotions and deploying moral courage, as well as engaging in the moral reasoning that accompanies judgements and decisions.

One of the most significant additions is the new international cases for discussion drawn from seven countries across the world, which are placed at the end of each chapter. They are designed to stimulate reflection and several questions for discussion are appended to each case, linked to the theme of the chapter and the subject matter of the case. Some of these cases are longer than those included within the chapters and give more detailed and sometimes personal information about the people involved. They range from an account from a high-profile child abuse case in Austria, where a social worker was initially given a suspended sentence and fined for neglect of professional duties, to the responses of professional associations of social workers in Argentina to a social worker discovered to have acted as an informant in the previous military dictatorship.

The overall rationale for the book, an overview of each chapter and guidance on the use of exercises, cases and further resources is given at the end of the Introduction.

Acknowledgements

The main stimulus for writing this book has been the dialogue and discussion generated through teaching ethics to trainee social workers and community and youth workers, particularly at Durham University and the University of York in Britain. I have also benefited greatly from periods as a visiting lecturer in higher education institutions in several countries, especially in Amiens, Bryn Mawr, Copenhagen, Lisbon, Malmö and Oulu, where students have generously shared their dilemmas and problems and staff their ideas on teaching ethics. The continuing work with colleagues in the European Social Ethics Project since 1998 has also been a constant source of inspiration and I would like to thank all past and present members of that group for their companionship and stimulation, particularly Kirsten Nøhr. In recent years, attendance at the conferences and seminars of FESET (Formation d'Educateurs Sociaux Européens/European Social Educator Training), the European Association of Schools of Social Work, the International Federation of Social Workers and the International Association of Schools of Social Work has furnished particularly useful and stimulating conversations on ethical topics. In 2010/11, the privilege of participating in two Japanese–British seminars on social work in Stirling and Tokyo broadened my horizons greatly, as have the comradely gatherings of the Social Work Action Network internationally and in Britain.

Above all, I would like to thank the social workers, community workers and youth workers who have been prepared to discuss their ethical dilemmas with me over the years, particularly students from Durham University and the University of York, practitioners from several agencies in the north of England, and social workers, professional associations and academics from across the world who have contributed the many case examples in the book. The majority of these contributors remain nameless, in order to preserve confidentiality in relation to service users and agencies. However, I am particularly grateful to the following people who have contributed in many ways to enhancing my understanding of social work and the many ethical challenges faced by practitioners across the world: Laura Acotto, Matthew Armstrong, Dimitrinka Boumbovska, Sema Buz, Chris Carroll, Fumihito Ito, Mark Jones, Vic Jupp, Jan Lefevre, Maria Maiss, Maria Moritz, Donna McAuliffe, Leonie Mendo, Marie-Geneviève Mounier, Atefeh Nikouei, Gertraud Pantucek, Larissa Raffles, İpen İlknur Ünlü, Abbas Ali Yazdani, Kate Yeong-Tsyr Wang and Maki Yajima.

I am also grateful to the International Federation of Social Workers and the professional associations across the world that provided copies of their ethical codes; to Kate Boardman, Trifon Boumbovski, Lieve van Espen, Lauelia Rolland-Fortin, Marie Sanders and Mea Wilkins for their translations of codes and cases; and to Katie Appleford, Vic Jupp and Helen Roberts for research assistance. I am grateful to the following for permission to use extracts from my previously published work: the *International Journal of Youth and Adolescence* for permission to use sections in Chapter 3 from an article concerning virtue ethics and the ethics of care in volume 9 (2000); the *Journal of Social Intervention: Theory and Practice* for permission to use the material in List 3.2 taken from an article in volume 20, issue 2 (2011); Routledge for permission to use a case (Case for discussion 4) from *Practising Social Work Ethics Around the World: Cases and Commentaries* (2012); and Palgrave Macmillan for permission to use some materials from *Ethics, Accountability and the Social Professions* (2004), including Table 3.1 and some of the material on the ethics of proximity in Chapter 3.

Many colleagues and friends have offered encouragement and been prepared to discuss aspects of the first, second, third and fourth editions of the book with me. The list is now getting too long to include everyone, but I am particularly grateful to: Hiroshi Ando, Mark Baldwin, Chris Beckett, Margaret Bell, Peter Beresford, Cynthia Bisman, Tim Bond, Helen Charnley, Derek Clifford, Lena Dominelli, Lorna Durrani, Ken Fairless, Iain Ferguson, Ann Gallagher, Arne Grønningsæter, Richard Hugman, Umme Imam, Fumihito Ito, Hiroshi Kosaka, Tony Jeffs, Juliet Koprowska, Michael Lavalette, Kate Leonard, Anne Marron, Una McCluskey, Audrey Mullender, Akira Namae, Andrew Orton, Frank Philippart, Alf Ronnby, Muriel Sawbridge, Maria Rosàrio do Serafim, Ruth Stark, Mark K. Smith, Fritz-Rüdiger Volz, Robin Williams and Man Yae-Yang.

I am grateful to the late Jo Campling for her enthusiastic support when I first presented the idea for this book to her, to Catherine

Gray and Kate Llewellyn at Palgrave Macmillan for their patience and encouragement and to three anonymous referees for their helpful comments on the first and third editions.

Finally, I would like to acknowledge my debt to my late father, Fred Banks, for first pointing me in the direction of philosophy and supporting my academic endeavours with a healthy combination of interest and scepticism.

SARAH BANKS

Introduction

CHAPTER OVERVIEW

This Introduction sets the scene for the rest of the book, briefly discussing some of the key terms ('social work', 'social workers', 'service users', 'values' and 'ethics'), the relationship between ethics, religion and politics, and then outlining the rationale, aims and structure of the book.

The current context of social work

Social work is the kind of occupation that is always in a state of change, as it is linked so closely to social welfare systems that shift with global economic trends and in response to government social and economic policies. In many countries in the global North with traditionally strong state welfare systems, for example in Western Europe, the role of the state as a direct provider of services is declining, resources for welfare are being reduced and new styles of management and accountability are being introduced. These changes have ethical implications for social work practitioners, as their role in allocating scarce resources becomes more challenging and demands for cost-effectiveness and measurable outcomes for service users and society are increasing. In countries where social work has recently been established or re-established as a occupation, or is in a state of development, for example China, Russia and the countries of Eastern Europe, questions about its role, purpose and public profile are prominent.

Social work is, therefore, a difficult occupation to encapsulate. It is located within and profoundly affected by diverse cultural, economic, political and policy contexts in different countries of the world. Social work embraces work in a number of sectors (public, private, independent, voluntary); it takes place in a multiplicity of settings (residential homes, neighbourhood offices, community development projects); practitioners perform a range of tasks (caring, controlling, empowering, campaigning, assessing, managing); and the work has a variety of purposes (redistribution of resources to those in need, social control and rehabilitation of the deviant, prevention or reduction of social problems, and empowerment of oppressed individuals and groups). Faced with such diverse roles and settings, some argue that it is the values of social work that hold it together. In this book I will explore what some of these values are and the ethical challenges social workers face in trying to put them into practice.

Terminology: 'social work', 'social workers' and 'service users'

Social work

There are many definitions of social work. These vary in emphasis according to the purpose for which they are written, the ideological viewpoint of the authors, the country and/or organization of origin and the level of generality or detail. As Healy (2001, p. 80) comments, there are both striking similarities and differences in social work practice around the world. Some of the similarities are due to the influence of North American and Western European education programmes and literature in countries where social work developed later or was influenced by former colonial links. The establishment of international professional organizations and the growing ease of global communications have also contributed to an increasing awareness of common and interconnected issues and problems. Yet, at the same time as social work has become established in a range of countries, so its methods and approaches have adapted to the local conditions and culture (the 'indigenization' of social work). So while it is possible for the International Federation of Social Workers (IFSW) and International Association of Schools of Social Work (IASSW) to produce a definition of social work that is designed to be applicable worldwide, it is a general statement of purpose and principle. It is acknowledged that the priorities of social work will vary between countries and time periods, depending on cultural, historical and socioeconomic conditions. The IFSW/IASSW (2000) definition of social work will, however, be used as a starting point for this book:

> The social work profession promotes social change, problem solving in human relationships and the empowerment and liberation of people to enhance well-being. Utilising theories of human

behaviour and social systems, social work intervenes at points where people interact with their environments. Principles of human rights and social justice are fundamental to social work.

The purpose of this statement is to unify social workers around the world, and to provide a common starting point for presenting social work to governments and other international and national agencies and bodies. The term 'profession' is used to describe social work, which instantly gives the occupation a status and implied unity. Reference is made to the use of theories relevant to social work interventions, which again serves to legitimize social work as a profession, based on a body of knowledge. Implicit in this is the fact that the theories need to be learned through an educational process and applied through expertise. The definition also focuses on the purposes of social work, referring to 'social change', 'empowerment' and 'liberation'. These terms indicate that social work is about more than just helping people to adapt to their environments. It is about enabling them to take action for themselves. The fact that the definition explicitly states that principles are fundamental highlights the importance of social workers having a commitment to a set of core values. The mention of 'human rights' and 'social justice' covers both issues of individual freedom of choice and action and the distribution of power and resources in society.

Social workers

The term 'social workers' is used in this book to refer to people who are paid, or contracted without payment in a professional capacity, to undertake the work just described. The IFSW/IASSW definition is followed by a commentary, which includes a fuller description of social work practice, suggesting that 'interventions range from primarily person-focused psychosocial processes to involvement in social policy, planning and development'. It is important to note that some of the activities that form part of these interventions, such as counselling or helping people obtain services and resources in the community, may be carried out by people who are not social workers, that is, volunteers, family members, other welfare professionals. But the placing of the interventions undertaken by social workers within a rubric of theory and specialized terminology indicates that the practices will only be recognized as social work if they can be constructed in this way. In Britain, the occupations of community work and youth work are organized separately from social work. This book includes some examples of neighbourhood-based work and work with young people that may not be regarded as social work in Britain, but would be in many other countries.

Service users

I have tended to adopt the term 'service users' to refer to the people who use social work services and/or have a professional relationship with a social worker or related professional. It is now in common usage in preference to 'clients', which can be interpreted as implying dependency in a social work context. It is also preferable to 'customer', which implies more choice over services than is usually available, or 'consumers', which suggests a passive role. One of the limitations of the term 'service users', however, is that it does not encompass those people deemed ineligible for a service who are nevertheless in need or assert a claim. A second limitation is that, like 'client', it defines and categorizes people in terms of one (often small) part of their lives that involves a relationship with a social worker or service provider, First and foremost, however, those who have contact with welfare services are *people*, but frequently we need a term to refer to people in their role as users of services or in a professional relationship with social workers. So I have continued to use the term 'service users' in spite of its limitations. Occasionally the term 'clients' is used, as this was until recently in common usage and some of the social work literature uses this term.

Terminology: 'ethics' and 'values'

It is also important to clarify the other terms in the title of the book – 'ethics' and 'values'.

Ethics

People use the term 'ethics' in a number of different ways, but perhaps the most important distinction to make is between ethics as synonymous with moral philosophy and ethics as moral norms or standards. Within each of these two broad types of usage there are also many variations, depending on what aspects of moral philosophy are stressed and whether 'moral norms' are seen as habits, preferences, rules, standards, principles or character traits, for example.

If we take the first usage of ethics, as moral philosophy, it is a singular term, used to describe a branch of philosophy concerned with the study of 'morality, moral problems and moral judgements' (Frankena, 1963, p. 3). This is the way most moral philosophers writing on ethics use the term. For example, Warnock (1998, p. 7) talks of 'ethics (or moral philosophy, as I prefer to call it)'. Exactly what is the nature and remit of moral philosophy is, of course, disputed. Often philosophers distinguish three types of ethics, as follows:

1. *Meta-ethics:* comprises critical and analytical thinking about the meaning and use of moral terms such as 'right', 'good' or 'duty', about whether moral judgements can be justified or what is the nature of morality, for example.
2. *Normative ethics:* attempts to give answers to moral questions and problems regarding, for example, what is the morally right course of action in a particular case, whether someone is a morally good person, or whether lying is always wrong.
3. *Descriptive ethics:* studies what people's moral opinions and beliefs are and how they act in relation to these, for example what views people in Britain have about whether assisted suicide, euthanasia or abortion are always morally wrong.

Some philosophers confine moral philosophy to meta-ethics only (for example Urmson, 1975, p. 99), but generally it is regarded as comprising both meta-ethics and normative ethics. Descriptive ethics, however, is usually regarded as outside the realm of moral philosophy, although not irrelevant, in that it comprises the kinds of empirical and historical inquiries that might be conducted by anthropologists, sociologists or historians. Clearly, in the context of professional ethics, we are interested in all three aspects of ethics, including descriptive ethics (what moral views social workers actually hold and how they behave in practice), although the purpose of this book is not to conduct an empirical inquiry.

The second usage of the term 'ethics' is as a plural term referring to the norms or standards of behaviour people follow concerning what is regarded as good or bad, right or wrong, or good and bad qualities of character. Commentators vary according to whether they regard ethics as norms, standards, rules, principles or character traits, and whether they regard them as internally developed by the moral agent, or externally imposed by an outside authority. A common use of this second sense of ethics is in the expression 'code of ethics', which is usually regarded as a set of principles, standards, rules of conduct or sometimes character traits required for ethical practice. A variant on this usage of ethics is to use the term synonymously with 'morality' to mean a system of moral norms or standards.

In English, we often use the terms 'ethics' and 'morals' interchangeably in this second sense. Indeed, as Edwards (1998, p. 41) points out, 'morals' is derived from the Latin *mores* and 'ethics' from the Greek *ethos*, both meaning habits or customs. It is in this interchangeable sense that I will use the terms 'ethics' and 'morals' in this book, along with the adjectives 'ethical' and 'moral'. However, it is important to point out that some commentators do distinguish between the two. Osborne (1998, pp. 221–2) makes the following distinction:

> Moral systems are systems of interdiction; they are ideologies, codes to which individuals must relate themselves. Ethics, on the other hand, might be considered in a more positive sense, not as codes of interdiction, not as external norms to which individuals must relate themselves, but as constructed norms of 'internal consistency' (cf. Deleuze, 1988: 23; Foucault, 1984). Morality, one could say, is about doing one's duty to others or doing one's duty by some moral norm; ethics is about doing one's duty to oneself.

This has resonances with the distinction made in some of the French literature between *la morale* and *l'éthique*. Bouquet (1999, p. 27) defines *la morale* as 'a set of universalisable values, absolute and imperative; it comprises duties'. She suggests that the term has become discredited through being confused with moralizing and through the recent rejection of a prescriptive morality, of dogmatism and universalism. Common usage is now substituting the term *éthique* for *morale*. She regards *l'éthique* as equally normative, but not categorical. It is principally associated with the subject and interior to the subject, that is, the moral agent, who is autonomous, free and responsible to herself for her acts. Bouquet defines *l'éthique* as 'the set of principles which are at the foundation of each person's conduct'.

However, such distinctions in the English-speaking literature are less common, and great care must be taken to ascertain how commentators distinguish 'ethics' and morals', if at all, since they do not all follow the same broad distinctions made by Osborne and Bouquet. For example, Bauman frequently talks of 'ethics' as the externally imposed codes prescribing correct behaviour universally

(1995, p. 11) and the 'moral impulse' or 'morality' as internal and 'autonomous' (1993, p. 46). No such distinctions will be made in this book. I will use the term 'ethics' in a broad sense. The following are my working definitions of ethics and professional ethics that I will use in this book:

> Broadly speaking, 'ethics' is about matters of right and wrong conduct, good and bad qualities of character and responsibilities attached to relationships. Although the subject matter of ethics is often said to be human welfare, the bigger picture also includes the flourishing of animals and the whole ecosystem. The term 'ethics' may be used in a singular sense to refer to the study of right and wrong norms of behaviour, good and bad qualities of character; or in a plural sense, to refer to the actual norms and qualities.

> Professional ethics concerns matters of right and wrong conduct, good and bad qualities of character and the professional responsibilties attached to relationships in a work context.

Values

The term 'values' is equally problematic, as it tends to be used rather vaguely and has a variety of meanings. Timms (1983, p. 107) cites a literature review that discovered 180 different definitions. In everyday usage, 'values' is often used to refer to one of or all religious, moral, cultural, political or ideological beliefs, principles, attitudes, opinions or preferences. For our purpose, 'values' can be regarded as particular types of belief that people hold about what is regarded as worthy or valuable. The use of the term 'belief' reflects the status that values have as stonger than mere opinions or preferences. Clearly, there are many different types of thing that can be regarded as valuable. Seedhouse (1998, p. 78) lists physical objects (for example furniture), aesthetic qualities (for example beauty), intangibles (for example creativity), principles (for example truth-telling), or ideologies (for example communism).

In the literature on professional values, it is frequently principles, and particularly ethical principles, relating to how people should be treated, what ideas or actions are worthy or unworthy, good or bad, right or wrong, that are regarded as values. For example, the IFSW/IASSW (2000) definition of social work includes 'respect for the equality, worth, and dignity of all people', 'human rights' and 'social justice' under the heading 'Values'.

However, some of the literature also includes what Seedhouse calls 'intangibles' as professional values, such as creativity or integrity, which we might regard as 'virtues' or character traits of workers. Furthermore, there is an increasing tendency to distinguish 'values' from 'principles' in some statements on professional ethics, with 'values' being used to encompass broad beliefs about the nature of the good society and the role of social work within this (belief in human dignity and worth, integrity in social work practice), and principles being general statements about actions that promote these values (treating people with respect, placing service users' needs first). I will use the term 'social work values' in a broad sense. The following are my working definitions of 'values' and 'social work values':

> 'Values' can be regarded as particular types of belief that people hold about what is regarded as worthy or valuable.

> The term 'social work values' refers to a range of beliefs about what is regarded as worthy or valuable in a social work context – general beliefs about the nature of the good society, general principles about how to achieve this through actions, and the desirable qualities or character traits of professional practitioners.

Professional values and personal values

A conceptual distinction is often made between professional values and personal values, in that personal values may not be shared by all members of an occupational group. For example, a person who works as a social worker may have a personal belief that abortion is wrong, but this is not one of the underlying principles of social work. Insofar as professional values are located within and influenced by broader societal values, then they may reflect particular ideological or political positions (for example liberalism or socialism). In some countries, where religion is deeply intertwined with culture and law (for example in countries where Islam is dominant), societal values will more explicitly reflect the prevailing religion. However, in most countries, lists of professional values do not usually include direct or overt statements of ideological, religious or political beliefs (as can be seen from the professional codes of ethics discussed in Chapter 4). Employing agencies' values are usually similar to those of the profession as a whole, although some specialist organizations may include explicit religious or ideological beliefs. A worker's personal values, however, may encompass all Seedhouse's range of categories, and may include religious as well as aesthetic and ideological beliefs.

Ethics, religion and politics

Given that particular religions and political ideologies are one source of values, I will briefly consider the nature of religion and politics, and how they relate to ethics.

Religion

Religion is a source of values and ethical norms for individuals, groups and societies. So the relationship between ethics and religion is that one component of a religion is a set of ethical norms about how to lead a good life. The study of these norms is one specialist branch of ethics – namely religious ethics. Just like 'ethics', the concept of 'religion' is complex and contested. The origins of the term are usually linked to the Latin verb *religare*, meaning to tie or bind. The term 'religion' is used in a variety of ways, but generally refers to a system of beliefs and practices for achieving the spiritualization of human beings in relation to a transcendent God or gods or other superhuman presence. According to Schweiker (2005a, p. 2):

> Most scholars agree that a religion includes several features: convictions about what is most important in life (experiences like birth, death, sex and sorrow), ritual actions, beliefs about the whence and whither of existence, codes of conduct, communal life, and also experiences of transcendence (e.g. enlightenment, redemption, mystical insight). However, these features of religion are disputed and bear different meanings in cultures and traditions.

If we accept this view, a religion will comprise, among other features, a set of norms (normative ethics, based on convictions and codes of conduct) usually construed as deriving ultimate authority from God/gods or another superhuman presence. There will also be a body of scholarship based on the study of beliefs and norms of each religion at a meta-ethical level and the development of systematic theories of religious ethics, for example Buddhist ethics, Christian ethics, Hindu ethics, Islamic ethics and so on. Religion may be one source of values for some social work agencies, social workers and social work service users. Religion needs to be taken into account both to understand the values and practices followed by people who are members of different religious traditions, and as a potential source of conflict when different religious values clash with each other and with secular norms (Crabtree et al., 2008; Furness and Gilligan, 2010). Religious foundations play a role in delivering social work, and, as Rommelspacher (2010) points out, in some parts of the world their influence is currently increasing, especially where state resources for welfare are limited or being curtailed.

Social work, with its origins in late nineteenth-century Western Europe and North America, is rooted in Judeo-Christian values, and was often delivered by explicitly religious organizations and foundations (Cree, 1995). However, as social work professionalized in the twentieth century and societies in the West became more secular, the state took a greater role in providing welfare services and the explicit religious values became less prominent. Yet many of the norms in society, and hence in social work, reflect the traditional Judeo-Christian focus on notions of individual duty. The export of western models of social work to many other countries across the world, and the dominance of western literature, has resulted in a social work practice (in some countries) that rests on an amalgam of different religious and secular values, deriving from both indigenous and external norms and cultures. These origins need to be recognized in order to understand different conceptions of what is regarded as right and good in different countries and cultures, and within one country where people of many different religious persuasions and people with no religious affiliation live together.

Politics

'Politics', derived from the Greek *politika*, concerns the affairs of state and the activities involved in government, such as the management, administration and exercise of authority. A political ideology is a system of ideas or way of thinking that relates to how societies should be governed. It may entail certain political beliefs about how state power should be exercised, how goods should be distributed and how citizens should contribute to maintaining a good society. Some people are members of political parties that propose specific policies for how societies should be governed (for example Green Party, Communist Party, Labour Party) and often espouse fundamental ideological beliefs about what kind of society we should live in (for example ecosocialism, Marxism, fascism, democratic socialism, republicanism). In some countries, political parties incorporate explicitly religious values as well (for example Christian Democrat Party, Islamic Coalition Party).

So how, then, does politics relate to ethics? Although there is a commonly accepted distinction between political matters (how to organize government) and ethical matters (how individuals should conduct themselves), they are clearly interrelated. This was assumed by the ancient Greek philosophers Plato and Aristotle, who maintained that personal morality, good citizenship and the best way to organize a state all fit together (Hughes, 2001, p. 13). Ethics is about the motivations, commitments and responsibilities of individuals to take action in accordance with what they think is good and/or right. It assumes human agency and responsibility. As Critchley (2007, p. 120) argues: 'we need ethics in order to decide what to do in a political situation'. Yet we also need politics to provide the content for ethics (matters of justice, power and control). In social work, which is often organized as part of state welfare services, matters of politics and ethics are inseparable, as will be discussed in Chapter 1.

Rationale and aims of the book

The discussion above suggests that it is both important and difficult to explore the nature of the ethical and value issues inherent in social work practice. It is important not just because social work is in a constant state of change, but also because social work is inherently political and social workers themselves are increasingly under moral attack from the press and public for the outcomes of their actions. Controversies over the handling of child abuse cases, for example, raise ethical questions about the duties and rights of social workers and the extent to which they should be blamed if a child dies or if children are removed from their families unnecessarily. Many social workers feel a sense of guilt and anxiety when having to make a difficult ethical decision. While such feelings are inevitable for anyone who makes difficult decisions and has a sense of moral responsibility, should social workers take all the blame for bad outcomes? One of the purposes of this book is to encourage social workers to locate their work in a broader political and economic context, to be clear about their own value positions, and hence to reduce some of the unnecessary feelings of guilt, blame and anxiety in making difficult ethical decisions and to strengthen their resolve to stand up for what they believe is right.

In the course of collecting material for this book, I have found that when social workers are asked to describe ethical difficulties in their practice, there is never any shortage of examples. The occurrence of ethical problems and dilemmas in social work is serious and common. There are numerous cases where the rights of parents have to be balanced against the rights of children, a social worker's duty to her employing agency conflicts with a duty to a service user, or an injustice is witnessed and it is difficult to take action, for example.

There are no easy answers to the ethical problems and dilemmas in social work practice. It is not possible (or desirable) to produce a rulebook that would enable social workers easily and quickly to resolve their ethical difficulties. If a social worker is facing a dilemma, then sometimes its resolution will entail making a choice between unwelcome alternatives, perhaps by careful consideration and deciding that one alternative is less unwelcome than the others. Having made the choice, the impact of the dilemma does not go away, for even the least unwelcome alternative is still unwelcome. The resolution of a dilemma often leaves a residue of guilt, blame or regret. This is where some of the main stresses for social workers lie; not just in having to make difficult choices and decisions, but having to take responsibility for the unwelcome nature or outcomes of the decisions, as Case example 0.1 illustrates.

Practice focus

Case example 0.1: Responding to a boy exhibiting disruptive behaviour

Peter is a 10-year-old boy whose parents are barely able to control his violent and disruptive behaviour, even after a lot of support from a school-based social worker and a range of professionals from healthcare and other agencies. The school-based social worker had worked with Peter and his parents for over a year, and supported them in undertaking a special programme for families of young people with behavioural difficulties. A case review has been scheduled involving the family and other professionals. The social worker says she is facing a dilemma about whether to recommend that Peter should be removed from the parental home – a decision that would go against the wishes of Peter and his parents and might cause further disruptive behaviour as a result of the move – or whether to recommend that he stay at home with further support – a course of action that would be contrary to the demands from neighbours and the school and might risk further violent and disruptive behaviour towards other children and neighbours.

Both suggested solutions to the dilemma have unwelcome consequences. The process of investigation, taking into account the legal and ethical rights of different parties, the risks involved in both courses of action, and the legal, procedural and ethical responsibilities of the social worker, is a complex one. Whatever course of action is taken, somebody's rights may be compromised and some of the consequences may be unwelcome. While this example has been framed as a dilemma (a choice between two alternatives), there may be other possibilities. Part of the social worker's attempt to resolve the dilemma may be to find a third option.

Case example 0.2 comes from a community and youth worker who took a challenging course of action, but it is not presented as a choice. She felt what she did was part of her role.

Practice focus

Case example 0.2: Responding to a local riot

Vicki is an experienced community and youth worker who lives and works in a poor neighbourhood in a large British city. One night she was at home watching a DVD. She was feeling a little nervous as the previous night there had been serious rioting on the streets in a neighbouring district, following the shooting by a police officer of a local resident. This had involved a lot of young people, who had set fire to properties, looted and vandalized shops and attacked and robbed people in the streets. On the evening in question, Vicki received a text message from a young person who regularly used the community centre where she worked. He said there had been clashes between young people and the police outside a local shop, which was now on fire. Vicky immediately sent text messages to all the staff and volunteers who worked at the community centre, asking them to meet her there in 30 minutes if they felt able to help. At that point, she did not know what she could do and she knew the situation was dangerous, but she also knew that as a community and youth worker committed to working with people in her local area, she could not stand by and do nothing. In fact, she and her colleagues went out onto the streets together, calling for calm, assisting people who were hurt and drawing young people they knew away from the blazing shop. The next day Vicki gave an interview to the local newspaper. She said she did not condone the violence, but she also explained that many of the young people in the area had poor experiences of school, few opportunities for work and little sense of belonging to a society where they felt valued. The summer activity programme at the centre had recently been cut due to the withdrawal of local authority funding.

Vicki did not experience a dilemma about whether or not to act, but what she did required moral and physical courage and close cooperation with colleagues. Vicki was not at work that night, but she took action in her capacity as a community and youth worker and as a local resident. She also felt it was important to speak out afterwards. If Vicki had been new to the job, had not lived in the area, or did not have good relationships with co-workers and volunteers, she might have hesitated more about what to do.

The aim of this book is not to tell social, youth or community workers how to make decisions or what roles they should take in particular circumstances, because I believe that would be both impossible and undesirable. It is impossible because of the complexity of social work practice; no rulebook could cover the variety of types of situation or local contexts (especially in different countries). It would be undesirable because it would suggest that social workers would simply have to follow the prescribed rules applying in each case and could in effect abrogate their individual responsibility for making judgements and decisions. Rather, the book aims to encourage critical thinking, reflection and reflexivity through exploring the nature of ethical problems and dilemmas in social work, how and why they arise, and what might be some alternative ways of tackling them according to different ethical theories and approaches. Through gaining a clearer understanding of what the problems and dilemmas are about, hopefully social workers can decide where they stand on some of the important ethical issues in the work, will have more confidence in justifying the ethical judgements and decisions they make, may feel less obliged to take the blame for the inevitable unwelcome outcomes of social work intervention, and may develop their moral courage and commitment to take actions to challenge the injustices they witness in their daily practice.

The structure of the book

Chapter 1 examines the nature of the ethical challenges inherent in social work and includes four brief case examples to illustrate some of the main issues relating to individual rights and welfare; public welfare; equality, difference and structural oppression; and professional roles and boundaries. The nature of social work as a human services profession, its links with state welfare systems and the problems of blame and guilt in social work are discussed. This chapter provides a basic orientation for the rest of the book. Chapters 2 and 3 cover a range of theoretical approaches to ethics, drawing on literature from moral philosophy and discussing its relevance to social work. These theoretical approaches are divided into principle-based ethics (Chapter 2, covering Kantian, utilitarian, radical and 'common morality' approaches) and character- and relationship-based ethics (Chapter 3, covering the ethics of virtue, care and proximity and postmodern ethics). These chapters are located near the beginning of the book, as the ethical theories and theoretical approaches they outline are referred to in later chapters. However, for those readers or teachers who prefer to start by looking at practical matters, the case examples given in Chapter 7 and at the end of each chapter can fruitfully be used to introduce the subject matter of ethics before reading Chapters 2 and 3.

Chapter 4 provides a bridge between the ethical theories of Chapters 2 and 3 and the discussion of policy and practice in the rest of the book. It explores the nature of professionalism with reference to social work, and the nature and functions of codes of ethics. Reference is made to debates about what is meant by the concept of a 'profession', whether the occupation of social work should strive to take on the trappings of a profession, and the advantages and limitations of codes of ethics. The discussion is illustrated with examples of codes of ethics from a variety of national professional associations for social work worldwide.

Chapters 5 and 6 explore the meaning and nature of service users' rights and social workers' responsibilities respectively. Chapter 5 offers a critical discussion of the concepts of 'rights' and 'human rights', then explores different conceptions of service users as 'persons', 'clients', 'consumers' and 'customers' and what this means for the framing and exercise of their rights. The growth of service user movements and the strengths and limitations of trends towards the personalization of care (including 'direct payments' to service users or 'cash for care') are covered. Chapter 6 considers the meaning of 'duties' and 'responsibilities' and discusses the implications of the growth of trends towards more standardized approaches and market principles in social work for the roles and responsibilities of social workers.

Chapter 7 focuses on ethical problems and dilemmas in practice, looking at the nature of ethical judgements, followed by a range of practice examples from students and practitioners. This is the most practice-focused chapter in the book.

The use of exercises, cases and further resources

At the end of each chapter, exercises called 'Putting it into practice' have been included that can be used by readers to focus their thoughts around particular issues, or by tutors and facilitators teaching or working with groups of social workers or students. A relevant 'case for discussion' is also included at the end of each chapter, with a series of questions designed to be used by individual readers to reflect on the issues raised by the case and by groups of practitioners and students in teaching and learning situations. These cases are longer than the case examples within the chapters, give more details of situations and people, and are drawn from accounts given by social work students and practitioners from different countries around the world. They are included as a way of encouraging readers to think about the commonalities and differences in the kinds of ethical challenges that arise for social workers globally. Within many of the chapters, one or two case examples are used to illustrate particular points. In Chapter 7, there are 10 case examples (largely from Britain), which illustrate a range of different types of ethical problems and dilemmas that arise for students, and for experienced practitioners, and how they can be tackled in practice. Details of the cases and all names of people involved have been changed to preserve anonymity.

Each chapter ends with annotated references for readers to pursue if they wish to explore further some of the issues raised.

CHAPTER 1

Ethical challenges in social work

CHAPTER OVERVIEW

This chapter explores how we conceive of the domain of the 'ethical', including discussion of the distinctions and relationships between ethical, technical and legal matters. It then discusses the nature of the ethical challenges inherent in social work, and how and why questions of ethics arise, linked to the place of social work as a human services profession largely within state-organized systems of welfare. Finally, consideration is given to the guilt and anxiety often felt by social workers and whether the blame allocated to them for outcomes of what are essentially moral decisions is justified. The chapter ends with an exercise to encourage identification of ethical issues and a case for discussion from Austria about a social worker who received a suspended sentence and fine for neglecting to perform her professional duties in relation to safeguarding a child.

Introduction

There is general agreement among social work practitioners and academics that questions of ethics, morals and values are an inevitable part of social work. The majority of social workers, when asked, have no difficulty in offering examples of ethical problems and dilemmas. The literature of social work is also very clear: 'Moral issues haunt social work', says Jordan (1990, p. 1); according to Reamer (1999, p. 3): 'social work is among the most value based of all professions'; while Healy (2001, p. 101) comments: 'value commitments and ethical principles are at the core of social work as a profession'.

In the Introduction, I discussed the meanings of the terms 'ethics' and 'values' and offered working definitions. I discussed the fact that religious and political values often form part of our sets of personal values and professional social work values. Before examining the nature of the ethical challenges that are inherent in social work, I will first consider how we demarcate the realm of the 'ethical' from related domains covering technical and legal matters.

The ethical, the technical and the legal

Frequently in the social work literature values are distinguished from knowledge, and ethical/moral issues from legal and technical matters. Such distinctions can be useful, as long as it is not implied that knowledge can be value-free, or that legal and technical decisions can be made without recourse to ethics. For example, when considering what action to take in relation to a person with a severe psychiatric problem, a social worker might say: 'It is essentially a legal question whether to detain this person in hospital under the mental health legislation.' Yet, as Braye and Preston-Shoot (2010) point out, the law is rarely clear, and has to be interpreted by the social worker. The law in Britain and many other countries tells us that if we make the technical (and ethical) judgement that the person concerned is suffering from a 'mental disorder', such that it is in the person's interest to be detained in hospital, then we have the legal powers to bring that about. Laws do not tell us what we ought to do, just what we can do. The laws in operation nationally and internationally themselves reflect the particular values and norms prevalent in the societies where they apply, some of which we may regard as immoral, for example in the case of laws that regulate immigration, abortion or human cloning. Most decisions in social work involve a complex interaction of ethical, political, technical and legal issues, all of which are interconnected. Our values will influence how we interpret the law.

Giving another example, when asked to assess the needs of an older person with mobility problems for home care support with shopping and cleaning, a social worker might say: 'It is a technical matter to decide whether this person is eligible for the home care service.' The social worker assesses the person according to the defined criteria and makes a judgement using her professional skill and knowledge. The social worker might only consider that ethical issues were involved if she had to consider whether she ought to recommend a particular service even though the person did not quite meet the criteria. This is a helpful distinction between the technical and the ethical. However, a judgement might be regarded as a technical one not because only technical questions of measurement and assessment were involved, but because the social worker chose to see it in that way, as she might if it were a relatively straightforward case that did not present any ethical problems or dilemmas. However, the process of assessing needs for a home care service is not devoid of ethical content. The criteria of need that determine who should get the service will be based on ethical judgements about social duties to reduce some of the disadvantages caused by disability, or about how to distribute a scarce resource efficiently and fairly, for example. The social worker may judge that the criteria are not fair or do not result in resources being allocated to the most needy people. This is what Jordan (1990, p. 1) means when he says that moral issues haunt social work.

Ethical issues, problems and dilemmas

The preceding discussion suggests that all aspects of social work have ethical dimensions, even if they are not always identified as such. It is important that social workers recognize this and are aware not only of their own power in relation to service users, but also of the source of their power and their contradictory roles within society. Very often we associate professional ethics with dilemmas and problems – the making of difficult judgements and decisions in cases where the rights, needs and interests of different parties conflict. But it is also important to see ethical issues as deeply embedded in the construction of social work as an occupation, its location within state systems of welfare and the everyday practice of its members. Thompson et al. (2000, pp. 6–9), writing about nursing ethics, distinguish ethical problems (difficult choices have to be made, but it is clear what is the right action to take) and ethical dilemmas (difficult choices have to be made and it is not clear what is the right course of action). Many of the case examples in this book are constructed as problems and dilemmas. However, I would argue that it is important also to see the whole of social work as comprising ethical dimensions and to focus on the ethical issues in practice as much as the ethical problems and dilemmas (Banks, 2009a).

In the light of the discussion above, it may be useful to distinguish between ethical issues, ethical problems and ethical dilemmas, as outlined in List 1.1.

List 1.1 Ethical issues, problems and dilemmas

1. *Ethical issues* pervade the social work task (including what appear to be 'legal' or 'technical' matters), in that social work frequently takes place in the context of state systems of welfare, premised on principles of social justice and public good, where social workers have professional power in the relationship with service users. So, although making a judgement about whether to recommend home care services for a person with a disability in a case that is straightforward may not involve a social worker in agonizing over a ethical dilemma, it is not devoid of ethical content.
2. *Ethical problems* arise when a social worker sees a situation as involving a difficult moral decision, but is clear what is the right course of action, for example when she decides to turn down the application of a very needy person for home care services because this person does not fit the criteria.
3. *Ethical dilemmas* occur when a social worker sees herself as facing a choice between two equally unwelcome alternatives, which may involve a conflict of ethical values, and it is not clear which choice will be the right one. For example, should the social worker bend the criteria for allocating home care services in order to help a very needy person, or stick to the rules and refuse the application of someone who really needs support. She is faced with a conflict between the interests of this individual and the public interest in having rules and criteria that apply to everyone.

What is regarded as a technical matter for one person (simply applying the rules) may be an ethical problem for another (a difficult choice, but it is clear what action should be taken) or a dilemma for a third person (there appears to be no solution). It depends on how each person sees the situation, how experienced they are at making ethical judgements and decisions and how they prioritize different values (see Banks and Williams, 2006 for a detailed discussion of practitioners' accounts of ethical issues, problems and dilemmas).

What are the ethical challenges in social work?

In collecting examples of ethical difficulties experienced by qualified and trainee social workers in Britain and various countries across the world, I identified four main themes, as summarized in List 1.2.

List 1.2 Ethical challenges in social work

1. *Individual rights and welfare:* service users' rights to make their own decisions and choices; social workers' responsibilities to promote the welfare of service users.
2. *Public welfare:* the rights and interests of parties other than service users; social workers' responsibilities to their employing agencies and to society; the promotion of the greatest good for the greatest number of people.
3. *Equality, difference and structural oppression:* balancing the promotion of equality with due regard to diversity; the social worker's responsibility to challenge oppression and to work for changes in agency policy and in society; managing religious and cultural differences and conflicts.
4. *Professional roles, boundaries and relationships:* deciding what role the social worker should take in particular situations (counsellor, controller, advocate, assessor, campaigner, ally or friend); considerations of issues of boundaries between personal, professional and political life.

Any categorization is obviously artificial, and does not do justice to the complexity of the issues within each category and the overlap between them. Frequently there are conflicts between rights, responsibilities and interests both within and between these categories. However, this framework may be a useful starting point for exploring issues of values and ethics in social work practice. Short case examples from four practitioners talking about everyday issues in their practice may illuminate our discussion.

Rights and welfare of the individual

Practice focus

Case example 1.1: Should I persuade Mrs Brown to accept help?

Mrs Brown, an 80-year-old woman, was referred to a social work agency by a local hospital after a fall at home. A student social worker visited her in her home to assess her needs and felt that Mrs Brown was finding it hard to look after herself – her house was dirty and untidy and it was clear that she was not eating much. She lived alone, and her son visited twice a week to deliver shopping. The social worker suggested to Mrs Brown that she should consider having a home care assistant to help her on a daily basis, but she categorically refused. The social worker met the son and it was clear he was not willing to offer any more support to his mother. The social worker visited Mrs Brown a second time, but Mrs Brown was still adamant she did not want any help. The social worker commented:

> It was difficult to know how far to try to persuade or even coerce Mrs Brown to accept the offer of a home care assistant, or whether just to leave her alone and hope she would manage to survive. This was one of my first cases as a student social worker and I felt very concerned for Mrs Brown's safety.

Here the focus of the student social worker's concern is the service user's welfare. The social worker wants to respect Mrs Brown's own choices about how to live her life, yet the worker also wants to ensure that Mrs Brown feeds herself properly and is checked on regularly in case she falls again. The social worker experiences a conflict between the promotion of Mrs Brown's welfare and her right to make her own choices.

Public welfare

Practice focus

Case example 1.2: Should we help the police to catch a sexually exploitative man?

Sally was a 12-year-old girl who looked much older. She had recently come into a care home because her parents felt her behaviour was out of control. She had been having sexual relations with a 50-year-old man who supplied her with money in return for sexual favours. On arrival at the residential care home, restrictions were placed on Sally's movements to prevent her from meeting this man. One day two police officers visited the care home to ask the staff to assist them in their attempt to arrest the man. One of the residential care workers made the following comment:

> The police were near to catching the man, and asked staff to lift restrictions on Sally leaving the [residential care] unit in the hope of catching him in the act. Should we have refused because we were allowing Sally to put herself at risk, or was catching the culprit and preventing further risk to herself and other girls a priority?

The care worker sees that it will be in the best interests of everyone if this man is caught, yet feels uneasy about using the young girl in this way, both because of the deception involved, and the responsibility if any harm comes to Sally when she is allowed out of the care home. This case is presented as involving making a decision about whether the public interest in catching the man outweighs the deception involved and the short-term risk to Sally.

Equality, difference and structural oppression

Practice focus

Case example 1.3: How can we ensure young Bangladeshi men have equal access to our services?

The staff of a drop-in centre for young people based in a small rural town in Wales were concerned that the young Bangladeshi people living in the neighbourhood were not using the centre. They made big efforts to make contact with the young people and eventually quite a large group of young men of Bangladeshi origin (from Muslim families) started to use the project, which offered a range of services including an IT suite, summer projects, outreach work and sexual health advice. The sexual health provision, which offered confidential advice, information and free condoms, was the most well-used service at the centre. The staff team was aware of potential issues with the use of this service by the young Bangladeshi men, as their religion forbids sex outside marriage and the service might be viewed as promoting promiscuous behaviour. However, they felt that young people from any background should be entitled to services that support their needs and issues.

According to one of the youth workers:

> It was the consensus among the staff that denial of any service to a young person who wanted to access it was a denial of their human rights and against the moral, ethical, theoretical and practical notions of anti-oppressive youth work. It was thus agreed that working towards what was right for a young person was a greater concern than respecting a community's religion or culture.

However, after a year, the young Bangladeshi men stopped coming. The sexual health worker received a complaint from the parents of one young man, as they had found condoms in his school bag. A community meeting was called at the mosque and all young Bangladeshi people were banned from accessing the project. A review was held at the youth centre, as there was concern that a whole community of young people were now not able to access the drop-in centre. Speaking about the situation four years later, the same youth worker commented:

> The main discussion was about what could have been done differently. At the time an agreed new strategy was never formulated and the dilemma about how to resolve the situation has remained ever since.

The staff team at this youth project was clearly committed to promoting equality of access and supporting all young people, regardless of their ethnic origin or religion, in exercising their rights to make their own choices and decisions. Yet, despite their best intentions and a brief period of 'success', no young Bangladeshi people are currently using the project. From the information given, it sounds like the approach of the youth workers – to support and promote the young people's freedom of choice – was too simplistic, given that the young people lived in a fairly tightknit community, where adherence to Muslim values was paramount. This case highlights the complexities of working with ethnic and religious diversity and the need for long-term neighbourhood work based on dialogue, bridge-building and compromise.

Professional boundaries and relationships

Practice focus

Case example 1.4: How can I maintain my professional boundaries without being too harsh?

A student social worker was undertaking a fieldwork placement in an agency working with families and children in the UK. A recently arrived Ethiopian woman with two young children was referred to the agency by the asylum seekers unit in the local social services department. This woman had recently been relocated to the area as part of a government policy of dispersal of asylum seekers, and seemed very depressed and isolated. Her seven-year-old daughter was reported to be withdrawn and unhappy at school and both mother and daughter cried during most of the first home visit. The student also felt that the family was being subjected to 'low level racism in the area' where they lived. The student visited the family at least once a fortnight over the next three months, during which time the situation improved and mother and daughter appeared much happier. When the student's placement was due to end, she reported feeling some discomfort about how the family viewed their relationship with her:

> I was aware that the woman viewed me as a friend, and although she was aware that I was a worker, when I told her that I would be finishing the placement soon, she became upset. She made a number of comments on numerous occasions asking me to visit her whenever I was in the area and invited me to her son's birthday party in four months time. I felt that I did not deal with this effectively, as I tended to use the fact that I did not live in the same city as an excuse for not being able to maintain contact, and I felt that this blurred the professional boundaries. I found it extremely difficult to maintain these boundaries and although I felt guilty for giving the impression of being a family friend, I also felt that it would be extremely harsh to tell her that she was a 'service user' rather than a friend.

This student obviously developed a good relationship with a very vulnerable family. As a student, she may have had a relatively small caseload and so could afford to spend time and energy with this family and to develop what was perceived (and/or desired) by the woman as a close and caring relationship. This case highlights the dangers of the caring role of the social worker being misunderstood and misinterpreted by service users and the importance of clarity at the outset and honesty during the course of a relationship. This situation was still concerning the student after the placement ended and had clearly caused her to reflect on what she might have done differently, as she commented: 'I didn't sit down and explain in an honest way.'

The above descriptions have simplified the issues arising in each case. In many cases, issues in all four categories arise. Some of the problems and dilemmas workers face are about balancing different sets of rights, interests, responsibilities and commitments. Social work is a complex activity, with many layers of duties and responsibilities, for example to one's own professional integrity, to service users, to the agency and to society. These often conflict and have to be balanced against each other. There are no easy answers to such ethical challenges. They are part of the everyday life of social workers. Some will handle them more easily than others, depending on experience, moral sensitivity and their own value positions. Often, it helps to discuss difficult cases with colleagues, or in supervision sessions, to gain a range of different perspectives on the issues involved and possible courses of action. For example, in discussing Case example 1.2, many students have said that the dilemma identified (whether to respond to the request of the police) would not arise for them, as it would be clear that the strategy proposed by the police was inappropriate (it could be regarded as 'entrapment' and hence might not stand up in court) and/or unethical (it involved treating Sally as a means to an end and breached the social work relationship of trust with her). Vignettes like the short case examples given here and longer cases like those at the end of each chapter can be useful as a focus for reflection and student discussions, to encourage rehearsal of issues and actions (see also the cases in Chapter 7; Banks, 2001a, 2005; Banks and Nøhr, 2012; Banks and Williams, 1999).

In the remaining sections of this chapter we will explore how and why questions of ethics are an integral part of social work practice.

Social work as a human services profession

Social work may be regarded as a 'human services' profession along with other occupations that focus on human relationships such as those in the field of healthcare, teaching and the law. Social workers have special powers, knowledge and expertise and must be trusted by service users to act in their best interests. The relationship between social workers and service users is an unequal one, in that social workers are more powerful. Social work, therefore, along with law, medicine, nursing, counselling and other similar professions, has a code of ethics that is designed, among other things, to protect service users from exploitation or misconduct. Some commentators have described the relationship between social workers and service users as 'fiduciary', that is, based on trust (Kutchins, 1991; Levy, 1976, pp. 55ff.).

While there are many similarities between social work and professions such as law and medicine, there are also several ways in which social work is different. The degree of individual autonomy exercised by social workers over how to perform their work and the scope of the decisions they can make tends to be more limited than that of doctors and lawyers. Many social workers are employed either directly or indirectly by local authorities or municipalities; they may have a social control function and therefore their primary aim is not straightforwardly to work in the best interests of the service user. In many countries, social work is part of a 'welfare state' or at least a state-organized system of welfare, which is itself based on contradictory principles and undergoing a process of questioning and change, as is the role of the profession generally.

Social work and state welfare systems

Social work may be delivered by public, voluntary/not-for-profit or private sector organizations or by individuals in private practice. Its services may be offered as part of the provision of state welfare or control, as services motivated by independent philanthropic concern, or as services to be purchased directly by customers/service users. In the UK and many other countries in the global North and West, from its charitable origins in the nineteenth century, social work grew rapidly in the mid-twentieth century largely as part of a state-organized and state-funded system for distributing goods and services to meet certain types of social need of individuals, families, groups and communities, and to cure, contain or control behaviour that was regarded as socially problematic or deviant. It became part of a state-sponsored welfare system that included a range of other social services, including education, health, social security and housing. These are collective services that, in principle, benefit the whole community. However, social services are often regarded as different from other public services (such as police, army, roads and refuse collection), in that they are seen as a means of transferring resources to people who are not able to meet their own needs independently, through, for example, sickness, old age, childhood, unemployment or disability. They are also a way of attempting to redress, in small-scale ways, the inequalities, social exclusion and discrimination faced by people in poverty and people whose differences and social circumstances are not well tolerated in society.

Developed state welfare systems are allied to capitalist economies and have a redistributive role through taxation, compulsory social insurance and the direct provision of services. They can be seen as compensating for defects in the market system in the allocation of goods and services. Even in countries like the USA and Japan with relatively weak welfare states, state social workers are employed in a range of settings from welfare offices to hospitals and courts of law. As state welfare systems contract, this results in more self-help, private sector and non-governmental organization (NGO) provision, although many of these organizations still rely on public funding or contracts with public bodies to deliver services.

Many commentators have analysed the nature of welfare states in terms of contradictions. Marshall (1972) saw the tensions inherent in welfare capitalism between the values of social justice and equality and the competitive individualism of the market, although he recognized that the aim of the welfare state was not to remove inequality of income, rather it was to eradicate poverty and give everyone equal status as citizens in society. According to O'Connor (1973, p. 6), welfare states have two contradictory functions in capitalist societies – accumulation (enabling private capital to remain profitable) and legitimation (of the existing economic and social order). Moon (1988, p. 12) succinctly summarizes the contradictory principles upon which the welfare state is based:

> The welfare state embraces the market, but at the same time seeks to limit and control it; it incorporates ideas of rights, especially rights to property and the fruits of one's labor, but asserts a right to welfare, a right to have one's basic needs met; it is based on a conception of the person as a responsible agent but recognizes as well that many of the conditions of one's life are due to circumstances beyond one's control; it is premised upon sentiments of sociability and common interest, but its very success

may undermine those sentiments; it seeks to provide security, but embraces as well a commitment to liberty.

Moon suggests that this is one reason why the concept of the welfare state appears to be so vulnerable to criticism. Others might disagree that it is the contradictions per se that make it vulnerable (Offe, 1984, Ch. 5), but there is no doubt that the whole concept of the welfare state – its aims, functions, methods and outcomes – is the subject of questioning and criticism from various quarters, both right and left (Pierson, 2006; Roger, 2000). The economic recession of the mid-1970s gave rise to a sustained critique of state welfare provision from rightwing politicians and theorists, and this was reinforced by the recession of the late 1980s/early 1990s and the economic crisis of the late 2000s. First, the burden of taxation and regulation imposed on capital was claimed to serve as a disincentive to investment. Second, welfare benefits and the collective power of trade unions were said to amount to a disincentive to work. The argument has also been made from a communitarian perspective that family values and responsibilities, a sense of community and moral obligation may, in fact, be undermined by systematic state welfare provision (Etzioni, 1995, 1997). Criticisms from the left tend to focus on the ineffectiveness and inefficiency of the welfare bureaucracies, which have done little to redistribute income between classes and do not tackle the fundamental causes of poverty and unemployment. Feminist and anti-racist critiques have been increasingly vocal as many aspects of the state welfare system have been shown to reinforce gender and race stereotyping, discrimination and oppression. The welfare state is also seen as a repressive instrument of social control, through individualizing problems and distinguishing between people who are deserving and undeserving.

These various critiques, along with fiscal pressures and demographic constraints, especially the increasing proportion of older people in the global North, have led to changes in welfare systems, often resulting in an increasing role for markets, private provision and new forms of management and governance, including service user and citizen involvement (see Clarke, 2004 and Chapters 5 and 6 for further discussion).

This account of social work as part of the state-organized welfare provision is important as it helps us understand how some of the ethical issues are inherent in the role of the social worker. Insofar as social work is what Johnson (1972) called a 'state-mediated profession', it is based on contradictions and societal ambivalence. Social work contributes towards expressing society's altruism (care) and enforcing societal norms (control); it champions individual rights as well as protecting the collective good. Social workers are regarded as wimps (caring for those who do not deserve it) and as bullies (wielding too much power over individuals and families). As the welfare state is questioned, undermined and reformed, so the role of social work is also subject to question and change. While systems of state welfare vary enormously in different parts of the world, and in some countries the majority of social workers are not employed by the state, social work is very often at least partially funded and hence controlled through government sources. Social work is intimately connected with politics, as resources for welfare services and the role of welfare professionals are linked to policies and programmes for the distribution of wealth, taxation and the conferring of citizenship.

Blame and guilt in social work

Social workers are often at the interface between the state and civil society, working with people who are needy, vulnerable, socially excluded or marginalized. In this position they frequently bear the brunt of blame for certain unpalatable societal problems such as child abuse. One of the most publicized areas of social work is child protection or safeguarding. In this context, if a bad outcome occurs, social workers usually get the blame. A bad outcome can be either that children left at home suffer or die, or that children are removed from home unnecessarily. Franklin (1989) demonstrates how the press often portray social workers either as indecisive wimps who fail to protect children from death, or as authoritarian bullies who unjustifiably snatch children from their parents. Either way, the social workers are to blame. As Franklin (1989, p. 1) comments:

> Press reporting of child abuse, paradoxically, rarely focuses upon the abuse of children. It quickly regresses into an attack on welfare professionals, particularly social workers who, in their turn, seem to have become a metaphor for the public sector.

Social workers can be seen as symbols of state welfare, simultaneously representing two of its much criticized facets – bungling inefficiency and authoritarian repression. All professionals are blamed, but social workers offer a soft target when their interventions fail and they are often pilloried in the press (Aldridge 1994,

p. 70; Butler and Drakeford, 2005). This may be connected partly with the more ambivalent and morally charged role that social workers play in society. For example, doctors treat people who are sick; and sickness might be regarded as an unfortunate state that generally affects individuals through no fault of their own. Social workers often work with people whom society regards as 'undeserving', idle, feckless or deviant. Social workers have a control as well as a care function. It is their job to protect society from deviant or morally dangerous people; if they fail to do this job, they are committing a moral crime. Physical and sexual abuse of children, particularly by their parents, is a threat to social stability and the idea of the family as a good and caring setting. Child abuse in families, therefore, must not happen. It must either be prevented by social workers (and therefore barely exist) or not exist at all. Social workers' vilification by the press and public is partly due to their role as welfare professionals in a society that is ambivalent about state welfare. It also reflects the particular role they play within state welfare systems, which includes both the care and the control of people whom the family or other state agencies cannot help and who may be regarded as difficult or deviant.

Taking the child protection role of social workers as an example, social workers tend to feel that they should not always take the blame in cases where children are abused or die. The situation is complex: resource constraints mean that social workers cannot always provide the services required; decisions regarding how to handle children at risk are usually taken by interprofessional groups at case reviews and are a shared responsibility; and assessing the nature of risk of child abuse is an uncertain art and even the most skilled and competent professionals who follow all the guidelines and procedures may find that a child dies. Obviously, if workers fail to follow the procedures correctly or neglect to carry out specified duties, then they are culpable. Yet if a worker does the best she can in the circumstances, surely she should not be blamed?

In a provocative article, Hollis and Howe (1990) argue that taking on the job of a social worker is rather like being asked to drive a car in the knowledge that its brakes are faulty. If someone takes on the role of social worker, then she must expect and accept moral blame when bad outcomes occur (as they inevitably will). Yet this analogy does not capture the complexity of social work practice. First, while this may not exonerate the social worker, it is important to note that it is not her job to service the car. Second, while she may be in the driving seat, there are plenty of others in the car map-reading or directing. Third, while objective observers like Hollis and Howe may claim that the brakes are faulty, the rest of society regards such a state as the norm, and is certainly not prepared to pay to improve the brakes. If social workers take moral responsibility, they are, in effect, allowing others to scapegoat them and avoid taking blame, and hence to avoid recognizing the variety of contributing factors that cause a child's death and the need to change some of these factors. Also, if social workers always take the blame for outcomes that are largely outside their control, they become personally and professionally undermined and stressed. It may be appropriate to take some responsibility, and hence blame, but certainly not all of it. Otherwise the retreat into 'defensive' social work (following rules and procedures) becomes even more necessary and appealing as a survival strategy.

One of the purposes of this book is to enable social workers to gain an understanding of the nature of ethical decision-making and hence to feel less unnecessary guilt and blame for the outcomes of decisions and actions with which they are involved. Very often in connection with ethical challenges in social work (and indeed the caring professions generally), the term 'dilemma' is used. As has already been noted, a dilemma is usually defined along the lines of 'a choice between two equally unwelcome alternatives', which seems to sum up quite well how it often feels to be a professional in a 'no-win' situation. Let us consider a child protection case, as briefly outlined in Case example 1.5.

Practice focus

Case example 1.5: A case review meeting about a child at risk

The father of a young baby has been violent to his partner (the baby's 17-year-old mother) on several occasions in the past. Recently the baby has suffered bruising three times. The mother explains that the baby fell from his cot twice and on one occasion her partner accidentally dropped him. Despite input from a social worker and health visitor, it has not proved possible to support the parents to any great extent in coping with looking after the baby. The social worker has been working with the mother for over a year, during which time the couple have split up several times. When the father is not present, the mother seems to cope quite well. The social worker is keen to give the young mother a chance to look after the baby, but is concerned about the risk to the child from the father. A case review meeting with the parents and the various professionals involved is called to consider what to do to ensure the baby is protected.

Very many factors will be taken into account during the case review in coming to a decision about what level of intervention is necessary and possible as well as legally and ethically justified in order to protect the baby. The professionals will be mindful of the infringement of parental rights and the potential damage and unhappiness that may be caused if the child is removed from the family. Yet if the child remains with the family, there is a chance that the child will suffer physical abuse from the father and may be injured or even die. The way to resolve the dilemma as identified above is to try to work out whether one of the alternatives is more unwelcome than the other and then act on that. Of course, participants in the case review also need to try to work out how likely it is that each of the unwelcome outcomes will occur, using various protocols and procedures for assessing and predicting risk. They might decide that it is more unwelcome (indeed, it would be tragic) for the child to die, than to be unhappy.

However, let us assume that the consensus of opinion at the case review is that it is highly unlikely that the father will seriously injure or kill the child. Participants also judge that there is scope for more intensive work with the parents to improve their parenting skills and to cope with some of the pressures that may lead to the baby suffering further harm. So it is decided to leave the child with the family. The professionals involved know it is a risk – a moral risk as well as a technical one – which is why the situation is described as a dilemma. There are not welcome outcomes, only less unwelcome ones; when the choice is the lesser of two evils, whichever one chooses is an 'evil'. This is a constant problem for the social workers and other professionals involved such cases. If the professionals have carefully thought through all aspects of the dilemma, and made a decision to act in order to try to avoid the worst outcome, then they have acted with professional integrity.

I will return to the issue of the guilt and blame felt by social workers in Chapter 7, in the light of the more detailed discussion of ethical and value issues in the next few chapters. In the meantime, the case for discussion at the end of this chapter gives an account of a case from Austria where a child died and the lead child protection social worker was found guilty by a court of neglecting her professional duties, given a suspended sentence and fined.

Conclusions

This chapter has set the scene for the discussion of questions of ethics in social work. I have argued that ethical problems and dilemmas are inherent in the practice of social work. The reasons for this arise from its role as a public service profession dealing with vulnerable and marginalized service users who need to be able to trust the worker and be protected from exploitation; and also from its position in many countries as part of state welfare provision, which is itself based on contradictory aims and values – care and control, capital accumulation and legitimation, protection of individual rights and promotion of public welfare – which cause tensions, dilemmas and conflicts. The current 'crises' of welfare capitalism, which entail a questioning of the role of state welfare, are increasing the tensions and dilemmas for social workers, who often find themselves the victims of media attacks and public blame. It was argued that this blame is often unjustified and it is important that social workers both understand the essential tensions in their role and consider how moral decisions are actually made in social work, in order that they are not consumed by unnecessary guilt about the unfortunate, tragic, or unwanted outcomes of cases in which they have been involved.

Putting it into practice

Identifying ethical issues

Aims of the exercise: to encourage readers to identify ethical issues in their own practice and to reflect on and clarify their own ethical stance.

1. Briefly describe a situation/incident/event in your experience as a practitioner that raised ethical challenges for you.
2. List the ethical issues involved in this situation.
3. What does your view of this situation/event tell you about the important values and ethical principles that underpin your practice as a social worker?

Practice focus

Case for discussion 1: A social worker is fined in a high-profile child abuse case in Austria[1]

A 17-month-old boy died of a brain oedema (swelling) in a hospital in Austria. Several months before his death, the boy was given medical treatment in two different hospitals. Suspicions were aroused that he might be subject to ill-treatment and sexual abuse. So the child protection team based in one of the hospitals, in accordance with its legal responsibility, informed the local childcare agency about its concerns. The childcare agency has a responsibility to assess and monitor cases where children are thought to be at risk.

When the childcare agency is informed about a case of suspected child abuse or neglect, it then follows prescribed standards for risk assessment. Two social workers have to contact the parent(s). Following this meeting, the case must be discussed with a supervisor at the start and at the end of the casework process, as a minimum. The social worker on the case must have personal contact with the child (at least once) and with the legal guardians (at least once). In the case of children under six years old, compulsory home visits have to be made. All children under three years old must be referred to a physician. The casework process must be accurately documented.

In this case, meetings were organized between childcare social workers and the boy, his mother and his mother's new boyfriend. The boyfriend lived in another district, which meant that a second childcare agency was also involved. This complicated the assessment process. There was some exchange of information with the hospitals involved and between the two childcare agencies in order to manage the risk assessment.

The boy's father, who was living separately from the family, had contact on several occasions with the childcare agency because he had a suspicion that the boy was being ill-treated by the mother's new boyfriend.

The doctors at the hospitals to which the boy had been sent, at the request of the mother, on two previous occasions did not

1. I am grateful to Gertraud Pantucek and Maria Maiss for providing this case and to Maria Moritz of Österreichischen Berufsverbands für SozialarbeiterInnen (OBDS, Austrian Association of Professional Social Workers) for additional information. Further details can be found at http://tirol.orf.at/stories/364104/ and the OBDS website: www.sozialarbeit.at/index.php?option=com_content&task=view&id=312&Itemid=427.

confirm the suspicion of ill-treatment by the new boyfriend. The boy's mother denied the suspicion. She explained that her son's wounds were caused by accidents.

The leading childcare agency decided that the risk for the child was not high enough to remove the child from the family. Instead, the mother was forbidden to visit her new boyfriend with the child, but the boyfriend was allowed to visit them both at their home.

This relatively 'mild' condition placed on the family was based on what is written down in the Austrian child protection law, which forms the basis of two core values followed within the childcare assessment process:

- Safeguarding the endangered child in an effective way by using the mildest method of intervention, in order to protect the parents' rights as legal guardians.
- Using the mildest method is judged necessary in order not to endanger cooperation between the social worker and parent(s) and others involved (new partners, grandparents).

Nevertheless, even the 'mildest method' (the condition that the mother and child should not visit the new boyfriend together) has to be monitored. This puts pressure on the family and endangers the cooperation built primarily on trust. It is not known how closely the condition was monitored in this case.

When the boy was hospitalized for the third time, he was so seriously injured that he died two days later. Following the court case, the boyfriend was sentenced to life imprisonment in an institution for mentally disordered offenders, for sexually abusing and causing the death of the boy. The boy's mother was sentenced to one year in prison for child neglect. Finally, for the first time in Austria, the social worker from the childcare agency who had worked with the family also stood trial and was given a suspended sentence and a fine of €1,200 for 'neglecting' to provide the professional help required. The social worker's supervisor appeared in court as a witness and confirmed that the social worker had followed all the steps of the assessment process correctly.

In the media reports on the verdicts, the Austrian Association of Professional Social Workers argued against charging social workers, denied that social workers were guilty, asked for the responsibility of other professionals involved to be taken into account and demanded additional resources in order to establish better working conditions.

As a direct consequence of this case, more crisis intervention centres, child protection teams in hospitals, and an obligatory period of fieldwork for young lawyers in childcare agencies have been installed. Furthermore, the childcare agency introduced a workshop for social workers on the following topic: how to protect and defend yourself in case of being on trial. This is a consequence of the fact that the pressure caused by negative and one-sided media reports led to a growing fear among social workers of being made publicly responsible for mistakes concerning the selection of interventions that could be judged to be too mild. This led to a significant increase in the removal of children from their families too quickly.

Afterword

After an appeal, the case was then heard by the supreme court. This process took almost a year. The social worker was found 'not guilty' by the higher court and the sentence imposed on the social worker was cancelled. There was very little coverage of this decision in the media.

Questions for discussion

1. What ethical issues does this case raise?
2. Do you think social workers who are judged to have neglected to fulfil their professional responsibilities in the way described here should be subject to fines and (potentially) prison sentences? What do you think should be counted as 'neglect of professional responsibilities'?
3. Do you agree with all or some of the arguments and demands of the Austrian Association of Professional Social Workers?
4. Why do you think there was little media coverage when the social worker was found 'not guilty'?
5. Although this case happened in Austria, do you recognize common features with similar cases in your own country?

Further resources

Dominelli, L. (2004) *Social Work: Theory and Practice for a Changing Profession*, Oxford, Polity Press.
Overview of the nature of social work, taking a global perspective, in the context of current uncertainties and challenges. Argues for a new relationship between social workers and service users based on ideas of citizenship, solidarity and reciprocity.

Smith, R. (2005) *Values and Practice in Children's Services*, Basingstoke, Palgrave Macmillan.
Offers a useful discussion of the different value positions inherent in laissez-faire and interventionist approaches to child protection, an account of practice dilemmas and a framework for action.

Warnock, M. (1998) *An Intelligent Person's Guide to Ethics*, London, Duckworth.
Written by a moral philosopher, who has herself been involved in the UK public policy-making process, and designed to introduce the layperson to ethical thinking covering topics such as death, birth, rights and freedom.

CHAPTER 2

Principle-based approaches to social work ethics

CHAPTER OVERVIEW

In this chapter I will discuss the nature of 'principles', give examples of principle-based ethics relevant for social work (Kantian, utilitarian and radical approaches), and consider the potential of a combined common morality approach to ethics that draws on principles relating to respect for human dignity and worth, the promotion of human welfare and promotion of social justice. The chapter concludes with an exercise to encourage reflection on ethical principles, and a case for discussion about a social worker using deception to 'rescue' an abused girl in Iran.

Introduction

This chapter and the next will explore a number of approaches that have been or could be taken to theorizing about ethics in social work. There are many ways of categorizing theoretical approaches to ethics. For the purposes of this discussion, I will divide the approaches into two broad kinds: those that focus on principles of action, which will be the subject of this chapter; and those that pay more attention to the character of the moral agents and their relationships with each other, which will be covered in the next chapter. I will draw on some of the theories of ethics developed by moral philosophers and on literature in other areas of professional ethics, particularly healthcare, to develop ideas that are less well explored in the context of social work. Some caution must be exercised in relating theories of moral philosophy to professional ethics. When writers on professional ethics talk of 'Kantian' or 'utilitarian' approaches, they are not necessarily taking on board the whole of the ethical theories of Kant or utilitarianism, but rather suggesting that their approaches to professional ethics have connections with some of the basic orientations to ethics found in those theories. The aim of these two chapters is to point out some of these connections to help to clarify the nature of different approaches to social work ethics.

The place of religious ethics

This chapter and Chapter 3 focus on the theoretical approaches to ethics that are most commonly drawn upon in the literature on social work ethics, which is largely a western literature, with a secular orientation. There are many more approaches that could be covered, including normative theories derived from many of the world's religions (see Holm and Bowker, 1994; Schweiker, 2005a; Singer, 1993). As noted in the Introduction, religions comprise many components, one of which may be a set of precepts about how to lead a good life (Schweiker, 2005b). In Christianity, for example, there are the Ten Commandments, in Islam the guidance found in the Qur'an, and in Buddhism the various precepts found in the Noble Eightfold Path. In developing a normative theory of ethics (a theory that prescribes what we ought to do) based on a religious tradition, some theorists may focus on these duties and develop systems of principles that underlie them. For example, Sardar (in Anees et al., 1992, quoted in Bennett, 1994, p. 108) argues that the eternal principles underlying Islamic codes include unity, human trusteeship, justice, worship, knowledge and public interest. Religious traditions also advocate certain goals or ends for human beings, which might include states such as happiness or blessedness, or qualities of character, such as the Buddhist virtues of unselfishness, benevolence and understanding (Keown, 2005, p. 292). In many religious traditions there are disputes between thinkers who prioritize duties, principles and rules and those who prioritize qualities of character and relationships (Schweiker, 2005b, p. 22).

One significant difference between religious and secular approaches to normative theories of ethics is that, in religious ethics, the authority for the principles is derived from God or some other spiritual source. In secular ethics, it may be derived from reason, intuition or cultural norms. Much early social work in the West was provided by religious organizations, motivated by Christian values. However, as social work professionalized and secularized and state involvement developed, overt reference to Christian values tended to be reduced, except in specific religious organizations offering social work.

Nevertheless, religious traditions clearly inform social mores and laws and hence also the construction of social work, as well as influencing the moral codes and actions of individuals, even in largely secular societies. In some parts of the world, the distinction between religious and secular life is scarcely applicable, as 'religious' beliefs and practices are deeply embedded in everyday life, as Mbiti (1989) argues in an African context (see also Gbadegesin, 2005). The separation of 'ethics' as an area of life and a topic for study is arguably a western construction.

In this chapter on principle-based approaches, I will focus on the kinds of modern liberal principles, based on assumptions of the individual as the fundamental unit in society, that underlie the majority of the literature on social work ethics. While presented as universal, these do not reflect the religious and cultural beliefs of people in many parts of the world where the extended family, tribe or community is the focus of attention and the notion of individual rights makes much less sense. Arguably, some of the approaches to ethics outlined in Chapter 3 (based on qualities of character and interpersonal relationships) fit better with more communal approaches to ethics, as do elements of the radical and anti-oppressive approaches in social work, covered towards the end of this chapter.

Principles

The most common approach to professional ethics is to articulate a set of general ethical principles that give guidance about how professionals should act. According to Beauchamp (1996, p. 80), a principle is:

> a fundamental standard of conduct on which many other standards and judgements depend. A principle is an essential norm in a system of thought or belief, forming a basis of moral reasoning in that system.

It is important to distinguish a principle from a rule, which is much more specific and narrower in scope. For example, 'respect people's rights to self-determination' would count as a principle because its scope is broad, in that it applies to all people in all circumstances. 'Respect the rights of service users to consult files', on the other hand, is more specific, in that it applies to people in a social work context who wish to see their files, and would therefore be regarded as a rule. Principle-based theories of ethics usually construe ethical reasoning and decision-making as a rational process of applying principles and derived rules to particular cases and/or justifying action with reference to relevant rules and principles (for clear examples of such approaches in medical and nursing ethics, see Beauchamp and Childress, 2009; Edwards, 1996). I will briefly look at three principle-based approaches, of which the first two can be loosely linked with Kantian and utilitarian approaches in moral philosophy, and the third with radical and anti-oppressive approaches in social work.

Respect and autonomy in the social work relationship: duty-based principles

Much of the literature on social work values and ethics has focused on lists of principles about how the social worker ought to treat the individual service user. Such lists of principles are often underpinned by one basic or ultimate principle formulated as 'respect for persons', which, it has been argued, is the foundation of social work ethics, and, indeed, any system of moral thinking (Plant, 1970). In western secular literature, this principle tends to be linked with Immanuel Kant (1724–1804), a German philosopher whose work is the main reference point for modern deontological (duty-based) theories of ethics. Kant developed his ethical theory based on the authority of reason. However, similar kinds of 'golden rule' can be identified in many religious traditions worldwide, ranging from Judaism's 'What is hateful to you, do not do unto your fellow human' to the Sikh principle 'No one is my enemy, and no one is a stranger. I get along with everyone' (Inter Faith Network for the UK, 2004).

Kant and respect for persons

Kant was one of the most influential philosophers of the Enlightenment period in eighteenth-century Europe. This was a time of growing urbanization, emerging industrialization and political revolutions, accompanied by the growth of systematized scientific knowledge, a questioning of religious authority and traditional and mythological modes of thinking. While the response of the British empiricist philosophers (particularly the Scottish thinkers, Hutcheson, Hume and Smith) was to develop theories of morality based on human sentiment and the emotions, Kant developed a moral philosophy based on human reason, founded on the ultimate principle of respect for persons.

Kant formulated his principle of respect for persons as a categorical imperative, that is, a command that must be adhered to, one version of which is: 'So act as to treat humanity, whether in your own person or that of any other, never solely as a means but always also as an end' (Kant, [1785]1964, p. 96). By this he meant that we should treat others as beings who have ends, that is, choices and desires, not just as objects or a means to our own ends. The individual person is intrinsically worthy of respect simply because she or he is a person, regardless of whether we like the person, whether they are useful to us or whether they have behaved badly towards us. According to Kantian philosophy, a 'person' is a being who is capable of rational thought and self-determined action, where 'rational' means the ability to give reasons for actions, and 'self-determining' entails having the ability to make decisions and wact according to one's own choices and desires. 'Respect' can be regarded as 'active sympathy' towards another human being (Downie and Telfer, 1969, 1980).

It is this aspect of Kantian moral philosophy, the principle of respect for persons, that has been the most influential in social work ethics. It focuses on the content of morality, explicitly stating how we should treat other people. Other features of Kant's theory are also important in relation to professional ethics. He did, in fact, formulate several other versions of his categorical imperative, one of which focuses on the importance of consistency and 'universalizability' in the form of moral judgements: 'Act only on that maxim through which you can at the same time will that it should become a universal law' (Kant, [1785]1964, p. 88). The example of promise-keeping can be used to illustrate this point. In order to obtain a loan, I may be tempted to promise to repay the money borrowed, although I have no intention of doing so. The maxim I might act on in this case might be something along the lines of: 'I will make a false promise if it will get me out of difficulty.' However, if I ask whether I could consistently will that this should become a universal principle applying to everybody, Kant's answer would be 'no'. For if everybody made false promises, the whole institution of promise-keeping would collapse and there would be no basis for obtaining loans at all. So if I could not will that everybody should do this, then such an action would be morally wrong. It is important to stress that, for Kant, making false promises is not wrong because of the consequences if everyone did so. Rather, his argument is that it would be logically inconsistent to will that everyone should do it, because I would then be making a promise in a world where promise-keeping no longer functioned.

This highlights an important feature of Kantian ethics, the stress on rationality and the importance of the will. According to Kant, the only good action is one that is done from a sense of duty – as opposed to inclination. We work out what is our duty through a process of logical reasoning. We are, like all our fellow human beings, rational and autonomous, that is, we are free to make our own decisions and choices; we ourselves make the moral law and give it to ourselves. However, this does not entail absolute freedom to act on desires or whims, nor on choices that are solely beneficial to ourselves as individuals. It is about acting on principles that we could will as universal laws – what O'Neill (2002, pp. 73–95) calls 'principled autonomy'.

There have been numerous criticisms as well as many defences and developments of Kantian ethics (for brief summaries, see Arrington, 1998, pp. 262–94; Norman, 1998, pp. 70–91; for the debate in social work, see Downie, 1989; Webb and McBeath, 1989, 1990). Many of the criticisms have tended to focus on Kant's formalism – his stress on the form of moral judgements as universalizable and consistent – at the expense of the content of morality, and on his moral absolutism (for example that lying is always wrong) and his stress on doing one's duty for its own sake as the only morally worthy motive. Few ethicists have developed in any detail a wholly Kantian approach to social work ethics, although Bowie's (1999) application of Kantian moral philosophy to business ethics gives some idea of how it might be achieved.

Discourse ethics as a development of Kantian ethics

'Discourse ethics', as developed by the contemporary German philosopher and social theorist Habermas (1929–), is sometimes discussed in the social work literature (Blaug, 1995; Gray and Lovatt, 2007; Houston, 2010; Hugman, 2005, pp. 125–39). Discourse ethics is also a formal system, developed from Kantian ethics, based on universal principles of moral reasoning enabling us to reach consensus on generalizable maxims (Habermas, 1990, pp. 116–94). However, Habermas's theory moves on from the Kantian notion of moral agents as individuals working out their moral duties in isolation, to a recognition of the intersubjective nature of morality, seeing universal moral principles as those that are validated in an ideal system of rational discourse, which would allow everyone concerned a 'fair' hearing and remove the distorting domination of wealth and power. These presuppositions, formulated as rules of discourse by Habermas (1990, p. 89, with original numbering of rules amended), are:

(1) Every subject with the competence to speak and act is allowed to take part in a discourse.
(2) a. Everyone is allowed to question any assertion whatsoever.
    b. Everyone is allowed to introduce any assertion whatever into the discourse.
    c. Everyone is allowed to express his attitudes, desires and needs.
(3) No speaker may be prevented, by internal or external coercion, from exercising his rights as laid down in (1) and (2).

According to Vetelsen (1994, p. 296), the basic principle of ethical validity is 'formulated in terms of *rational, universal* and *uncoerced consensus*'. Accordingly, only those norms that could be agreed to by all concerned participants in a practical discourse may claim validity (Habermas, 1990, p. 93). Habermas's speech situation is an ideal one, but, he argues, in accomplishing a speech act, we act as if it were real.

Given that a key feature of discourse ethics is intersubjective communication, based on structures that promote rational consensus, such as allowing everyone concerned a 'fair' hearing and removing the distorting domination of wealth and power, it is not surprising that it has been suggested that it may have promise for the social professions. Several writers on social work ethics have proposed developing a discourse ethics with more content than simply the formal rules of communication, sometimes aligning it with virtue ethics, or at least arguing that moral deliberation along the lines proposed by Habermas enhances virtue in social work (Gray and Lovatt, 2007; Houston 2003, 2010).

Respect for persons and the social work relationship

In social work, the main element of Kantian moral philosophy that has been influential is the principle of respect for persons, which has been used to underpin a set of general principles relating to the relationship between the individual social worker and service user. The lists of principles of the social worker–service user relationship developed for social work are often adaptations or modifications of the seven principles developed by Biestek, an American Catholic priest, in the late 1950s (Biestek, 1961, first published in 1957). These principles have been surprisingly influential, especially given two factors. First, Biestek did not intend them as ethical principles per se. Indeed, he seemed to regard them primarily as principles for effective practice – instrumental to the social worker's purpose of 'helping the client achieve a better adjustment between himself and his environment' (Biestek, 1961, p. 12). Second, his emphasis was primarily on the voluntary one-to-one casework relationship, where the service user initiates the contact by coming to the agency and relates individually to a social worker. This is somewhat removed from the complexities of modern social work, which may include compulsory intervention within a statutory framework and work with families, groups and communities. However, since the principles have been so influential, it may be useful to summarize them here.

List 2.1 A summary of Biestek's casework principles

1. *Individualization* is the recognition of each service user's unique qualities, based upon the rights of human beings to be treated not just as a human being but as this human being.
2. *Purposeful expression of feelings* is the recognition of service users' need to express their feelings (especially negative ones) freely. The caseworker should listen purposefully without condemnation and provide encouragement when therapeutically useful.
3. *Controlled emotional involvement* is the caseworker's sensitivity to service users' feelings, an understanding of their meaning and a purposeful, appropriate response to them.
4. *Acceptance* entails the caseworker perceiving and dealing with service users as they really are, including their strengths and weaknesses, congenial and uncongenial qualities, maintaining throughout a sense of their innate dignity and personal worth.
5. *Nonjudgemental attitude* entails that it is not part of the casework function to assign guilt or innocence or degrees of service user responsibility for causation of problems, although evaluative judgements can be made about the attitudes, standards or actions of service users, that is, the caseworker does not judge service users themselves, but their behaviour.
6. *Service user self-determination* is the recognition of the right and need of service users to freedom in making their own choices and decisions in the casework process. Caseworkers have a duty to respect that need and help activate service users' potential for

self-direction. Biestek stresses, however, that service users' rights to self-determination are limited by their capacity for positive and constructive decision-making, by civil and moral law and by the function of the agency.

7. *Confidentiality* is the preservation of secret information concerning the service user which is disclosed in the professional relationship. Biestek describes confidentiality as based upon a basic right of service users and as an ethical obligation for the social worker, as well as being essential for effective casework service. However, service users' rights are not absolute and may be limited by a higher duty to self, and by the rights of other individuals, the social worker, agency or community.

Source: Adapted from Biestek, 1961

During the 1960s and 70s, many other theorists adopted modified versions of Biestek's list of principles, often with the addition of the ultimate or basic principle of 'respect for persons' (see, for example, Butrym, 1976; CCETSW, 1976; Moffet, 1968; Plant, 1970; Ragg, 1977). A key theme running through all these principles could be identified as the Kantian theme of *respect for the individual person as a self-determining being*. It is significant that the first principle on the list, and one which was taken on board by all the other writers mentioned, is 'individualization' – the recognition of each service user's unique qualities based upon the right of human beings to be treated as individuals with personal differences. The other important principle that has also been adopted by all the other writers is 'service user self-determination' – a recognition of service users' rights to freedom in making their own decisions and choices. Many of the subsequent writers did, in fact, include in their lists the basic or ultimate principle of 'respect for persons', and although Biestek himself did not include this, his principles are compatible with it. Some of Biestek's principles directly follow from this ultimate principle, not just service user self-determination, but also acceptance, nonjudgementalism and confidentiality. Accepting a service user as she is, rather then stereotyping or categorizing, is obviously part of respecting the innate worth and dignity of every human being. Similarly with nonjudgementalism – the social worker should not judge the person as unworthy, evil or inadequate. Breaking confidence would violate the principle of respect for persons, because it would entail not respecting the service user's wishes – treating her, perhaps, as a means to an end.

Commentators on social work ethics and values in the 1980s tended to be critical of the 'list approach' and the focus solely on the nature of the social worker–service user relationship. There are a number of reasons why the kinds of lists of principles suggested by Biestek and others have been regarded as unsatisfactory. First, such broad general principles can be variously interpreted, and there are confusions both within and between writers using the same terminology. McDermott (1975) indicates, for example, that the term 'self-determination' has been defined persuasively in social work and that the favourable connotations of freedom from constraint are used to justify what amounts to a recommendation that the social worker should decide what service users' real interests are and may be justified in promoting them against their will – a tendency that can be seen in Biestek's formulation. In fact, self-determination can mean all things to all people, from maintaining that each individual should be completely free to do whatever they want (a version of negative freedom, which might be associated with a libertarian interpretation of Kantian philosophy based on respect for persons), to justifying fairly large-scale intervention from the state to enable individuals to become more self-determining or self-realizing (a version of positive freedom that might be associated with Hegelian or Marxist ethics). Within social work, interpretations at the negative end of the spectrum would tend to advocate freedom from restraint unless another's interests are threatened; whereas on a more positive view, a further clause is often added, 'and/or unless the person's own interests are threatened'. The concepts of principled and relational autonomy developed more recently by moral philosophers and feminist theorists (see Mackenzie and Stoljar, 2000; O'Neill, 2002) are attempts to reclaim 'autonomy' as a concept from the clutches of an extreme libertarian, individualistic and masculinist political philosophy.

Similar problems regarding meaning arise for the principles of nonjudgementalism, acceptance and confidentiality. For example, Stalley (1978) argues that nonjudgementalism appears to be about refraining from making moral judgements about a person's character, yet, at the same time, social workers have a responsibility to society to help service users, and to maintain their own moral integrity by making moral judgements. This raises the question of where we draw the lines around these principles, which can only be answered in relation to other principles within a more systematic framework of moral beliefs and principles. This is complicated by the second difficulty arising from such lists of principles, namely, that very little indication is given of the status of the different principles. Some appear to be methods for effective practice (for example purposeful expression of feelings), others might be regarded as professional standards (for example confidentiality), others might be classified as general moral principles (such as self-determination) and one (respect for persons) has been characterized as the basic presupposition of any morality.

A third criticism of lists of principles is based on the fact that many writers do not rank the principles and no indication is given of what to do in cases of conflicting principles. We may well ask what criteria are to be used for judging whether to promote a service user's self-determination at the expense of revealing a confidential secret. Some theorists do state, following Downie and Telfer (1969), that their sets of principles follow directly from one ultimate principle, respect for persons. If this were the case, then respect for persons could be referred to in cases of conflict. However, apart from Plant (1970), and to some extent the Central Council for Education and Training in Social Work (CCETSW, 1976), little detail is given as to how respect for persons can actually be used to justify the other principles, or how it can be used in actual moral decision-making to arbitrate between principles. While Downie and Telfer do articulate a moral system for social work based on respect for persons, they do not derive from it the kinds of principles suggested by Biestek as relevant to social work. This may not be surprising, since these principles, if regarded as moral principles, are certainly not complete for social work. Indeed, as Biestek envisaged them, they were more a set of principles for effective casework, focusing on the *content of the relationship* – how the individual service user should be treated by the social worker. Insofar as moral matters were involved for Biestek, these centred around notions of individual rights/liberties, rather than the questions of social justice and responsibility, which attention to the *context of the agency and society* generally would raise for the social worker.

Promoting welfare and justice in society: utilitarian principles

Writers on social work ethics in the later part of the twentieth century were critical of the lists of principles focusing on the individual worker–service user relationship within a broadly Kantian ethical framework, pointing out that other types of moral principles also influence social work practice (Banks, 1990; Clark, 2000; Clark with Asquith, 1985; Horne, 1999; Rhodes, 1986). Social workers are not autonomous professionals whose guiding ethical principles are solely about respecting and promoting the self-determination of service users. They are usually employed by agencies, work within the constraints of legal and procedural rules and must also work to promote the public good or the wellbeing of society in general. Other types of ethical principles concerned with utility (promoting the greatest good) and justice (distributing the good(s) as widely and/or fairly as possible) are important. There may be conflicts between the rights or interests of different people, for example a parent and a child, a confused older man and his carer. Within a Kantian framework, it is difficult to decide whose right to self-determination has priority. The Kantian approach also advocates always following one's duty, no matter what the outcome. For example, lying is always wrong, because it would involve manipulating people and failing to treat them with proper respect – even if by lying a life could be saved. Such an approach fails to take account of how social workers actually do behave. Very often they have to look to the consequences of their actions and weigh up which action would be least harmful or most beneficial to a particular service user, and which action would benefit most people or use resources most efficiently. This kind of ethical theory has been termed 'utilitarianism' (see Mill, [1863]1972; Shaw, 1999), which is the most well-known type of consequentialist theory – where morality is based on weighing up the consequences of actions.

J.S. Mill and utilitarianism

The systematic development of utilitarianism is generally associated with Jeremy Bentham (1748–1832) and John Stuart Mill (1806–73), British philosophers and social reformers. The basic idea of utilitarianism is that the right action is that which produces the greatest balance of good over evil – the principle of utility. However, so many philosophers have added so many qualifications and modifications to enable this doctrine to capture more and more of our ordinary conceptions of morality that any discussion of what is known as utilitarianism becomes complicated. First, Bentham (1789) and some recent philosophers equate the good with happiness (the sum of pleasures) and the bad with unhappiness (the sum of pains), espousing what has been called *hedonistic utilitarianism* (see Plamenatz, 1966; Smart and Williams, 1973). Others, notably Mill ([1863]1972), claim that the good consists of other things besides happiness (for example virtue, knowledge, truth, beauty), a view known as *ideal utilitarianism*. Second, some philosophers espouse what has been called *act utilitarianism*, which involves deciding the rightness of each action with reference directly to the principle of utility (Smart and Williams, 1973). Others advocate *rule utilitarianism*, claiming that we do in fact use rules to speed up the process of moral reasoning and decision-making, and that the rules themselves are tested and justified with reference to the principle of utility (Downie, 1971). For example, we adhere to the rule of promise-keeping despite the fact that on some occasions it might produce a greater balance of evil over good, because promise-keeping as a whole generally produces good. This has often been regarded as the most plausible account of utilitarianism and not surprisingly tends to result in the articulation of rules and principles, such as promise-keeping, truth-telling, not stealing, respecting autonomy, that would also be prominent in a Kantian system. However, utilitarians would have less tendency to regard these rules as absolute in the way Kant did. They would test their efficacy against the consequences they tend to produce and they might be more willing to admit of exceptions if this resulted in greater utility.

However, the principle of utility on its own tells us nothing about whose good we should promote, that is, about the distribution of the good. If we could choose between an action that produced a large amount of good (let us assume we are talking about happiness) for two people and nothing for eight people, and an action that produced slightly less total happiness, but distributed it equally between ten people, would we choose the former? This led Bentham to introduce his proviso – everyone to count for one and no one for more than one – and to Mill's formulation of the principle of utility as the greatest good for the greatest number. Here we seem to have a principle against which conflicts between derived principles and rules (if we are rule utilitarians) or between particular actions (if we are act utilitarians) can be decided. However, as critics have pointed out, we now have, in effect, two principles, utility (urging us to produce as much good as possible) and justice (as equality of treatment, urging us to distribute it as widely as possible), which themselves may conflict. As Raphael (1981) suggests, the most difficult conflicts in life are between these two principles: he gives the example of whether the government should give large grants to engineering students in the national interest (utility) or the same amount to each student for the sake of fairness (justice). This difficulty does not mean that utilitarianism cannot be defended as a system of morality, but if we accept it, it does mean that it cannot be regarded as a system that is founded on one ultimate principle, which can be used to decide all conflicts between other principles, rules or alternative courses of action.

Contemporary utilitarianism

Utilitarianism in various forms has a number of modern adherents, who have attempted to develop more sophisticated and robust versions that can withstand the criticisms discussed earlier (see Shaw, 1999). As Driver (2009, pp. 16–17) comments, in the latter part of the twentieth century, many philosophers have tended to identify their theories as 'consequentialist' rather than 'utilitarian' in order to distance themselves from the classical utilitarianism of Bentham and Mill. One of the most well-known contemporary utilitarians is the philosopher Peter Singer, who espouses a version of utilitarianism known as *preference utilitarianism* (see also Hare, 1981). On this account, right actions are those that fulfil the interests or preferences of the parties involved. This includes not just human beings, but all sentient beings (including animals). However, the focus on preferences gives priority to beings capable of determining their interests, hence lower weight to children, people with impaired mental functioning or fetuses, for example. He develops a system for working out how the interests of living beings should be weighed against each other, and justifies different treatment for different interests. His views have generated a great deal of controversy, especially those on abortion, euthanasia and infanticide (Singer, 1994, 2011). For example, he argues that killing a newborn baby (who lacks rationality, autonomy and consciousness) can never be equivalent to killing a person (assuming a person is a being who wants to continue living). He also argues that people living in the developed world have a moral obligation to give to charitable causes that help relieve poverty and suffering in those parts of the world where it can make much more difference to the interests of human beings in terms of the avoidance of pain, needs for food and shelter and the pursuit of their own projects (Singer, 2009). Singer himself reports giving 25% of what he earns to NGOs, mainly Oxfam (www.princeton.edu/~psinger/faq.html).

Approaches to social work ethics that are explicitly and wholly utilitarian have not been well developed, partly because such approaches do not lend themselves to taking account of the personal relationship element of social work that has always been regarded as so crucial, and the weight given to the dignity of all humans, regardless of mental or other capacities. Although Downie and Telfer (1980) attempt to develop a form of ideal rule utilitarianism for social work and medicine, insofar as they ground this in the principle of respect for persons, I would categorize it more as a combined Kantian-utilitarian approach, which will be considered later in this chapter. However, in social work practice, the focus on outcomes, impact and risk assessment in practice ultimately draws on utilitarian values (promotion of individual and public welfare) as justification.

Commitments to emancipation and social justice: the challenge of radical and anti-oppressive principles

Both Kantian and utilitarian theories of ethics are premised on the assumption of the human being as a freely acting individual. Individuals are the basic unit of analysis, and they can make choices about how to act, and hence can and should take moral responsibility for their actions, for which they can be either praised or blamed. These theories of ethics reflect the twin values of freedom and individualism that lie at the heart of western capitalist societies. During the 1970s, a radical movement within social work developed based on a growing awareness that treating each service user as an individual and seeing the problems faced by that person, such as poverty, homelessness, mental illness, as belonging to them was, in effect, 'blaming the victims' for the structural inequalities in society. Radical social work at this time tended to be based on Marxist theory (see Corrigan and Leonard, 1978), which regards humans as essentially social beings and the idea of human freedom as a myth.

The literature on radical social work of the 1970s and 80s pays little attention to ethics per se. Indeed, Marx himself regarded morality as a 'bourgeois illusion', part of the prevailing ideology promoted by the ruling classes to control and dominate (see Lukes, 1987; Marx and Engels, [1848]1969). Further, a key theme of radical social work at that time, although not always expressed very clearly, is 'praxis', the notion of 'committed action'. On this view, it makes no sense to regard values, theory and practice as separate. The radical social work approach acknowledged social workers' role as agents of social control on behalf of an oppressive state, and called on them to raise the consciousness of the people they worked with, to encourage collective action for social change and build alliances with working-class and trade union organizations (Bailey and Brake, 1975; Brake and Bailey, 1980; Corrigan and Leonard, 1978; Galper, 1980). Although the radical social work literature of the 1970s and early 1980s did not itself seem to influence the literature on social work values and ethics of the same period, the broadening of the understanding of oppression created by the feminist and anti-racist movements of the 1980s began to find its way into the lists of social work values in the mid-1980s. While the contributions from feminist and anti-racist theorists are often highly critical of the Marxist-inspired radical social work, with its preoccupation with class at the expense of other social divisions (Ahmad, 1990; Day, 1992; Dominelli, 1997; Dominelli and McLeod, 1989; Shah, 1989), they can nevertheless be seen to have grown out of, and alongside, the radical social work movement of the 1970s. The collections of articles on radical social work in the 1980s included substantial contributions from feminist and black perspectives (Brake and Bailey, 1980; Langan and Lee, 1989).

While such approaches to social work have not been concerned with articulating ethical principles per se, a moral/political stance is embedded in the commitment to working for social change. The more recent literature on radical, anti-oppressive, structural and critical social work identifies values such as equality, collectivism/ community and social justice as central to emancipatory forms of social work (see, for example, Clifford and Burke, 2009; Dominelli, 2002; Ferguson, 2008; Ferguson and Woodward, 2009; Lavalette, 2011; Mullaly, 1997). Social justice in particular has been stressed in social work and in its broadest interpretation also embraces equality in all its senses of equal treatment, access to services and equality of outcome or result. Social justice is based on the idea of distributing resources in society according to need (as opposed to desert or merit), challenging existing power structures and oppressive institutions and actions. The recent resurgence of radical social work, especially through the Social Work Action Network (www. socialworkfuture.org), formed in 2007 in Britain but with international membership, takes social justice as a key value and some of the literature takes some account of ethics. Ferguson (2008, p. 132), for example, speaks of 'reclaiming ethics'. In a slightly different vein, Clifford and Burke (2009) have developed a book-length account of anti-oppressive ethics, which draws on Marxist, structural analyses as well as identity-based and care ethics.

Insofar as anti-oppressive and emancipatory approaches to social work are based on structural analyses of society, then we can see them as fitting into principle-based approaches to ethics, which articulate universal, abstract principles. Other versions of anti-oppressive practice may be more focused on issues of identity, diversity and culture, including poststructuralist and discourse approaches (discussed in Chapter 3), or may balance structural and cultural approaches (critical postmodern approaches, also covered in Chapter 3; see Fook, 2002; Ife, 1999; Leonard, 1997; Pease and Fook, 1999). I will continue to use the term 'radical' to refer to approaches premised on a commitment to structural social change, which includes certain versions of 'anti-oppressive', 'emancipatory', 'critical' and 'transformatory' social work.

From the point of view of traditional social work, the early radical approaches were criticized for focusing less on the here and now – the immediate and pressing problems facing individuals – and more on the creation of a better society in the future. This might involve treating individual service users as a means to an end, and not respecting their own current expressions of needs and wants. In the short term, Marxist and neo-Marxist approaches could be interpreted as recommending a utilitarian approach – using people as a means to an end, for the greater good of humanity as a whole. However, more recent versions of radical and transformatory social work do propose working on micro-changes at an individual and local level (Adams et al., 2005; Clifford and Burke, 2009; Ferguson 2008; Langan and Lee, 1989, p. 8).

'Common morality' approaches to ethics

So far we have looked at three different theoretical approaches to ethics, each of which entails a focus on different types of principle. Beauchamp and Childress (2009), in their work on bioethics, propose what they call a 'common morality' approach based on four principles. I will briefly outline how they develop this within what I identify as a 'Kantian-utilitarian' framework, before going on to consider how such an approach in social work might also include 'radical' principles based around social justice.

Kantian-utilitarian principles

The earlier discussion of Kantian and utilitarian theories of ethics suggests that neither of these can furnish us with one ultimate principle for determining the rightness and wrongness of actions. Both Kantianism and utilitarianism, being idealized theoretical systems of morality, inevitably fail to take account of certain aspects of our ordinary moral thinking. The Kantian system tends to emphasize the individual person and their rights and duties, particularly the principles of liberty and justice (as desert); while utilitarianism stresses the notion of the public good, looking to the consequences of actions with respect to the principles of utility and justice (as equal treatment). Kantian ethical theory has a tendency to advocate rigidly following what is thought to be one's duty for its own sake, whereas utilitarianism focuses on amounts of good and evil in the abstract as opposed to the people who will experience the pleasure or whatever. Taken to its extreme, the Kantian doctrine might entail, for example, that, in a particular case, it was morally right to keep a promise even if this resulted in many people suffering, because the consequences or general utility would not be taken into account; whereas utilitarianism might entail that it was right to kill an innocent person for the good of society, because individual liberty would not be taken into account.

Insofar as Kantians and utilitarians have attempted to modify their views to account for such cases, they become less distinct, at least in practice, even though they may be unwilling to relinquish the basic emphasis of their outlook. Interestingly, in the field of professional ethics, several influential theorists have advocated an approach that combines Kantian and utilitarian principles, recognizing that, in our ordinary moral thinking, we do, in fact, draw on both. In *Caring and Curing*, which covers medicine and social work, Downie and Telfer (1980) advocate a form of ideal rule utilitarianism based on the ultimate principle of respect for persons. They argue that the principle of utility presupposes the principle of respect for persons. This argument is elaborated in their earlier book, *Respect for Persons* (1969, pp. 38–9). Taking Mill's formulation of the principle of utility (that right actions promote happiness), they claim that the reason we organize action to maximize happiness is because happiness matters; and it is unintelligible to suppose that happiness matters unless the people whose happiness is in question matter; and to say that they matter in this way is to say that they are objects of respect. The logic of Downie and Telfer's argument may be questioned. For example, we might ask whether individual persons are the only beings capable of experiencing happiness (what about groups or animals?) and indeed whether this sense of people mattering (being valued in themselves) is equivalent to being worthy of respect, which Downie and Telfer interpret as an active sympathy towards others as rational and self-determining agents. However, the important point to note is that they develop a framework for moral thinking that combines Kantian and utilitarian principles, such as liberty, equality, utility and fraternity (Downie, 1971), although by retaining respect for persons as the ultimate principle, they still seem to be propounding a foundationalist ethical theory, that is, an ethical theory grounded in one ultimate principle.

Beauchamp and Childress (2009), on the other hand, in developing a principle-based approach for bioethics, explicitly eschew such foundationalist aspirations. They advocate what they call a 'common morality' theory that is pluralistic (based on two or more non-absolute moral principles) and relies on 'ordinary shared moral beliefs' for its starting content (Beauchamp and Childress, 2009, p. 387). Any ethical theory that cannot be made consistent with the shared moral beliefs falls under suspicion. Beauchamp and Childress advocate four principles that they claim are usually accepted by rival moral theories: autonomy, beneficence, nonmaleficence and justice. These principles have been influential in medical and healthcare ethics and other related fields. Since a common morality approach has not been developed in any depth for social work, I will outline the four principles and briefly summarize Beauchamp and Childress's approach. The four principles are outlined in List 2.2.

List 2.2 Beauchamp and Childress's four principles of biomedical ethics

1. *Autonomy:* The obligation to respect the decision-making capacities of individual people.
2. *Nonmaleficence:* The obligation to avoid causing harm to others.
3. *Beneficence:* The obligation to provide benefits and balance benefits against risks.
4. *Justice:* Obligations of fairness in the distribution of benefits and risks.

Source: Based on Beauchamp and Childress, 2009

Although common morality ethics relies on ordinary shared beliefs for its content, Beauchamp and Childress stress that their principles are universal standards. They make use of Rawls' (1973, pp. 46–50) notion of 'considered judgements' as a starting point for ethical theory. These are the moral convictions in which we have the highest confidence and which we believe to have the lowest level of bias. Examples might include judgements about the wrongness of racial discrimination, religious intolerance and political repression. However, such judgements are only provisional fixed points and are liable to revision – a process Rawls terms 'reflective equilibrium'. This involves adjusting considered judgements so that they coincide and are rendered as coherent as possible. For example, there is a longstanding rule in medicine about putting the patient's interests first. Beauchamp and Childress (2009, p. 382) state that this needs to be made as coherent as possible with other considered judgements about clinical teaching responsibilities and responsibilities to patients' families.

Principles and rules will never be perfectly coherent and will certainly conflict. They also need to be interpreted (what meanings do they have?), specified (when and how do they apply?) and balanced (which should have priority in certain types of cases?). According to Beauchamp and Childress (2009, p. 384):

> moral thinking is analogous to the process of evaluating scientific statements such as hypotheses. Science is neither strictly inductivist (involving only observation and experimentation), nor strictly deductivist (using mathematics and a priori premises).

Following Ross's (1930) account of prima facie duties, they describe their four principles as prima facie principles, that is, we have a duty to uphold each of these principles unless it conflicts with or is overborne by another. When we face conflicts between, say, respecting a person's request for confidentiality (autonomy) and saving that person's life (beneficence), then we have to make a judgement that involves interpreting the principles in the light of this situation, specifying how and why they apply and balancing them against each other. There is no ultimate principle or set of rules that can tell us how to do this in every possible type of case.

Kantian-utilitarian-radical principles in social work

A common morality approach as such has not been explicitly developed for social work ethics in the level of detail offered by Beauchamp and Childress for bioethics. However, in the lists of ethical principles put forward for social work in recent literature, we can detect a range of principles of Kantian, utilitarian and radical origin, which are based on different underlying assumptions about the nature of human beings and society, have the potential for conflict and must be weighed against each other in making decisions in particular cases. Figure 2.1 summarizes the Kantian, utilitarian and radical approaches to social work ethics.

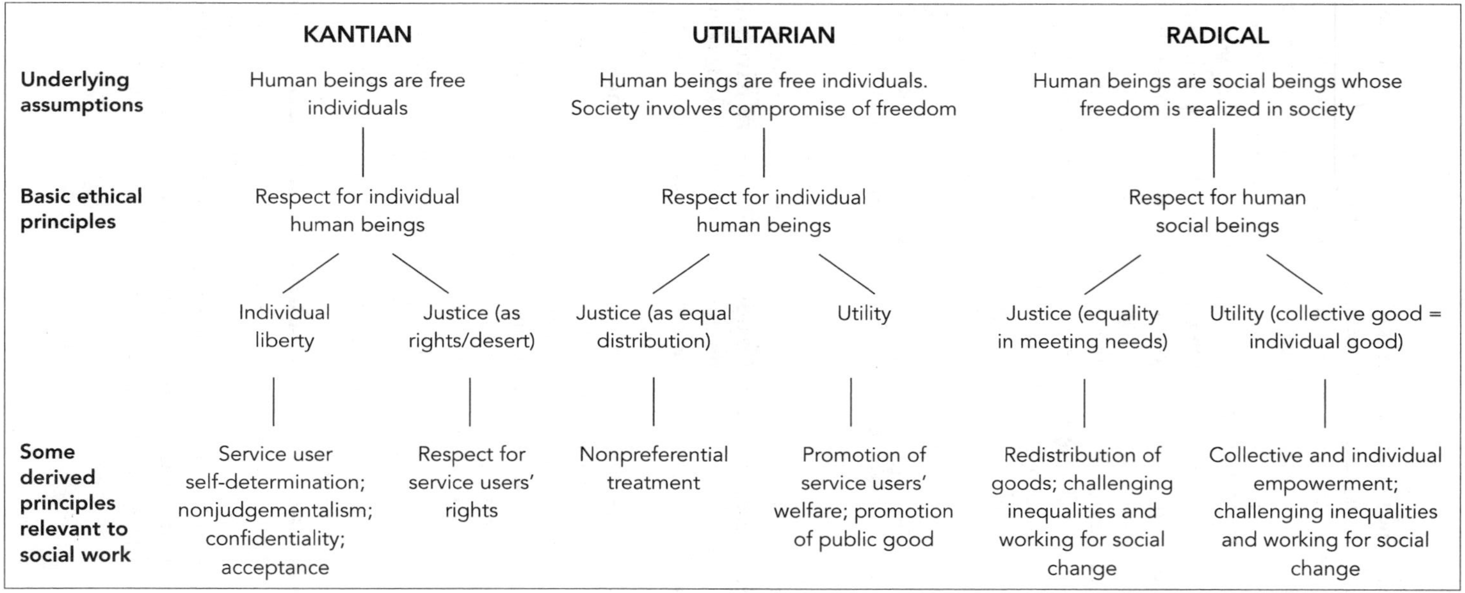

	KANTIAN	UTILITARIAN	RADICAL
Underlying assumptions	Human beings are free individuals	Human beings are free individuals. Society involves compromise of freedom	Human beings are social beings whose freedom is realized in society
Basic ethical principles	Respect for individual human beings	Respect for individual human beings	Respect for human social beings
	Individual liberty — Justice (as rights/desert)	Justice (as equal distribution) — Utility	Justice (equality in meeting needs) — Utility (collective good = individual good)
Some derived principles relevant to social work	Service user self-determination; nonjudgementalism; confidentiality; acceptance — Respect for service users' rights	Nonpreferential treatment — Promotion of service users' welfare; promotion of public good	Redistribution of goods; challenging inequalities and working for social change — Collective and individual empowerment; challenging inequalities and working for social change

Figure 2.1 Kantian, utilitarian and radical approaches to social work ethics

One difference between the kinds of principles proposed for medicine and healthcare more generally and those of social work is the stronger emphasis in social work on *social* justice, with radical overtones. According to the International Federation of Social Workers and the International Association of Schools of Social Work (IFSW/IASSW, 2004), principles of human rights and social justice lie at the heart of social work. Although the values and principles stated as important for social work in the professional literature and in codes of ethics vary in how they are expressed, I have identified three basic general principles that commonly occur. These are summarized in List 2.3. The principles are generic and complex, that is, they each could be regarded as clusters of related principles, and could be described as values (broad beliefs about the nature of the good society) as defined in the Introduction. However, I have presented them as principles (fundamental norms of action for putting values into practice) along the same lines as Beachamp and Childress's principles of biomedical ethics.

List 2.3 Ethical principles for social work

1. *Respect for the dignity and worth of all human beings:* The obligation to respect each human being as an individual, to treat all people as equally valuable and to respect and promote the human rights of individuals and groups to self-determination (particularly users of social worker services).
2. *Promotion of welfare or wellbeing:* The obligation to bring about benefits for service users and for society more generally, balancing benefits against risks of harm.
3. *Promotion of social justice:* The obligation to work to remove damaging inequalities between people and groups and to promote the fair distribution of goods and services among people and groups.

If we start to flesh out and interpret these principles, it soon becomes clear that each one contains a cluster of subprinciples and can be interpreted in many different ways.

Dignity and worth of all human beings
Dignity is a frequently used concept and has been categorized by Macklin (2003) as overused and 'a useless concept'. However, 'respect for dignity' is frequently stated as a principle in codes of ethics, and also underpins the UN Universal Declaration of Human Rights (1948). As Macklin states, it tends to be used in these kinds of contexts to mean 'respect for persons and their autonomy'. Indeed, this principle is reminiscent of Kant's ultimate principle of 'respect for persons', which entails treating people as ends in themselves and never as a means to an end. It entails that every human being should be treated in this way, regardless of who they are or what they have done. In Kant's scheme, the term 'person' is used rather than 'human being'. As discussed earlier, Kant regarded a 'person' as essentially a rational and self-determining being, hence parentalist or controlling treatment might be justified if someone is regarded as lacking the capacity for self-determination. So the use of 'human being' rather than 'person' in List 2.3 emphasizes the dignity that belongs to each human as a human being, regardless of their capacities, and also suggests that people have dignity, regardless of whether they are respected by others.

In a social work context, 'self-determination' or autonomy is a crucial concept and has various meanings, which have been discussed earlier, including:

- *negative:* allowing people to do as they choose, that is, not interfering in people's freely chosen course of action
- *positive:* creating the conditions that enable people to become more self-determining, that is, helping people to reach a state where they have the capacity to see what choices might be available.

Recent emphasis on the participation of service users in decision-making and empowerment – the development of service users' skills and self-confidence so they can participate more in society – is a manifestation of negative and positive self-determination. Self-determination in both senses has, for a long time, been one of the fundamental principles stated for social work practice, often phrased as 'client self-determination'. Yet while the social worker may sometimes be able to focus largely on one individual service user and take on the role of advocate for the service user's rights, often the social worker has to take into account the rights of significant others in a situation. In the interests of justice, it may not always be morally right to promote one service user's rights at the expense of those of others. Furthermore, the focus of attention may not always be on individuals. The social worker may be involved in working with groups of people to enable them to exert their collective rights, for example Muslim teenagers in a particular neighbourhood. Implementing this broad principle relies on us interpreting the meaning of 'human being'.

Welfare or wellbeing

The concept of 'welfare' embraces both individual welfare (the wellbeing of individual people) and social welfare, which can be interpreted as the sum of all individuals' welfare, or as some communal or collective wellbeing, not necessarily reducible to the sum of all individuals' welfare. Promoting someone's 'good' or welfare is also open to interpretation depending on what we think counts as human welfare (happiness, pleasure, wealth, satisfaction, as discussed earlier in the context of utilitarianism) and whether we adopt our own view of what a person's welfare is or the person's own conception of their welfare. It is dependent on cultural views about what are the basic human needs or capabilities and what is a good quality of life. The ideal is for professionals and service users to work together to determine what courses of action would be beneficial or least harmful. There are debates about what counts as minimum standards for a decent human life, for example food, shelter, social interaction, and what counts as a decent standard of living in a particular society or social context, for example in terms of levels of income or welfare benefits, or access to consumer goods. Recently, attention has been paid to measuring 'wellbeing'. Measures generally include psychological, economic, physical and social dimensions, with the recognition that these are interrelated and that many aspects of wellbeing are essentially subjective.

Much of modern social work is explicitly about ensuring that the 'best interests' of particular service user groups are served, for example children in child protection work. While it is hard to define 'best interests', as these are relative to age, maturity and other circumstances, generally 'best interests' broadly describes the wellbeing of the persons concerned (see UNHCR, 2008, p. 14). Codes of ethics generally stress the social worker's duty to work in the interests of service users. Often it is the social worker's view of what service users' interests are that is regarded as important. However, as with the concept of self-determination, while in some cases it may be clear-cut that it is the service user's interests the social worker should be protecting, in other cases the social worker has to consider the interests of significant others and the 'public interest', for example through preventing reoffending in work with young offenders. These various interests may conflict.

Social justice

Social justice is generally regarded as being about the distribution of advantages and disadvantages in society. As used in a social work context, the principle of social justice links with both utilitarian and radical approaches to ethics. It embraces the concepts of equality and justice – both of which are essentially contested and which themselves may frequently be in tension, depending on which versions are at stake. In earlier editions of *Ethics and Values in Social Work* (Banks, 1995, 2001b), I separated equality and distributive justice. However, there is a tendency in the social welfare literature to encompass both these principles in the complex concept of 'social justice'.

According to Spicker (1988, p. 125), equality means 'the removal of disadvantage'. This can be interpreted in many ways, including:

- *Equal treatment:* preventing disadvantage in access to services, including treatment without prejudice or favour. For example, in Britain it should not be the case that a middle-class white man seeking resources for his elderly mother is dealt with more quickly than a black woman seeking similar support.
- *Equal opportunity:* the removal of disadvantage in competition with others, giving people the means to achieve socially desired ends. For example, a British social worker may arrange for an interpreter for a Bengali-speaking woman so that she can express her needs in detail and have the same opportunity as an English-speaking service user to receive the services she requires.
- *Equality of result:* in which disadvantages are removed altogether. For example, the residential home that would provide the best quality care for two older service users with similar needs is very expensive. The service user with a rich son who is prepared to pay is able to go to this home; the service user who is poor is not. To achieve equality of result might entail the state or some agency acting on its behalf paying the full fee for the poorer service user, or, to avoid stigmatization, the state providing free high-quality care for all people with similar needs.

Social workers are concerned to promote all three forms of equality, although equality of treatment is much easier to achieve than equality of opportunity or result. Equality of treatment would follow logically from the principle of respect for persons. Equality of opportunity and of result require some more positive action to redress existing disadvantages, and may require additional resources or changes in government policy. To achieve equality of result will require structural changes in society – challenging certain people's existing rights to wealth, property and power. It is this type of principle that underpins some of the more radical and anti-oppressive approaches to social work (Ferguson, 2008; Ferguson and Lavalette, 2009; Ferguson and Woodward, 2009). It is also what Young (2008) is referring to in her concept of 'structural injustice' or 'positional difference' – meaning that people's group social positioning, such as class, gender, ethnicity, entails that institutions and practices limit their opportunities to achieve wellbeing. Young (2008, p. 79) distinguishes injustice by virtue of structural inequality from culture-based injustice, which entails people not being free to express themselves, associate with others or socialize their children in the cultural ways they value.

The other key concept embedded in the principle of social justice is 'distributive justice', which is about distributing goods according to certain rules and criteria. The criteria for distribution may be selected according to people's already existing rights, for example property rights, desert and need. Although justice and equality are linked, and some commentators argue that equality is subsumed within justice, this depends on which concept of justice is being used. A concept of justice based on property rights or desert may result in inequality. Rawls' (1973) concept of justice, for example, is based on two principles: equality in the assignment of basic needs and resources; and social and economic inequalities only insofar as there are compensating benefits for everyone, especially the least advantaged. Distributive justice is a central focus in social work, especially for those working in the public sector, in that social workers are responsible for distributing public resources, whether they be counselling, care or money, according to certain criteria based variously on rights, desert and need. It is becoming more central in the present climate as resource allocation becomes an increasingly common role for social workers and they are finding themselves unable to meet the pressing needs of people facing disadvantage and distress.

Conclusions

In this chapter we have explored some of the philosophical foundations of approaches to social work ethics. We have argued that principle-based approaches have tended to dominate professional ethics, that the traditional principles of the profession have been broadly 'Kantian', resting on the doctrine of respecting the individual as a rational and self-determining human being and focusing on the form and content of the social worker–service user relationship. However, the context in which social work is practised, often as part of a welfare bureaucracy with a social control and resource-rationing function (based on more utilitarian values), also places ethical duties on social workers that may conflict with their duties to the service user as an individual. Issues relating to the fairness of the distribution of welfare and challenging existing inequalities and injustices are also important in social work, based on radical and anti-oppressive values. It was argued that a combined Kantian-utilitarian-radical approach might better encapsulate our everyday moral thinking in social work, and that a set of key principles might comprise respecting the dignity, worth and self-determination of human beings (particularly service users), promoting the welfare of service users and society generally, and promoting social justice for service users and in society generally.

This is similar to the 'common morality' approach advocated by Beauchamp and Childress (2009) for biomedical ethics. However, in social work, the emphasis on *social* justice is much greater. This feature of social work values distinguishes social work from other caring professions, such as medicine and nursing, with which social workers increasingly have to work in multidisciplinary and interdisciplinary contexts. It is a source of strength and distinctiveness, while also potentially leading to conflict and misunderstanding, as social workers are more committed to anti-oppressive approaches to practice and working for progressive change in society (see Banks, 2004a, Ch. 5 for a discussion of interprofessional ethics). Social workers require, therefore, not only a good understanding of the concepts and principles of social justice, human dignity and welfare, but also the confidence, commitment, motivation and skills to put these principles into practice in difficult and challenging contexts. Issues of motivation, commitment and qualities of character are the subject of the next chapter.

Putting it into practice

Reflecting on ethical principles

Aims of the exercise: to encourage readers to reflect critically on the stated ethical principles of social work in the light of their own value commitments.

1. List what you think are the important ethical principles *you* hold as a social worker.
2. How do they compare with those in List 2.3?
3. From what you have read in this chapter and elsewhere, can you suggest any modifications/additions to List 2.3?

Practice focus

Case for discussion 2: Using deception to remove a child in Iran

This case comes from a social worker who works for the social emergency service Line 123 in a city in Iran. Line 123 is a government agency that intervenes in emergency situations, especially cases relating to child abuse, wife abuse and suicide. It is available in many cities in Iran as an on-call service, and also as a full-time patrol service with a team comprising a social worker and a psychologist. The patrol service has a vehicle (a van) so they can be present in situations where trouble arises or they can search for clients, such as runaway girls.

On one occasion, a call was made to Line 123 by a neighbour reporting an urgent child abuse case. When the emergency team arrived, the neighbour who had called Line 123 came out and described the situation. The social worker on duty was a woman with four years' experience as a social worker, who had spent two years working for Line 123. The neighbour told the social worker that she had heard a loud painful lament from her neighbour's child. This frequently happened. Living next door there was a single mother with a nine-year-old child. The mother, as was diagnosed later, had episodes of paranoia, and regarded her daughter as her enemy. The mother punished her child frequently for trivial reasons. At such times, neighbours would come to rescue the child and hide her until the mother became calm.

Finally, the female neighbours, disappointed with the mother, decided to call Line 123 to try to solve the problem once and for all.

The standard procedure in such cases is to remove the custody rights from the mother by a court order and to send the child to a supportive residential home until such time as a legal decision is made about the mother. The whole of the process must be done with the awareness of the family.

However, in this case, there was an obstacle – the mother. The neighbours and the social worker decided that the mission had to be carried out secretly, without the mother being aware. They believed that if she knew, she would possibly kill her young child or take her to a place out of the social worker's reach before the court order was put in place.

So the social worker decided to make a good plan to remove the child from her home, with the cooperation of her colleague, a psychologist. The social worker informed her colleague of her plan and they started to put it into action. The child was hidden in the home of one of the neighbours. The psychologist went to speak to the mother, and the social worker, secretly, with the help of one of the female neighbours, kidnapped the child and took her quickly to the van to convey her to a safe place. She would inform the mother afterwards.

The ethical challenge for the social worker was whether she should make the mother aware in advance about the proposal that her daughter should be removed. On the one hand, if the mother was told, it was feared that she might kill or seriously injure the child. Yet to remove the child without telling the mother is against the principle of client consent.

Questions for discussion

1. What ethical principles are relevant in this case?
2. What arguments could be used to justify the use of deception in this case? Rehearse the arguments from a duty-based perspective (Kantian theory), from a perspective based on the promotion of good consequences (utilitarian theory), and from a radical perspective based on social justice.
3. From your own perspective, do you think it was ethically acceptable to deceive the mother in this case?
4. Are there any features of this case, for example the role of neighbours in working with the social worker, that you think might possibly be distinctive to social work in the Iranian cultural context?

Further resources

Boss, J. (2010) *Ethics for Life: A Text with Readings*, 5th edn, New York, McGraw Hill.
Useful background on various ethical theories, written in a clear, practical style. Has biographical details of key thinkers, selected readings from key texts and includes discussion of religion and cultural relativism.

Ferguson, I. and Woodward, R. (2009) *Radical Social Work in Practice: Making a Difference*, Bristol, The Policy Press.
Clearly written textbook advocating a radical approach to social work based on social justice.

Lafollette, H. (ed.) (2000) *The Blackwell Guide to Ethical Theory*, Oxford, Blackwell.
Useful edited collection with chapters on a range of major ethical theories.

Stanford Encyclopedia of Philosophy, http://plato.stanford.edu.
An open access encyclopedia that is frequently updated and contains detailed refereed articles written by recognized experts on key philosophers, philosophical concepts and theories – including much material relevant to philosophical ethics.

CHAPTER 3

Character and relationship-based approaches to social work ethics

CHAPTER OVERVIEW

This chapter discusses a number of approaches to ethics that focus attention on people rather than actions, including virtue ethics, the ethics of care, the ethics of proximity and postmodern ethics. The chapter concludes by arguing for a holistic account of ethics that combines a range of different types of values, including principles, character and relationships. At the end of the chapter, there is an exercise to encourage readers to explore character and emotion, and a case for discussion about the relationship of social workers in Bulgaria with a young girl.

Introduction

There have been many critiques of 'principlism' in professional ethics, particularly the version developed by Beauchamp and Childress (2009), and indeed of Kantian and utilitarian approaches to morality and Marxist/neo-Marxist versions of radical social work. These critiques have come from several directions, arguing that a principle-based approach to ethics (including professional ethics) places too much stress on actions (as opposed to the person doing the action), the rational and impartial nature of ethical decision-making, the universality of principles, and, in the case of Kantianism and utilitarianism, on the individual person as a rational and self-determining agent. Principle-based approaches ignore important features of the moral life and moral judgements, including the character, motives and emotions of the moral agent, the particular contexts in which judgements are made, and the particular relationships and commitments people have to each other. Insofar as they assume the individual as the basic unit, they do not reflect the actual norms and practices of many cultures in many parts of the world where the family and community are primary.

I will now consider several alternatives to the principle-based approach to ethics, namely virtue ethics, the ethics of care, the ethics of proximity and postmodern ethics. There are many other overlapping and interrelated ethical theories and theoretical approaches to ethics that could be covered (for example existentialist ethics, situation ethics, ecological ethics, dialogical ethics or narrative ethics), as well as religious ethics (for example Confucian ethics, Islamic ethics or Hindu ethics). However, the purpose here is not to produce a complex 'map', but rather to explore the possibilities of a selection of approaches (for further discussion of ethical approaches relevant to social work, see Banks, 2004a; Gray and Webb, 2010; Hugman, 2005).

Table 3.1 summarizes some of the main differences between the principle-based approaches outlined in Chapter 2 and the character and relationship-based approaches covered in this chapter.

Table 3.1 Approaches to ethics: some generalizations

Principle-based ethics (impartial, detached approaches)	Ethics of character and relationships (partial, situated approaches)
Ethics as universal	Ethics as particular, relative to context, time, place
Ethics involves generalizations	Ethics is specific
Ethics involves abstraction	Ethics is concrete and contextual
Ethics requires impartiality	Ethics is about partiality
Ethics is based on principles	Ethics is based on qualities of character (virtues), relationships or proximity to the other person
Ethics is about duty or justice	Ethics is about character, care or responsiveness
Focus on action: What should I do?	Focus on character: How should I live? Focus on response: How should I respond?
Ethics involves principled decision-making, moving deductively from general principles to what to do in particular cases	Ethics involves a character trait or disposition to act for the good and the ability to make good judgements (phronesis), or an attitude of care, attentiveness, or a response towards a particular other

Ethical decisions should be justified through a process of reasoning with reference to universal/general principles	Ethics is not about justification, but about acting upon a disposition to live well and act in accordance with what makes for the good; genuinely caring and authentically responding to the other
Moral agent as rational	Moral agent has emotions as well as rationality
Moral agent as isolated individual; an 'unencumbered self'	Moral agent as a person with a history, responsibilities, particular commitments, part of a community; an 'embedded self'
Separation of the right and the good. Focus on the right	Focus on the good; and/or inseparability of the right and the good

Source: Adapted from Banks, 2004a, p. 77

The importance of character in the professional role: virtue-based approaches

In recent years, there has been a revival of virtue ethics in the field of philosophical ethics (Adams, 2006; Crisp, 1996; Crisp and Slote, 1997; Hursthouse, 1999; MacIntyre, 1985; Slote, 1992; Statman, 1997; Swanton, 2003). While there are many versions, including that stemming from Aristotle ([350 BCE]1954) and those contained within many religious traditions (including Buddhist, Confucian, African or medieval Christian), what they have in common is a focus on the character or dispositions of moral agents as opposed to abstract obligations, duties or principles for action. One of the reasons suggested for the growing popularity of virtue ethics is the failure of the attempts of Kantians and utilitarians to articulate sets of principles for right action. As Statman (1997, p. 6) comments:

> principles are just too abstract to provide helpful guidance in the complicated situations met in everyday ethics. These situations typically involve conflicting considerations, to which principle-ethics either offers no solution, or formulates higher order principles of preference, which, again, are too abstract and vague to offer any real help.

Virtue ethics is an approach 'according to which the basic judgements in ethics are judgements about character' (Statman, 1997, p. 7). In Hursthouse's version of virtue ethics, an action is right if it is what a virtuous agent would do in the circumstances; a virtue is 'a character trait a human being needs to flourish or live well' (Hursthouse, 1997, p. 229). What counts as 'living well' or 'flourishing' then becomes an important question in deciding what characteristics count as virtues. Some virtue theorists argue that these vary according to different time periods and cultures, for example the kinds of characteristics cultivated as virtues in ancient Greece may not all be applicable in twenty-first-century Europe or other parts of the world; others claim that there are universal virtues. Nevertheless, the kinds of dispositions usually regarded as virtues include courage, integrity, honesty, truthfulness, loyalty, wisdom and kindness. Virtuous people tell the truth, it is argued, not because of some abstract principle stating 'you shall not lie', or because on this occasion telling the truth will produce a good result, but because they do not want to be the sorts of people who tell lies. Virtue ethics also tends to emphasize the particular relationships people have with each other. It could be argued that it makes more sense to see my kindness towards my best friend as arising out of the fact that I have a relationship of friendship with her, I like her and care about her, rather than from some abstract moral principle about promoting the welfare of others.

If we are to develop a virtue-based ethics for social work, we need to consider what are the virtues of the social worker. In one sense, they should reflect the virtues recognized in society at large. According to MacIntyre (1985, p. 191), the virtues are relative to culture and role; they are qualities 'the possession and exercise of which tends to enable us to achieve those goods which are internal to practices'. While not all virtue theorists adopt this kind of view, the importance of roles and the idea of virtues as relative to 'practices' or communities of practitioners are useful if we are to attempt to articulate a virtue-based theory for professional ethics. We would have to ask ourselves what it means to be a 'good social worker'. 'Good' would be internal to the role of social worker and would be defined by the community of practitioners who do social work.

There have been some recent attempts to develop a virtue-based approach in the context of professional ethics; for example, Solomon (1992, 1997) does so for business ethics, Oakley and Cocking (2001) for medical and legal ethics, and Armstrong (2007) for nursing ethics. There is also some interest in social work (Houston,

2003; McBeath and Webb, 2002), and Banks and Gallagher (2009) have developed a virtue-based approach for health and social care. As Rhodes (1986, p. 42) claims:

> a virtue-based ethics seems particularly appropriate to professions, because the ethical issues so often focus on the nature of the relationships and our responsibilities in those relationships – to the client, other colleagues, our supervisors, the agency itself. What sort of person ought a 'professional' social worker to be? What is human excellence in that context?

Table 3.2 A selection of virtues for social workers drawn from recent literature

Rhodes (1986)	Compassion, detached caring, warmth, honesty, moral courage, hopefulness, humility
Bowles et al. (2006)	Open-mindedness, practical reasoning, moral courage, reflectiveness/critical reflection, empathy, integrity/commitment to social work values, discretion, tolerance/valuing diversity, good judgement/'wisdom'
Akademikerförbundet SSR (2006)	Integrity, critical self-insight, responsibility, courage/moral courage, a sense of justice, balanced judgement, tolerance/broadmindedness, empathy/sensitivity and a basic attitude of respect, friendliness and equality in relation to others
Banks and Gallagher (2009)	Professional wisdom, courage, respectfulness, care, trustworthiness, justice and professional integrity

However, there are few developed accounts of the specific virtues relevant for social work. Rhodes (1986, pp. 42–3) briefly touches on the kinds of virtues that might be appropriate for social work, identifying from textbooks on social workers' responsibilities virtues such as compassion, detached caring, warmth and honesty. She also suggests some additional virtues that might seem appropriate: a certain kind of moral courage, hopefulness and humility. In their textbook on social work ethics, Bowles et al. (2006) identify the virtues of open-mindedness, practical reasoning, moral courage, reflectiveness/critical reflection, empathy, integrity/commitment to social work values, discretion, tolerance/valuing diversity, good judgement/'wisdom'. Interestingly, the code of ethics produced by one of the Swedish associations for social workers (Akademikerförbundet SSR, 2006) also highlights the importance of ethical traits of character and produces a list: integrity, critical self-insight, responsibility, courage/moral courage, a sense of justice, balanced judgement, tolerance/broadmindedness, empathy/sensitivity and a basic attitude of respect, friendliness and equality in relation to others. Banks and Gallagher (2009) select seven virtues that they regard as important in health and social care, while acknowledging that this is a partial selection: professional wisdom, courage, respectfulness, care, justice, trustworthiness and professional integrity. These different sets of virtues are summarized in Table 3.2 (see previous page).

Interestingly, the only virtue mentioned in all four lists is (moral) courage. The fact that these textbooks select different virtues, most of which would equally apply to nonprofessional people living their everyday lives, and certainly to many other professions in addition to social work, suggests that simply producing and studying lists of virtues may not be particularly useful in helping us to identify what counts as a good social worker – as opposed to a good nurse, or a good human being. These virtues need to be lived out within the framework of a specific core purpose or service ideal for a profession. In social work, this core purpose is arguably about promoting social welfare or wellbeing, while in nursing (and other healthcare professions), it is about promoting health. To demonstrate this, I will take the virtues identified by Banks and Gallagher and briefly elaborate on them for social work (see List 3.1).

List 3.1 Some virtues for social work

1. *Professional wisdom* is the excellence by which professionals deliberate well about what to do in their working lives. A person of professional wisdom has a capacity to engage in practical reasoning, which includes the ability to perceive and appreciate ethically salient features of situations, the exercise of ethical imagination, and reflective and deliberative capabilities (to make judgements and act). This process of reasoning is used to make the appropriate practical choices that constitute good social work.
2. *Courage* is, according to Aristotle ([350 BCE]1954, 1115a6), 'a mean with regard to feelings of fear and confidence'. By this he

means that a courageous person, when facing situations of risk and danger, is neither cowardly and lacking in confidence, nor foolhardy and overconfident. We need to know what is the right thing to fear and how much to fear. Courage is a complex virtue, with distinctions often being made between moral, physical and psychological courage. Moral courage may be required in social work to face dangerous and risky situations or to communicate unwelcome news to service users or colleagues.

3. *Respectfulness* towards someone or something entails acknowledging the value of the person or thing, preserving and/or not destroying it, and engaging with what is valued. Respectful social workers make use of the self in developing relationships and getting to know and understand the perspective of those people with whom they work.

4. *Care* is about how one person relates to others, related to the goal of enhancing the existence of the others. In a social work context, a caring person is one who has a motive of attentiveness towards particular others for whom the professional takes responsibility, and competence in giving care, tailored to the responses of the person cared for.

5. *Trustworthiness* is about not letting others down. A trustworthy person in a social work role is someone who behaves as relied upon, is aware and accepts that they are liable to be held responsible for this behaviour, and is able to give a plausible performance as a reliable and responsible person.

6. *Justice* is associated with the fair allocation of benefits and burdens, and relies on a capacity to make good judgements in weighing up how people should be treated. A just person in a social work context is someone who has a disposition to act fairly in relation to individuals to whom she or he owes a particular obligation and to act in a way that promotes and reflects just social arrangements.

7. *Professional integrity.* In Aristotelian ethics, integrity was not regarded as a virtue per se, but as the holding together of all the virtues as a whole. In the context of professional practice, it is often used to mean the overarching capacity or disposition to hold true to the values of the profession and to balance the other virtues. It might be regarded as a kind of moral competence or capacity that people use to make sense of their ideals and actions as a whole and act accordingly (see Banks, 2004b and 2010 for a more detailed discussion of professional integrity in social work).

Source: Drawn from Banks and Gallagher, 2009

There is no doubt that developing certain traits of character and being a certain sort of person is important in professional ethics, even if academic writing on professional ethics has tended to focus more attention on the articulation of general ethical principles and their use in rational moral decision-making. Indeed, many codes of ethics stress the kind of person a professional should be, as well as listing principles of ethical action, although, interestingly, few codes in the caring professions contain more than passing references to character traits, which is probably a reflection of the fact that the current focus of attention is still towards principles and actions. Actions are more concrete and measurable than traits of character. However, a number of recent codes of ethics produced by professional associations for social work include 'integrity' as a value – defined variously as comprising honesty, reliability and impartiality.

These kinds of statements relate to certain views about what it means to be a professional. A virtue ethicist would argue that it is less important that professionals claim to abide by explicit sets of rules, for example stating that they will not discriminate on grounds of religion and gender, or that they will not exploit service users, than that they are particular types of people who have a disposition to act justly and in a trustworthy fashion. They are trustworthy, and therefore act in a trustworthy fashion, not because of a rule devised by their professional association, but because being trustworthy is part of what it means to be a good professional. However, this still leaves terms like 'trustworthy', 'just', 'honest' and 'competent' to be explored.

Lists of virtues can be criticized in the same way as lists of values or ethical principles as being abstract and unhelpful in making everyday ethical decisions. It could also be argued that virtue ethics can be subsumed within principle-based ethics; that being a just person simply consists of a disposition to act justly. Therefore our moral judgements must be grounded in judgements about people's actions rather than their characters. This is an area that warrants much more discussion in the context of professional ethics. But it is interesting to note that even Beauchamp and Childress, often held up as the major exponents of principlism in professional ethics, introduced a whole chapter relating to virtues in professional life into the fourth edition of their *Principles of Biomedical Ethics*, acknowledging that:

> Principles require judgement, which in turn depends on character, moral discernment, and a person's sense of responsibility and accountability … Often what counts most in the moral life is not consistent adherence to principles and rules, but reliable

character, moral good sense, and emotional responsiveness. (Beauchamp and Childress, 1994, p. 462)

In their fifth and sixth editions, this chapter, renamed 'Moral character', comes as a precursor to the coverage of principles (Beauchamp and Childress, 2001, 2009).

The caring relationship between professional and service user: the 'ethics of care'

The theme of emotional responsiveness is a key element in what has been termed the 'ethics of care' or 'an ethic of care', which has been particularly associated with feminist approaches to ethics. While Beauchamp and Childress (2009) include care as a virtue, the majority of the proponents of care ethics have not located themselves within the virtue ethics tradition, although they do share the rejection of impartial principle-based approaches to ethics and a concern with particularities and relationships. While 'care' or 'caring' can be regarded as a quality of character and features in lists of virtues for social care and health, it is care as a *relationship* and/or as a *practice* that is the main focus of attention of care ethicists. Noddings (2002, pp. 20–1) is keen to make the distinction between care as a virtue and care as an attribute of relation. She points out that is it possible for someone to care sincerely (in the virtue sense) and yet not connect with the person receiving the care. It is this *connection* that is the focus of attention of the ethics of care. Ruddick (1989), Tronto (1993), Sevenhuijsen (1998) and others characterize care as a *social practice* – a collective human activity, with a distinct purpose, based on shared values – rather than a relationship per se, although clearly a practice in this sense entails interrelationships between practitioners. Indeed, according to Held (2006, p. 20), the ethics of care 'focuses on social relations and the social practices and values that sustain them'.

Recent developments of care ethics owe much to the empirical work of the psychologist Gilligan (1982), who identified two 'moral voices' in her interviews with people about how they conceptualized and spoke about moral dilemmas. She contrasts what she calls the 'ethic of care' with the 'ethic of justice'. The ethic of justice refers to principle-based approaches to ethics, including Kantian and utilitarian moralities, which are based on a system of individualized rights and duties, emphasizing abstract moral principles, impartiality and rationality. Gilligan argues that this is a male-oriented system of morality, which does not take account of approaches to ethics that tend to be adopted by women. The latter would emphasize responsibility rather than duty and relationships rather than principles – an 'ethic of care'. The distinction between the ethics of care and justice is summarized in Table 3.3, which is based on material from Farley (1993).

Table 3.3 The ethics of justice and care

	Justice	Care
Key value	Justice – reinforces separation of persons	Care – represents connectedness
Appeal to	Principles	Relationships
Focus on	Social contracts, ranked order of values, duty, individual freedom	Cooperation, communication, caring, relationship between persons

Gilligan herself is equivocal about the extent to which an ethic of care should be regarded as a 'female' or 'feminine' ethics, although others in this tradition (such as Noddings, 1984) explicitly adopt this kind of view. It should be noted that Gilligan and some of those following her use the singular term 'ethic' both to refer to a distinctive moral voice and a more detailed philosophical approach to ethics. However, over time, with the more systematic development of these ideas, many writers are now using the term 'ethics of care'. I will use the term 'ethics of care' in this book to refer to a developed philosophical approach to ethics, retaining the term 'ethic' when referring to the work of Gilligan or others who use this term.

Many feminists have argued that it is both dangerous and misleading to attribute an 'ethic of care' (as a distinctive moral voice) simply to women (see Farley, 1993; Groenhout, 2004; Hekman, 1995; Koehn, 1998; Okin, 1994; Sevenhuijsen, 1998; Tronto, 1993). It may tend to reinforce essentialist views of women as 'merely' carers and leave unquestioned whether the caring role itself can have a negative and damaging effect on carers. Furthermore, as Tronto (1993, p. 84) argues, research has shown that African Americans, for example, adopt a view of the self that stresses a sense of cooperation, interdependence and collective responsibility, as opposed to the ethic of justice. Li (1994) argues that the concept of care is similar to the concept of *jen* in Confucian ethics. Indeed, prevailing cultures and values in many countries of the global South and East also have this stress on relationships and responsibilities (Gyekye, 2010), as do many of the world's religions, such as Buddhism and Confucianism. This is developed for social work in Graham's (1999, 2002) account of an African-centred paradigm that emphasizes values relating to the importance of interpersonal relationships, a holistic view of the interconnnect-edness of all things, and the collective nature of identity. Tronto argues that an ethic of justice represents the dominant mode of moral thinking that reflects the power structure in society (in the global North) and tends to marginalize and exclude the experience of women, black people, working-class and other oppressed groups.

Interest in care ethics has been relatively slow to develop in social work compared with nursing, where a body of literature grew quite quickly from the 1990s (for example Allmark, 1995; Bowden, 1997; Bradshaw, 1996; Hanford, 1994; Kuhse, 1997). The philosophical work of Noddings (1984, 2002), who argues that the caring relation-ship is ethically basic, has been particularly influential in nursing, where it has been used both as a basis for the nurse–patient relation-ship and to provide a theoretical basis for nursing ethics. According to Noddings (1984, p. 30), caring involves 'feeling with' the other, which she explicitly distinguishes from empathy (putting oneself in the other's shoes). She describes caring as 'receiving the other into myself' or what she calls 'engrossment' (p. 33). She talks of this as the 'subjective-receptive' mode in which we see clearly what we have received from the other. She distinguishes this from instrumental thinking – the use of reasoning to work out what to do once we have committed ourselves to doing something – but claims that rationality 'does not of necessity mark either the initial impulse or the action that is undertaken' (p. 36). Noddings (1984) develops her thinking in some depth to show how her approach applies to caring for strangers and for people for whom we do not naturally care; she also applies it particularly to the teacher–pupil relationship. Noddings is sceptical of the value of principles and rules per se and focuses on the concrete features of particular situations and our relationships to other people. She gives as an example Abraham's willingness to sacrifice his son Isaac: 'under the gaze of an abstract and untouchable God, he would destroy *this* touchable child whose real eyes were turned upon him in trust, love and fear' (p. 43).

While Noddings and other care ethicists have drawn our attention to important aspects of morality often lacking in traditional ethical theories, many critics question whether the ethic of care is sufficient to offer a complete account of either ethics in general or nursing ethics in particular. Kuhse (1997, p. 45) suggests that 'dispositional care' – an emotional response, a concern for the other, attentiveness and responsiveness to the needs of the other – is a necessary but not sufficient condition for nursing ethics, arguing that an adequate ethics needs impartiality or justice as well as care. It is important that we are attentive to the nature of situations and sensitive to people's feelings, needs and the potential for hurt or harm. Kuhse gives an example taken from Blum (1988), where two adults are watching children playing in a park. One adult does not see that one of the children is being too rough and is in danger of harming the other child. The other adult, being more attentive and sensitive, does, and hence sees the need to intervene. This enables the second adult to act on the principle 'protect children from harm'.

These arguments suggest that care alone is not sufficient for an adequate ethics. As Kuhse (1997) also points out, caring can some-times be harmful (overbearing or stifling for the person on the receiving end), it can be narrow and parochial (as with the mother who only cares for her own child), and its focus only on the mainte-nance of the caring relationship means it can result in us failing to challenge racism or lying (if, as in an example given by Noddings, my father is racist and I put my care for him above all else). Care ethics, in focusing on the one-to-one relationship, does not help us in deciding how to allocate scarce resources between different patients or service users, or in judging matters of policy. Issues of fairness, justice and equality are an equally important aspect of a profession-al's role, a feature that is perhaps even more evident in social work than in nursing. While Noddings has responses to these criticisms, particularly in her later work where she argues that 'caring-about' others may provide the link between caring and justice, she neverthe-less regards the relationship of 'caring-for' another as the 'natural, desired state'. 'Caring-about' is emotionally derived from 'caring-for' and must serve 'caring-for' to achieve its objectives (Noddings, 2002, p. 22). As she herself acknowledges, she 'inverts Kantian priorities' in grounding justice in caring. This account, in effect, claims that justice is derivable from and reducible to care.

In contrast to the version of the ethics of care developed by Noddings, Tronto (1993, p. 166) explicitly rejects what she calls the 'false dichotomy' between care and justice. She argues that care is a necessary but not sufficient account of moral life and that to address the problems with care requires 'a concept of justice, a democratic and open opportunity for discussion, and more equal access to power' (p. 155). She goes on to develop what she calls a 'political theory of care', where care is valued as a political ideal in the context of democratic institutions. Tronto's (1993) account of the nature of care, how this relates to an ethic of care and her argument for care as a political ideal have been influential in some of the social work literature that is now beginning to address the ethics of care (Banks, 2004a, Ch. 3; Clifford, 2002; Hugman, 2005, pp. 67–85; Koggel and Orme, 2010; Orme, 2002; Parton, 2003; Rauner, 2000; Steckley and Smith, 2011; Ward, 2011). This has been reinforced by the work of Sevenhuijsen (1998), who further developed the concept of a political ethics of care theoretically and in relation to the analysis of Dutch and South African social policy, and by Tronto's (2001, 2010) later writings, where she explicitly addresses issues relating to professional caring and organizational contexts.

One of the most influential aspects of Tronto's care ethics is her account of the four phases of care (caring about, taking care of, care giving and care receiving), for each of which she develops four corresponding elements of an ethic of care and a fifth element, 'integrity', which holds all the elements together. These five elements are summarized in List 3.2.

List 3.2 Tronto's five elements of the ethics of care

1. *Attentiveness:* noticing the need for care in the first place – actively seeking awareness of others and their needs and points of view (relates to caring about).
2. *Responsibility:* assuming responsibility for care – with responsibility being embedded in a set of implicit cultural practices, rather than a set of formal rules or series of promises (relates to taking care of).
3. *Competence:* the actual work of care that needs to be done – one's ability to do something about another's needs (relates to care giving).
4. *Responsiveness:* the response of the person who is cared for to the care – remaining alert to the possibilities of abuse that arise from the care receiver's vulnerability (relates to care receiving).
5. *The integrity of care:* according to Tronto, good care requires that the four phases fit together as a whole, which involves knowledge of the context of the care process and making judgements about conflicting needs and strategies. These judgements require an assessment of needs in a social and political, as well as personal, context.

Source: Based on Tronto, 1993, pp. 127–36

In the context of professional ethics, it can be argued that an ethics of care that can take into account the particularity of each situation, people's relationships with each other, cooperation, communication and caring is important and complementary to the ethics of justice, which stresses universal principles, individual freedom, social contracts and duty. An overemphasis in professional ethics on the latter may result in overregulation, a damaging impartiality and neutrality, and a mindless following of rules for their own sake. As Baier (1995, p. 48) comments, justice is found to be too 'cold' and 'it is "warmer" more communitarian virtues and social ideals that are being called in to supplement it'. Yet, at the same time, in the delivery of publicly funded and organized services, universally applicable rules are an important part of what defines the work of the professionals delivering these services. It is not expected that a professional worker will give preferential treatment to her neighbour's daughter over and above a stranger, for example, although she might in everyday life. The ethics of care and justice are not mutually exclusive, but are, as Mendus (1993, p. 18) argues, 'complementary facets of any realistic account of morality'.

Responding to the call of the other: the ethics of proximity

Some recent care theorists have made connections between the ethics of care and versions of both virtue ethics and Levinas's ethics of proximity (see Groenhout, 2004). For the latter, the focus on moral perception or sensitivity is important, generated initially in the face-to-face encounter with another person. In common with the ethics of care and virtue ethics, this approach to ethics shares a dissatisfaction with the abstraction from context required by principle-based ethical theories. It does have resonances with the ethics of care, insofar as it emphasizes the face-to-face relationship with the other, but the approaches of thinkers who develop an ethics of proximity originate in a different tradition, and lack the contextuality and situatedness of the feminist accounts of moral agency described earlier. This tradition includes the existentialists and phenomenologists of Continental Europe – Kierkegaard, Sartre, Buber, Husserl, Heidegger – and the later developments and critiques offered by Danish philosopher Løgstrup and Lithuanian/French philosopher Levinas. According to these philosophers, ethics arises from an experiential basis – not from abstract and universalizing theorizing. As Vetlesen (1997, p. 5) comments, the 'human dyad' (the 'I–thou' relationship between two people) is regarded as the basic seat of concern and responsibility. Therefore the cognitive and emotional abilities needed for adopting a moral point of view are: 'fostered in a setting of proximity, in interaction with close and, as one might say, irreplaceable others'.

Hand (1989, p. v) describes Levinas, a Lithuanian-born Jewish French philosopher, as 'one of the most profound, exacting and original philosophers of twentieth-century Europe'. It is not easy, therefore, to summarize his thought, which places ethics as first philosophy, prior to ontology – the study of being – and incorporates some of his religious thinking. Levinas takes as his starting point 'pre-reflective self-consciousness', which cannot be controlled by will and exists without attributes or aims, as 'a pure passivity' with no name, no situation, no status (Levinas, 1989, p. 80). He says that one has to respond to one's right to be, 'not by referring to some abstract and anonymous law, or judicial entity, but because of one's fear for the Other' (p. 82). He speaks of the 'irruption' of the face of the 'Other', in its nakedness, vulnerability, 'like a shot "at point blank range"' (p. 83):

> The Other becomes my neighbour precisely through the way the face summons me, calls for me, begs for me, and in so doing recalls my responsibility, and calls me into question.

Levinas refers to a 'guiltless responsibility' that goes beyond what I may or may not have done to the 'Other', 'as if I were devoted to the other man before being devoted to myself'. To be oneself, therefore, is to be *for the 'Other'*. In the face of the 'Other', Levinas (1989, p. 84) claims, I am inescapably responsible and consequently 'the unique and chosen one'. He speaks of the 'uniqueness of the non-interchangeable'. For Levinas, the relationship with the 'Other' is not a reciprocal one, concerned with what each may give and take (see Levinas, 1997), rather, it is a readiness to give unconditionally and is non-negotiable. As Vetlesen (1997, p. 10) comments: 'morality is not an option but a predicament, part and parcel of human existence. The Other commits me to being-for-him by his sheer co-existence.'

But we may well ask, as Vetlesen does (1997, p. 9), what about justice, goodness, happiness – the subject matter that usually defines ethics? These all matter, Vetlesen says, but they come later. Morality, as Levinas understands it, is not for the sake of anything. It defines us. And this is why he characterizes ethics as first philosophy. Llewelyn

(1995, p. 4), in his study of Levinas's work, notes that the term 'ethics' is used by Levinas in a different way to that classically employed by, for example, Aristotle or Kant. He suggests that it might be less misleading to call it 'proto-ethics'. He points out that Levinas is concerned with the 'genealogy of ethics'. We may conclude, therefore, that what Levinas calls 'ethics' is, perhaps, best seen as a starting point for ethics – it is certainly not an ethical theory.

There is a small but recently growing literature on Levinas and the ethics of proximity in relation to ethics in some professions, especially business and healthcare (for example Bevan and Corvellec, 2007; Clancy and Svensson, 2007; Nortvedt and Nordhaug, 2008). There are also some contributions on the relevance of Levinasian ethics for social work. Tascón (2010, p. 94), for example, calls for an ethics of responsibility (based on Levinas) 'that is beyond the borders of defined rules and roles and that instead relies on a response from the human-to-human', while Rossiter (2011, p. 490) talks of 'unsettled practice' and urges social workers to 'leave ourselves open to revelation from the Other'. But these appeals to the philosophy of Levinas are less about presenting an alternative theory of ethics for social work, and more a challenge to rethink the nature of social work and the inevitable distance that professionalism and managerialism brings to the relationship between social workers and service users.

The work of Bauman (1993, 1995, 2008) has also been influential in social work (see Smith, 2011). In his work on postmodern ethics, Bauman draws on the thinking of Levinas. Bauman describes the demise of ethics – as externally imposed principles and rules by which we can live our lives – in postmodern society, and suggests that what we are left with is 'the moral impulse', the demand of the other for our response. This refers to Levinas's description of the face of 'the Other' (the other human being), which summons my responsibility. Husband (1995, p. 9) considers this approach in a social work context, but acknowledges that 'the pure individuality of the moral impulse would render it an anarchic basis for organised systems of care in contemporary society'.

Diversity, narrative and constructionism: postmodern ethics?

As mentioned in the previous section, Bauman's postmodern ethics draws on the philosophy of Levinas. I am using the term 'postmodern ethics' as a broad heading covering a number of recent trends in the ethics and social work literature that have been loosely labelled as 'postmodernist', but in fact cover a variety of overlapping and inter-connected themes, including, in some cases, an interest in the ethics of virtue, care and proximity. Postmodernism is often associated with what Lyotard (1984, p. xxiv) calls an 'incredulity toward metanarratives', that is, a rejection of 'grand theories' designed to offer universal explanations or prescriptions for action. Instead, there is a focus on locally relevant 'theories' that work in specific fields or circumstances, and a preoccupation with discrete and meas-urable competences to perform particular tasks (Bauman, 1992, 1993, 1995, 1997; Harvey, 1990; Irving, 1994; Jameson, 1991; Leonard, 1997). In the context of ethical theories, this has led some commentators to speak of 'the end of ethics' (Caputo, 2000) – assuming ethics to be about foundationalist, all-encompassing and universally applicable theories of right and wrong, good or bad. Others have developed a 'postmodern ethics'.

In a social work context, a concern with fragmentation and postmodernism generally (Chambon, 1994; Chambon and Irving, 1994; Pardeck et al., 1994; Parton, 1994), diversity and difference (Briskman and Noble, 1999; Rossiter et al., 2000), small narra-tives (the service users' stories), constructionist accounts of knowl-edge and values (Milner, 2001; Parton and O'Byrne, 2000), empirical ethics, conversation and discourse analysis (see Hall et al., 1997, 2006; Taylor and White, 2000) are all evident in some recent writings.

While the approaches listed above are quite varied, and many are not explictly about ethics, what they have in common – and this is shared with some versions of the ethics of virtue, care and prox-imity – is an 'anti-foundationalism', that is, they have abandoned the search for a secure and all-encompassing foundation for ethics, such as Kant's categorical imperative or utilitarian principles, and indeed for any knowledge. All knowledges and values are partic-ular, situated and subject to revision. The concern with diversity and difference was a reaction partly against liberal free choice approaches to ethics, such as Kantianism and utilitarianism, which failed to take full account of the power held and used by dominant groups in society to oppress and subjugate others. It was also a reac-tion against the totalizing discourses of some of the universalist approaches of Marxism, feminism and anti-racist movements, which tended to focus on one type of oppression, such as class, ethnicity, gender, sexuality, age or ability, rather than see them as experienced together and in interaction, contributing to complex and shifting identities, particular to each individual and context. In social work, a concern with diversity – differences shared because of collective experiences – has led to a focus on the development of cultural competence, religious literacy and spiritual sensitivity, for example, as ways of ensuring that practitioners take account of diverse experiences and values and work alongside service users as co-producers of services and co-constructors of reality.

Constructionist approaches, which are becoming increasingly popular in some of the social work literature (for example Hall et al., 1997, 2003; Parton, 2002; Parton and O'Byrne, 2000), are based on the notion that there is no objective 'reality' existing independently of the human subject, but rather humans construct reality through discourse – language and ways of thinking (see Velody and Williams, 1998). This leads to an interest in language, in particular to the examination of who has the power to define dominant discourses, and a concern with 'deconstruction', that is, showing how knowledge and values are made, changed, developed and challenged in the context of particular power relations, cultures and historical time periods. The work of Foucault (1984, 1999) on the power of discourse, practices of surveillance and technologies of the self is particularly relevant to social work (Chambon et al., 1999).

One implication of poststructuralist and postmodernist thinking for professional ethics is a shift from a concern with the development of abstract principles and their application to practice through a process of reasoning, towards the study of the actual practices that people perform – what social workers, service users, managers and policy-makers do on a day-to-day basis – and the interrogation of institutional frameworks, professional cultures and norms. It may lead to the empirical study of social work interactions using conversation and discourse analysis, involving a detailed study of turn-taking in conversation, and including an examination of people's performances of moral blameworthiness, credibility, professional identity, trust and so on (see Hall et al., 1997, 2006; Taylor and White, 2000; White and Stancombe, 2003).

Parton and O'Byrne (2000) and Milner (2001) have developed 'solution-focused' approaches to social work, stressing the importance of the co-construction of selves and stories by service users and workers, advocating practice based on the role of narratives in empowering service users. One of the features of constructionist approaches in social work is a focus on the reflexivity of practitioners – developing a critical awareness of how they themselves are working within professional discourses that construct service users and social problems in certain kinds of ways, for example as victims or as involving child abuse.

At the same time, there is also a degree of wariness about some constructionist and postmodern perspectives. As Ife (1999, p. 215) comments:

> For the left to be spending its energies on analysing and deconstructing discourses of power, praising relativism and claiming that the era of unified visions of social justice is past, often in extremely inaccessible language, is very convenient for those who wish to pursue an ideology of greed, selfishness, increased inequality and a denial of human rights in the interests of free markets and private profit.

This kind of criticism applies particularly to postmodernists of the 'sceptical' variety (Rosenau, 1992, p. 15), who offer a 'pessimistic, negative, gloomy assessment' of the postmodern age as one of fragmentation, malaise and absence of moral parameters. In the social welfare field, however, the tendency has generally been to offer affirmative and critical postmodern perspectives, which recognize the fragmentation and diversity of the postmodern condition, yet are open to positive political action (a good example is Leonard, 1997).

The fragmentation of value

Each of these different approaches to ethics, including the principle-based approaches discussed in Chapter 2, has something to offer, but none seems to be complete on its own. Regardless of whether we believe professional ethics is socially constructed as a discourse and a practice, there is no doubt that principles and rules play an important role and that one of the expectations of a professional is that she should act impartially, without favouritism, treating people in similar circumstances in similar ways and giving a reasoned account of why she acted as she did. Principles are frequently invoked in professional decision-making. Yet it seems equally important that professionals are educated to develop attitudes and dispositions that make them the kinds of people who are honest, trustworthy, caring, sensitive, discerning and critically reflexive, and that they pay attention to the context of each situation and the special relationships they have with people. Surely all these are features of any comprehensive picture of what it is to be moral and to act morally?

Nagel (1979), noting the practical conflicts that often occur in moral decision-making, especially in the case of dilemmas, suggests that these arise because there are several fundamentally different types of value that cannot be ranked or weighed against each other on a single scale. Although he does not explicitly relate the types of value to particular theories of ethics, I think it is possible to make some connections, shown here in brackets:

1. *General rights* that everyone has that function as constraints on action, such as rights to liberty or freedom from coercion (related to Kantian principles)
2. *Utility*, which takes into account the effects of what one does on everyone's welfare (a utilitarian focus on the ends of human action)
3. *Perfectionist ends* or values, that is, the intrinsic value of certain achievements or creations apart from their value to individuals who experience or use them (a non-utilitarian focus on the ends of human action, which may allow for religious values)
4. *Specific obligations* to other people or institutions that arise out of deliberate undertakings or special relationships (virtue and care approaches)
5. *Commitments to one's own projects* and undertakings (personal commitments that may link with the virtue ethicist's idea of desiring to be a certain sort of person or pursuing excellence. This is different from self-interest).

Nagel argues that sometimes there is only one significant factor in a moral decision, for example personal obligation, and this makes things easier. On other occasions, decision-making may be insulated against the influence of more than one type of factor, for example in the judicial system which tries to limit itself to claims of right. But on many occasions, several different types of value are pertinent, and according to Nagel (1979, p. 134), there can be no system for ranking these values because they are fundamentally incommensurable:

> Human beings are subject to moral and other motivational claims of very different kinds. This is because they are complex creatures who can view the world from many perspectives – individual, relational, impersonal, ideal, etc. – and each perspective presents a different set of claims.

However, we nevertheless do have to make decisions when faced with conflicting and incommensurable claims. This requires good judgement, what Aristotle ([350 BCE]/1954) called 'practical wisdom', which Nagel (1979, p. 135) claims reveals itself over time in individual decisions rather than in the enunciation of general principles. 'Good judgement' could be regarded as a characteristic of the professional. Indeed, the concept of 'professional wisdom' has been developed to capture the practical wisdom required by practitioners in a professional context (see Banks and Gallagher, 2009, pp. 72–95). It can be linked with the notion of the reflective and reflexive practitioner, requiring, among other things, the ability to learn from and reflect on experience, a sensitivity to people's feelings and situations, attentiveness to the features of situations and an ability to reason.

Elements of professional ethics: principles, character, care and relationships

Nagel's argument for the fragmentation of value seems plausible in relation to ethics in general. But how does it fit with professional ethics? Could professional ethics fall into a category like the judicial system, which, by its very nature, is artificially insulated from certain types of value? Although there has tended to be an emphasis on principles in the form of general rights based on Kantian principles, we have seen how utilitarian principles are also important, and character traits and specific obligations, while underplayed, are relevant considerations in professional ethics. Indeed, Beauchamp and Childress (2001), while adopting 'principlism' in relation to bioethics, nevertheless reject the assumption that one must defend a single type of moral theory that is solely principle based, virtue based and so on. According to Beauchamp and Childress (2001, p. 408):

> In everyday moral reasoning, we effortlessly blend appeals to principles, rules, rights, virtues, passions, analogies, paradigms, narratives and parables ... To assign priority to one of these moral categories as the key ingredient in the moral life is a dubious project of certain writers in ethics who wish to refashion in their own image what is most central in the moral life.

So why do Beauchamp and Childress pay such a lot of attention to principles in their book? The answer may be because principles provide a useful framework for discussing and analysing ethical issues in professional practice. When a professional actually makes a decision in real life, then a whole range of factors will influence the decision-making process (see O'Sullivan, 2010), including the emotional response of the practitioner, the quality of the relationships she has with the people involved, her appraisal of the particular circumstances of the situation (including the feelings and attitudes of others involved), as well as consideration of her general obligations as a professional, the rights of the service users involved and many other aspects. However, in writing and teaching about ethical decision-making, we are not in the real-life situation and cannot actually see the people concerned or feel the emotions generated. So the focus inevitably tends to be on the general principles involved in cases like this – on the rights and duties that pertain and how they might apply in such a case (a principle-based common morality approach). To examine the principle of 'respect for the self-determination of the service user', for example to look at what it means or how it might apply in practice and what exceptions there might be, is one way of developing critical thinking about ethical decision-making. It is important to acknowledge that ethical principles are only one aspect of what is involved in decision-making.

What if we wanted to adopt a virtue-based approach to teaching professional ethics? If we want social workers in training to develop the virtues of honesty, respectfulness, trustworthiness or compassion, how is this to be done? It might involve examination of these characteristics and asking questions, such as: What does it mean to say someone is honest? How would an honest person act in this situation? We might ask whether this would be very different from exploring what is meant by the principle of honesty and how we can implement it in practice. The difference would be in the focus on the character and motivation of the moral agent, which might encourage the social worker to question issues about her own identity and dispositions. But looking to what principles she espouses and when she might make exceptions to them might have a similar effect.

Surely there is something more to a virtue ethics approach than this? Virtue ethics is about developing good character and good judgement in professionals, what we might call 'moral education'. An important part of this is having role models, teachers in both academic institutions and practice settings. According to Statman (1997, p. 13):

> Becoming a good person is not a matter of learning or 'applying' principles, but of imitating some models. We learn to be virtuous in the same way we learn to dance, to cook, and to play football – by watching people who are competent in these areas and trying to do the same.

This probably helps to explain why textbooks on practical ethics do not tend to adopt a virtue-based approach, that is, because virtues are largely developed in other ways. However, I think it is possible to acknowledge the importance of developing virtues through moral exemplars and imitating role models, while acknowledging the role of ethical principles and rules. Following Statman's analogy, if we want to improve our skills in football, apart from being coached and watching people playing, we may also read books on the principles of good football and we certainly need to study the rules of the game. The two approaches are surely complementary.

The real danger of the principle-based approach would be if it degenerated into a focus on rules, which are more specific and determined than principles. This would then turn professional ethics into a matter of learning the rules and how to implement them, rather than a process of critical and responsible reflection. But principles are not the same as rules, and it requires a lot of work to examine what they mean and how and when they apply. It also requires the development of the faculty of good judgement. In this sense, both virtue-based and principle-based approaches require the development of skilled, critical and reflective practitioners. A virtue-based approach is a good corrective to the tendency to adopt a rule-based approach to professional ethics, because we want professionals to become more than simply rule-following automata. We want to develop people who respect confidentiality because they are the kind of people who are trustworthy and respectful in all aspects of life, not just because their agency or professional association has laid down a rule to this effect. Yet not everyone is virtuous, and it is not as easy to change or develop people's characters as it is for people to be required to follow a rule. Rules are action oriented and take account of the fact that people in professional roles should behave in certain kinds of ways, even if they do this out of duty rather than because they have a disposition to act in such ways. Specific rules are needed precisely because people are not always virtuous and because they may not always have the capacity (or be trusted) to make good judgements. But the growth of more and more rules and the emphasis on the specific competences of social workers to act in certain ways should not lure us away from the need to develop workers of integrity and trustworthiness. This is why consideration of virtue ethics is important, because it emphasizes the moral education and development of the professional, as opposed to simply training in competences for work.

Further exploration of the ethics of care and the role of emotions, such as empathy and compassion, is also important in a social work context (see Hugman 2005, pp. 48–84 for a useful discussion). Hugman (1998a, p. 95) distinguishes between caring as work (concerned with doing and action) and caring as commitment (to do with being and attitude). He argues that the tendency to focus on quantifiable aspects of welfare practice precludes caring as attitude/commitment, because caring comes to be seen solely in terms of 'the tasks performed'. The ethics of care offers a challenge to this tendency to separate attitude and action. Edwards (1996, p. 155), for example, while arguing for the primacy of principle-based ethics in nursing, nevertheless acknowledges an important role for the kinds of considerations that are of concern to care-based theorists. He points out that there is a difference between a cool, detached application of principles and the implementation of principles 'in a manner which is infused with care'. These arguments do not necessarily distinguish between care as a virtue and care as a relation, as the two are inevitably intertwined. However, the emphasis on care as a relation in the ethics of care is what makes it highly relevant in the context of social work.

Towards a situated ethics of social justice

'Care' is certainly one of the distinctive values that lies at the heart of social work, even if its asymmetricality and association with parentalism – caring for someone on the carer's terms – means that it often does not feature in statements of values and ethical principles. In this respect, Tronto's (1994) conception of a political ethics of care is a useful one, as this focuses on human relationships in the context of structures of power and oppression. It takes account of the commitment in social work to social justice. However, in seeking to outline proposals for a set of values for progressive social work, I have preferred to speak instead of a 'situated ethics of social justice' (Banks, 2011a). Although this may be hardly distinguishable from a political ethics of care, it is significant that it takes 'social justice' as its starting point (qualified by the term 'situated') rather than care (qualified by 'political'). Hence, it emphasizes the social justice mission of social work. List 3.3 is a preliminary attempt to develop an ethical framework for social work, drawing on the insights from previous chapters.

List 3.3 Preliminary values for a situated ethics of social justice for social work

- *Radical social justice:* Social workers need to take seriously the social justice agenda contained within international and other definitions and descriptions of social work as being about working for equality of outcomes and challenging unjust policies and practices. We need to be alert to the variety of formulations of social justice, such as the more liberal reformist focus on equal opportunities, and hold onto a conception that embraces a call to challenge the oppression of individuals, groups and cultures.
- *Empathic solidarity:* Part of the role of social workers is to situate themselves in relation to the hopes, fears, pains and pleasures of other people, specifically service users. Empathy on its own, however, is not enough. It needs to lead to the development of a sense of solidarity and commitment to collective action for social change. This empathic solidarity requires abilities of critical analysis and an aspirational or hopeful attitude – this involves seeing the bigger picture, questioning received ideas and seeing the possibility for another kind of world.
- *Relational autonomy:* It is important that social workers claim power as moral agents to work for progressive micro-level and macro-level social change. However, we need to reframe individual professional autonomy as 'relational autonomy'. This involves recognizing that autonomy is both defined and pursued in a social context (including structures of oppression) and this influences the opportunities an individual has to develop and exercise autonomy. In social work, the exercise of professional autonomy is also based on 'power with' others, including service users.
- *Collective responsibility for resistance:* Social workers should take responsibility for good and just practice, and for resisting bad and unjust practice and policies. This is the counterpart to claiming autonomy. But in seeing their autonomy as relational, that is, in the context of oppressive and constraining structures and institutions, it is important that they resist the 'responsibilization' of social workers, service users and people in poverty. This means social workers should actively resist, with service users and other allies, the placing of responsibility for the causes and solutions of social problems with individuals,

families and communities. This responsibility is shared with all fellow citizens and the responsibility for taking action is also collective as well as individual. This could also be termed 'relational responsibility'.

- *Moral courage:* Moral courage is a quality or disposition to act in situations where such actions are difficult, uncomfortable or fear-inducing. Many aspects of social work require moral courage – knocking on the door of the house of a family whose child is under threat of removal, or challenging a racist comment by a service user. Moral courage is also required to speak out about inadequate resources and policies that impact disproportionately on people who are in need or difficulty.

- *Working in and with complexity and contradictions:* In social work, complexity, uncertainty, ambivalence and contradictions need to be acknowledged and used, along with the recognition that ethics is not about simple dilemmas, that is, choices between two courses of action. Ethical being and action require hard work on the part of social workers – a process of constantly negotiating and working out what roles to take, questioning what they are doing and why, and being alert to the dominance of the managerialist and neoliberal agendas. It entails working in the spaces between the contradictions of care and control, prevention and enforcement, empathy and equity. Ethics is definitely not about simply following rules – it is about questioning and challenging, feeling and acting.

Source: Adapted from Banks, 2011a

These values are a mixture of principles of action and moral qualities, premised on a relational worldview. This list is a preliminary statement, which is not designed to replace existing sets of values articulated in the social work literature and codes of ethics. Indeed, these values are not new – they are old values that have been reworked and restated in order to remind us of their importance and to reclaim them from dilution or cooption by managerialism, market principles or other negative trends in society. Versions of these values can be found in the international statement on ethics in social work (IFSW/IASSW, 2004), and in many national codes of ethics and other literature, as we will see in the next chapter. But when placed in a code of ethics in the middle of a whole range of other exhortations, injunctions and standards in documents of 30–50 pages, their significance can be lost, or they can be regarded as another example of social work's radical rhetoric that means little in practice, or is untranslatable into practice.

Conclusions

Although not well developed as yet for social work, we have discussed the merits and importance of character, relationship-based, proximity and postmodern approaches as a counterbalance to the detached rationality and impartiality of principle-based ethics. The development of good character, good judgement, reflexivity, the capacity to care and to be morally sensitive to the particularities of situations are equally important aspects of ethical being and acting. Social workers often work with very vulnerable people who enter into relationships of trust with them. It is therefore important that social workers take account of the unique circumstances of each person's life, recognize and respect diversity, express care and compassion, exhibit empathy, and act in ways that honour the trust placed in them by the people with whom they work. In this sense, social work has a lot in common with other 'caring' professionals, particularly those in the health and education field, with whom social workers are increasingly working in interprofessional contexts. However, some aspects of the qualities of character and nature of professional relationships appropriate for many other professionals with whom social workers collaborate (such as the police or doctors) are also different, which means that it is important to be clear in interprofessional contexts about professional values, so that social workers can play a distinctive role that complements and sometimes challenges that of other professionals. Here their commitment to a situated ethics of social justice is important. This is illustrated in Case example 7.12, about a childcare team manager who holds firm in her support of a young woman with whom she has a long-standing professional relationship against the demands of health-care professionals (see also Banks, 2004a, Ch. 5). The case for discussion at the end of this chapter illustrates how social workers in Bulgaria express both their caring relationship with a child and a commitment to individual justice for the child as part of a mission to achieve social justice in society.

Putting it into practice

Exploring character and emotion through a role-play and/or reflection

Aims of the exercise: to consider the role of emotion, qualities of character, caring relationships and professional power in a social work encounter.

Scenario
Take as a starting point a scenario where a 15-year-old young man meets a female social worker for the first time in a local social work office. He has come to ask for help with looking after his mother, who is severely depressed. The young man is an only child and has been giving quite a lot of support to his mother since his father left home a year ago. He says he is now very worried about his mother, as during the past few weeks, she has been spending most of the time in bed, eating very little and crying a lot. He has been missing school in order to stay with her and has been advised by his neighbour to come to the social work agency for support. He bursts into tears during the meeting with the social worker.

Group role-play
Act out this scenario with two people taking the roles of social worker and the young man. The rest of the group should act as observers. The 'actors' should imagine themselves in these roles and act out a first encounter between the two people lasting 5–10 minutes. The teacher/facilitator or another group member should take responsibility for stopping the role-play at a suitable point and debriefing the two participants, by asking how it felt for them in the roles and being prepared to talk them through any disturbing emotions it may have raised for them. Other group members should observe the encounter carefully, noting what the participants said, their tones of voice, body language and nonverbal communication. Questions to consider might include:

1. Did the social worker convey, perform and/or develop various qualities of character, emotions, relationships, positions or statuses, for example trustworthiness, compassion, empathy, moral sensitivity, a caring relationship, professional distance, professional expertise? Different observers could be asked to look for different features of the conversation.
2. How was this accomplished?

3. What emotions, positions or claims, for example despair, victim, hero, did the young man convey or perform?
4. How was power manifested in the relationship?

Individual reflection or group reflection instead of role-play
Imagine yourself first as the social worker, then as the young man in the scenario described above. Consider what emotions, relationships and performances might be generated by the meeting in the social work office and how you would recognize these. How might these be constrained or influenced by the agency context in which the encounter takes place and the professional role of the social worker?

Discussion
What do you think were the specifically ethical dimensions of this encounter? Does it help us to separate out the ethical aspects of a situation? Can we view this encounter both from the perspective of an ethics of care and an ethics of principles/justice? How do the two perspectives interrelate?

Practice focus

Case for discussion 3: The life of a child and the heart of a child protection department in Bulgaria

The material for this case was contributed by the head of a child protection department in Bulgaria. It is a story about the relationship between nine-year-old Julietta and the social workers who work for the child protection department in her home town.

Julietta is a young girl with eyes that are brown and a little bit sad. She has long auburn hair, long legs and a thin body. She now lives in a children's village some distance away from the home where she grew up with her mother and grandmother. She was placed in the children's village at the age of eight when her grandmother, who had been looking after her since she was four years old, was hospitalized. The child protection department had been involved with the family for five years, since the grandmother contacted them to report that her daughter (Julietta's mother, a single parent) was incapable of taking adequate care of the child. The three of them lived in a four-room apartment owned by Julietta's mother. The apartment had been donated to the mother by the grandmother in exchange for a promise to take care of her when she grew old.

When first contacted by the grandmother, the social workers undertook a thorough investigation and attempted to work with the mother to help her see that the child was often not washed, not properly dressed for the season and sometimes had not eaten during the whole day. The mother did not allow the grandmother to feed Julietta. According to neighbours, screaming was sometimes heard from the apartment in the late evenings, which the social workers thought might be a sign of violence. The child protection department decided to give parental responsibility for Julietta to her grandmother. Given that there was a warm relationship between the mother and the child, and considering that there was no direct threat to Julietta's life (only to her health), the child protection department boldly decided to take on the heavy responsibility of maintaining and supporting the contact between the mother and child. Julietta loved her mother and the mother adored the child, but the mother was slowly losing the ability to take care of herself and her daughter. The mother had been raped many years ago and had experienced psychiatric problems since that time, which were growing worse.

For four years the child protection department worked to ensure Julietta received good care. However, the social workers did not see any possibility to return Julietta to the care of her mother, who did not regularly follow her treatment and was judged unable fully to take care of Julietta. The child protection department strongly supported the relationship between the mother and the daughter, as the social workers judged that the child needed to know her roots. The social workers fought to convince the mother to take her medicines regularly in the interest of her child. Some kind of a result was achieved. Julietta and her mother got along perfectly well, but only insofar as the mother played games and went on walks with her, and picked her up from the kindergarden and later from school.

As the grandmother grew older, both women started to argue more often. The grandmother feared that her daughter would not take care of her, so she started to annul the donation of the apartment to her daughter, intending instead to donate the apartment to Julietta. Eventually, the mother's condition deteriorated so much that she was placed, under compulsion, in a psychiatric institution for three months.

One night, not long afterwards, the grandmother was hit on the head and fell down unconscious in the street. Some people 'rescued' her and took her to hospital. A woman she did not know took care of her. The woman stated that she had no place to live, but if the grandmother took her in, in exchange she would take care of the old woman. The grandmother agreed to this arrangement. Somehow, the grandmother obtained a proxy agreement from her daughter and sold the apartment to relatives of the woman who was caring for her. She believed that with the money from the four-room apartment, she would be able to buy two apartments – one for her and her carer and another one for Julietta. However, she never received the money from the people who 'bought' her apartment, only the promise that as soon as they found two apartments at the right price, they would buy them for her.

While the grandmother was in hospital, nobody was taking care of Julietta and it became urgent to find a place for her. There were no other close relatives. Her father had never recognized her. The foster families were all taken. As a last resort, the child protection department contacted the children's village in another town and Julietta was given a place there. This is how the child began a new page of her life away from her mother and grandmother.

Representatives from the child protection department often visit the village. They take walks and talk to Julietta, play with the other children, exchange information with the village staff and do their best to ease Julietta's adaptation to the new environment. When she asks questions about her mother, the social workers can only shed a tear in secret on their way back, thinking about the child and the destiny of her family. On one occasion, she asked about her favourite Barbie doll that she used to fall asleep with back home. The child described it vividly and visually. The social workers, driven by purely human feelings (rather than work duties), began a crazy search for a Barbie doll that was the same as Julietta's. They were only able to find one with curly hair, not straight. They bought some other things and prepared a package for the child, explaining that they had made Barbie's hair curly on purpose, so she could have a new look. When Julietta saw it in the village, she firmly stated that this was not her Barbie because hers had different eye lashes. Nevertheless, in the end, she said: 'Well, this one can also be mine.'

In the course of their work with Julietta and her grandmother, the child protection department uncovered the fraud that had been committed on the grandmother. Her apartment had been sold with either a fake or an invalid proxy (since her daughter, Julietta's mother, was under compulsory detention in a psychiatric institution). This was clearly a matter relating to a private property transaction, which was not part of the remit of the child protection department, especially as Julietta was not the direct owner of the property. However, Julietta's mother was the owner, and consequently the child's interests were seriously affected. According to the head of the department:

> The ethics of the child protection department employees do not allow them to remain silent, even when there is a case of organized crime and personal threats are involved. Our high sense of responsibility did not allow us to just let the prosecution lawyers know about the fraud and forget about the case.

> Our social work continued with Julietta in order to ensure that the child was growing up and her needs were met – such as a house, food, clothes, personal space, education, health, emotional comfort, having an adult close to her in the village and the realization of her identity as a person. Along with all this we started gathering documents in order to prove the fraud, since our final aim was to get the apartment back for the mother and her child.

> Are we going to be able to save one child from the consequences of the actions of organized crime groups? The last word belongs to the prosecution and to the court. An official investigation is taking place. We believe in the Bulgarian justice system especially when we witness good cooperation on many levels in this particular case.

This is a real story about a child with living parents, but because of circumstances beyond her control she lives without parents, relatives or a family home. This is also a short story about the hearts of the child protection department employees. In this story, there is no citation of the relevant laws, professional duties and all the official requirements that form part of child protection work. It does not reflect the whole activity of the child protection department. It only shows the human face of the department employees. This is the face, the ethics and values of the department. This is a part of the everyday life of the department that responds to the question: 'How do we help people within the boundaries of the law?' instead of 'How do we use the law to deny help to people?'

> We do not believe we are the only ones. It is probably the same in other departments in the country – where social workers have good knowledge of the laws, empathy and humanity. It is probably the same across the world, because by just applying the law one cannot reach children's hearts – one cannot reach unconventional, creative, bold and nevertheless right decisions in the interest of the child.

Questions for discussion

1. What is your immediate reaction to this case?
2. On the basis of the comments made by the head of the child protection department, what moral qualities or 'virtues' do you think she would look for in her staff?
3. Can you give an account of this case in terms of the ethics of care? How helpful do you find Tronto's five elements of care in contributing to your understanding of the human relationships in this case?
4. As the head of the child protection department acknowledges, the social workers and the department went beyond their official duties in this case. What are the strengths and limitations of this approach? From the information you are given about the ethos of the child protection department in this case, how does it compare with the Japanese welfare office in Case for discussion 7?

Further resources

Boss, J. (2010) *Ethics for Life: A Text with Readings,* 5th edn, New York, McGraw Hill.
Useful background on various ethical theories, written in a clear, practical style. Has biographical details of key thinkers, selected readings from key texts and includes discussion of religion and cultural relativism. Useful sections on virtue and care ethics.

Hugman, R. (2005) *New Approaches in Ethics for the Caring Professions,* Basingstoke Palgrave Macmillan.
Useful chapters that critically evaluate the ethics of compassion, care, postmodernity and constructionism in relation to the caring professions.

Taylor, C. and White, S. (2000) *Practising Reflexivity in Health and Welfare,* Buckingham, Open University Press.
Takes a social constructionist approach to analysing the discourses of professional practice in health and social care. Uses transcripts of professional conversations and documents and includes consideration of how professionals bring off and negotiate professional identity and authority.

CHAPTER 4

Principles into practice: professionalism and codes of ethics

CHAPTER OVERVIEW

This chapter will discuss the nature of professionalism, followed by an examination of the form, function and content of written codes of ethics as a way of capturing key ethical principles and moral qualities for social work and specifying their implementation in practice. The discussion is illustrated through the examination of codes of ethics collected from professional associations of social workers from different countries, consideration of the advantages and limitations of codes of ethics and the growing trends towards professional regulation. At the end of this chapter, there is an exercise about analysing codes of ethics, and a case for discussion is presented about defending a social worker's duty of professional secrecy in France.

Introduction

Chapters 2 and 3 discussed a variety of ethical theories and theoretical approaches that give accounts of the foundations of ethics and/or outline views about which values are important in leading ethically good lives. I indicated how these theoretical approaches have influenced statements of values for social work and how they have been regarded as relevant for the understanding of the role of social workers. This chapter looks at how values and principles for social work are constructed in professional codes of ethics and practice.

The traditional model of professionalism and trait theory

Earlier chapters have taken for granted that social work is a recognizable occupation and that people who belong to this occupation share certain sets of common values. I have occasionally used the term 'profession' to describe social work, but have not critically examined what this means. 'Professionalism' is, however, a contested and contestable concept, both in its own right, and as applied to social work. So I will briefly discuss various approaches to the study of professions as a precursor to examining an important source of statements of occupational values – namely, professional codes of ethics.

In many countries across the world, the occupation of social work has a national code of ethics, generally produced by a professional association. This is often said to be one of the defining features of a profession, according to the traditional model of professionalism (Koehn, 1994). On this 'traditional' view, a profession is an occupation, the members of which are committed to service to their clients. Professionals have special expertise, which they use for the good of their clients and for the public good. They also have considerable autonomy to make professional judgements and act upon them. In becoming members of the profession, they pledge themselves to be trustworthy and to put the interests of their clients and the public above their own interests. The 'pledge' (promise) made by members of a profession may be implicit, but more often it takes the form of a code of ethics. The Hippocratic oath in medicine, which until recently physicians used to swear on joining the profession, is a good example of an early version of such a public pledge.

In the 1960s and 70s, there was much debate about whether social work was a profession in the traditional sense just described (Etzioni, 1969; Toren, 1972). The 'trait' theory of professionalism was popular, which maintained that to be regarded as a profession, an occupation must possess certain characteristics. A commonly quoted list of ideal attributes of a profession was that of Greenwood (1957), which is outlined in List 4.1.

List 4.1 Ideal attributes of a profession

1. A basis of systematic theory.
2. Authority recognized by the clientele of the professional group.
3. Broader community sanction and approval of this authority.
4. A code of ethics regulating relationships of professionals with service users and colleagues.
5. A professional culture sustained by formal professional associations.

Source: Drawn from Greenwood, 1957

At this time, social work was often referred to as a 'semi-profession' because while it met some of these criteria (in some countries it had codes of ethics and professional associations, and claims were being made for a social work 'knowledge base'), it did not meet them all fully. Certainly, 'broad community sanction' and approval of social workers' authority was (and arguably still is) comparatively weak.

However, there has been considerable criticism of the 'trait theory' of professionalism (see, for example, Abbott and Meerabeau, 1998; Freidson, 1994, 2001; Hugman, 1991; Johnson, 1972; Koehn, 1994; Larson, 1977). First, there is disagreement over what the essential characteristics of a profession are. Some commentators speak of 'state licensing' rather than 'community sanction', 'esoteric knowledge' rather than 'systematic theory', and a 'public pledge' as opposed to a 'code of ethics' (see Koehn, 1994, p. 40). Others add additional criteria such as professional education and qualification (Millerson, 1964). According to Koehn (1994), there is only one defensible trait of professionalism, and this is the public pledge that professionals make to render assistance to those in need. Koehn argues that the other traits are neither necessary nor sufficient to define a professional.

Another criticism of the trait theory is that it is modelled on the old-established professions, such as medicine and the law, defining any occupation that does not share the same characteristics as less than a profession. Commentators have pointed out how the 'caring professions', such as social work, nursing and occupational therapy, have tended traditionally to be women's occupations and have been denied full professional status partly for this reason. Caring work (meaning caring for others) is thought to be women's work; it has less status and prestige and does not require special knowledge and skills. Medicine is not a 'caring profession' in the same way. Although medicine is based on a commitment to serve patients, this entails caring *about* them, not *for* them. It is the nurses who care for patients in performing the everyday tasks of bathing or feeding (Hugman, 1991, p. 17).

Some have argued that an alternative set of traits is needed for the 'people work' professionals, which takes account of their location in bureaucratic settings (as 'bureau-professionals' with limited autonomy over their work) and 'their affective knowledge based on intuitive interpersonal understanding' (Holmes, 1981, p. 27). However, this would perpetuate the trait model of professionalism, which has not been useful in developing our understanding of the nature and role of professions in society. As Johnson (1972, p. 29) points out, professions have developed in different ways depending on historical and cultural factors and variations in the role of governments and academic institutions. There is no one set of traits that uniquely characterizes a profession, nor one set of stages through which an occupational group passes to reach this end point of 'professionalism'. There are big differences in these respects in the development of professions between countries, as well as between professions in the same country (see Burrage and Torstendahl, 1990). Siegrist (1994, p. 8) argues that it is important to examine professions in terms of the complex interactions between the nation state, government and legislation, which vary between countries and change over time.

Professionalism and power

Johnson (1972) and others following him (Hugman, 1991; Wilding, 1982) focus instead on power as a factor in the success of an occupation in achieving status in society and see professionalism as a peculiar type of occupational control whereby a community of practitioners defines the relationship between professional and service user. Alternatives to the trait theory offer a much more self-interested view of professionalism, which focuses on the way individuals come together to create a relatively 'closed' occupational group and make claims about credentials and status (see Collins, 1990). Hugman argues that the language of professionalism often obscures the issue of power. Talk of the service ideal, trust, expertise, colleague control and public accountability appeals to the sentiments embodied in the trait approach, but can be interpreted as 'occupational bids for status and privilege' (Hugman, 1991, p. 6). On this analysis, it would be more useful to explore the reasons behind and the process of the professionalization of social work than to debate whether it could be regarded as a profession in the terms delineated by trait theory. Nevertheless, although discredited, trait theory is still influential, in that occupations continue to make claims to certain attributes in order to affirm their professional status, with a particular emphasis on developing codes of ethics.

While 'caring professionals', including social workers, may not be regarded as full professionals in many people's eyes, and are given less status and recognition than, for example, doctors, they do wield considerable power, particularly over service users. And this aspect of professionalism – the claim to expert knowledge, the control not just of resources, but also the power to define the terms of the professional–service user relationship – has been strongly attacked from many quarters, ranging from right to left. Ivan Illich, writing in the 1970s, referred to the 'disabling professions', arguing that power and control over individuals' lives has been taken away by so-called 'experts', such as doctors, teachers or social workers (Illich et al., 1977). Professions can be seen as protective and exclusive groups, seeking to retain power over their own occupations and hence over service users (Wilding, 1982). These criticisms may be levelled at social work, regardless of whether one regards it simply as an occupation, an aspirant profession, a semi-profession or a profession.

Democratic professionalism

Within social work in Britain, from the 1980s, the idea of a 'new professionalism' emerged, entailing an increasing focus on partnership with service users and with viewing service users as experts on their own lives and issues (for further discussion of the 'new professionalism' or 'democratic professionalism', see Chapter 5). Similar ideas were advocated by American author Freidson (1994, pp. 9–10), who in defending professionalism from recent critiques, talked of a professionalism reborn, 'stripped of the compromising institutions that assure workers a living, a professionalism expressed purely as dedication to the committed practice of a complex craft that is of value to others'. This is an attempt to renew and reassert the traditional notion of professionals as having a selfless commitment to the public good and being morally trustworthy, while acknowledging that claims to exclusive scientific expertise and relatively strong autonomy in their decision-making need to be modified (for further discussion of 'democratic' or 'civic' professionalism, see Dzur, 2008; Sullivan, 2005).

The traditional notion of professionalism has come under the critical scrutiny not just of academics, but also service user movements, the public and governments, accompanied in many countries by strong deprofessionalizing trends linked to campaigns for service users' rights, and the growth of consumerism and managerialism (Banks, 2004a; Dominelli, 1996; Exworthy and Halford, 1999; Freidson, 2001; Lymbery, 2000). These trends will be discussed more fully in Chapters 5 and 6. In the meantime, it is important to note that the development of codes of ethics in social work reflects some of these trends. Codes have developed from short oaths to include longer 'rulebooks' that prescribe specific behaviour in specific circumstances, partly as a way of demonstrating to sceptical publics that there are sound mechanisms for ensuring the competent and ethical practice of individual professionals (see Banks, 2003, 2011a).

Professional associations, regulatory bodies and 'colleges'

In most countries of the world, it is professional associations (independent membership bodies that social workers join voluntarily) that develop codes of ethics, hold disciplinary hearings in cases of professional misconduct and offer professional guidance and support to members. Sometimes these associations play a role as trade unions as well and work to protect members' employment rights and levels of salary. In several countries, including the UK, statutory regulatory bodies have been established for social work, the functions of which include maintaining a register of qualified professionals with the power to remove people from the register in cases of proven incompetence or unethical behaviour. This usually entails that 'social worker' becomes a protected title (as only those registered can practise as social workers) and these regulatory bodies take on a major role in licensing social workers and disciplining them on grounds of professional misconduct. There is a slow trend in social work towards statutory regulation. It is difficult to achieve as governments have to be persuaded of the value of and need for the regulation of social work. Many in the profession are sceptical of the benefits and it is costly to administer. The South African Council for Social Service Professions (SACSSP) is an example of a relatively long-established statutory regulatory body, originally set up as the Council for Social Work in 1978 (see Mazibuko and Gray, 2004; SACSSP, 2006). Examples of recently established regulatory bodies include those set up in the four countries of the UK in 2001 and the registration board set up in New Zealand in 2003 (Beddoe and Duke, 2009; Orme and Rennie, 2006).

Such developments are welcomed by some people as further moves towards gaining occupational recognition and status, but this comes at the price of increasing state control and a focus on controlling the conduct of individual social workers (McLaughlin, 2007, 2010; Webster, 2010). The autonomy of the profession, and of the professional associations, is reduced in the interests of maintaining and developing the credibility of the profession and standardizing practice. Moves in England towards the development of a college of social work, one of the recommendations of a government-sponsored review of social work (Social Work Task Force, 2009), continue this trend towards attempting to establish social work as a credible and higher status profession with consistent standards, high-level professional development and advanced education opportunities (www.collegeofsocialwork.org). The establishment of a college of social work as an independent voice for social work, developed and led by social workers, sparked a conflict with the British Association of Social Workers, leading to a later agreement to work together, as the new college was clearly encroaching on some of its functions (Dawson, 2011). In Australia, on the other hand, the Australian Association of Social Workers has itself recently set up the Australian College of Social Work as a focus for specialist and advanced practice, with one of its explicit aims being to provide 'identity, status and recognition for social workers and the profession' (www.aasw.asn.au/acsw).

Professional codes of ethics for social work

In 1994, 2000 and 2005, I undertook surveys of the codes of ethics of member associations of the International Federation of Social Workers (IFSW) (see Banks, 1995, 2001b, 2005). For the purpose of this chapter, in discussing changes in the form and content of codes of ethics, I will draw on these surveys (especially the 2005 survey, which included 31 codes), supplemented by more recent versions of some codes of ethics taken from the IFSW website (www.ifsw.org) and the websites of selected professional associations. The IFSW itself has a statement of ethical principles, which, when revised in 2004, was developed as a shared statement with the International Association of Schools of Social Work (IASSW) (IFSW/IASSW, 2004). This outlines general ethical principles for social work worldwide, based on human rights and social justice, followed by a short section on professional conduct. The statement on ethics is intended to provide a framework for national associations to develop their own more detailed codes to fit local circumstances. While this statement is not called a 'code of ethics', it fulfils many of the functions of a code of ethics at an international level, although the IFSW does not get involved in disciplining individual social workers since its members are national associations.

The term 'code of ethics' is used to cover quite a broad range of different types of codes of conduct or behaviour. Millerson (1964, p. 149), writing in the 1960s about professionalism in general, regarded 'professional ethics' as a part of what is entailed by 'professional conduct', dividing professional conduct into professional practice and professional ethics, as follows:

1. *Professional practice:* relates to the adoption of schedules of uniform professional fees and charges, standard forms of contract, regulation of competition for projects
2. *Professional ethics:* concerned with moral directives guiding the relationship between the professional and others and designed to distinguish right from wrong action. A professional ethic may be a formal code or an informal understanding.

While the early codes of ethics for social work and other professions focused almost exclusively on what Millerson defined as 'professional ethics' and often took the form of short statements of principles or oaths, in recent years codes of ethics have tended to expand to include 'professional practice' matters. The first code in the USA developed by Mary Richmond in the 1920s for the American Association of Social Workers was apparently 'a very simple, brief code'; and the first code of the National Association of Social Workers (NASW, published in 1960, following the formation of NASW in 1955) was only one page long (Brill, 1998). According to Reamer (1999), the 1960 NASW code comprised a short series of abstract first-person proclamations. This is in marked contrast to the 1996 version of 27 pages (still in operation with only minor revisions) comprising a short section on ethical principles, followed by 156 standards. The first code of the British Association of Social Workers (BASW, 1975) was also a relatively brief document of seven pages (of which four pages comprised commentary), with the 2002 version running to 16 pages (BASW, 2002).

Generally, these longer documents are still called 'codes of ethics', although they are often divided into sections, with more specific standards or rules concerning particular practice settings and matters of fees, advertising or etiquette and so on towards the end. In some cases, however, there may be two separate booklets, with one entitled 'code of ethics' and the other 'guidelines for ethical practice' or 'code of practice' (see, for example, Canadian Association of Social Workers, 2005a, 2005b; Irish Association of Social Workers, 2006, 2009). However, we should be cautious in reading too much into the titles of these documents as they do not necessarily conform to Millerson's distinctions between 'professional ethics' and 'professional practice'. For example, the code of the Hong Kong Social Workers Association (1998) includes ethical principles but is called a 'code of practice'.

Some commentators have highlighted the contrasts between the codes produced by state-sponsored regulatory bodies (often called 'codes of practice' or 'codes of conduct') and the codes of ethics of professional associations (Reamer and Shardlow, 2009; Webster, 2010). Much of the content is, however, very similar. For example, the code of practice developed in the UK for the regulatory bodies (General Social Care Council, 2002) was relatively short and did not include a greater focus on 'professional practice' issues than the BASW code of the same date, which was, in fact, longer. Similar comments apply to the code produced by New Zealand's Social Workers Registration Board (2008). However, one of the main differences is that the explicit aim of the codes of the regulatory bodies is to set minimum standards to which social workers should practise. The codes of the professional associations often include principles and standards that are aspirational or aiming towards 'best practice'. In the next section, I will focus particularly on the ethical codes of the professional associations rather than the regulatory bodies.

The components of codes of ethics

Although codes vary in form and content, there are several types of statement that feature in all or some of them, as outlined in List 4.2.

List 4.2 Ingredients of codes of ethics

1. *Statements about the core purpose or service ideal of the profession:* for example 'the primary mission of the social work profession is to enhance human wellbeing'.
2. *Statements about the character/attributes of the professional:* for example 'professional practitioners should be honest, trustworthy and reliable'.
3. *Statements about the values on which the profession is based:* for example 'human dignity and worth', 'social justice'.
4. *Ethical principles:* general statements of ethical principles underpinning the work, for example 'respect for the autonomy of service users', 'promotion of human welfare'.
5. *Ethical rules:* some general dos and don'ts, sometimes framed as 'standards', for example 'do not permit knowledge to be used for discriminatory policies', 'protect all confidential information'.

6. *Principles of professional practice:* general statements about how to achieve what is intended for the good of the service user, for example 'collaboration with colleagues'.

7. *Rules of professional practice:* specific guidance relating to professional practice, for example 'declare a bequest in a client's will', 'advertising should not claim superiority'.

Source: Adapted from Banks, 2004a, p. 109

Many codes, but not all, have some kind of preamble, which may state the core purpose and broad aims of the profession. Reference is frequently made to the IFSW/IASSW (2000) definition of social work and sometimes to various UN declarations and conventions on human rights. Current codes of ethics for social work contain relatively few statements about the character (or virtues) of practitioners, but some references can be found, along the lines of 'the social worker should maintain honesty', for example. In some codes, there is a statement of values – fundamental beliefs about what is valuable or worthy in life – prior to the outlining of the ethical principles related to these values. In other cases, no distinction is made between 'values' and 'principles'.

The codes largely comprise principles and rules. List 4.2 distinguishes between principles and rules, and between content that is primarily ethical in nature and that which relates to professional practice. Principles have a much broader scope than rules, tending to apply to all people in all circumstances, although in the case of social work, principles often apply to 'all service users'. So, for example, 'social workers should respect the autonomy of service users' is an ethical principle, whereas 'social workers should not disclose confidential information to third-party payers unless clients have authorized such disclosure' might be regarded as an ethical rule. 'Ethical' content relates to attitudes, rights and duties about human welfare, such as respecting human dignity and promoting social justice, whereas 'professional practice' matters have less direct ethical content and may even include issues of 'professional etiquette', such as how to dress and how to advertise. While codes vary greatly in their wording and the types of rule or 'standard' they include, the ethical principles are often variations on the following: respect for persons, respect for and promotion of the autonomy of service users, promotion of human welfare, social justice, and professional integrity.

If we analyse the codes in terms of the theoretical approaches outlined in Chapters 2 and 3, the general conclusion is that they are predominantly principle based as opposed to character and relationship based, with a greater emphasis on Kantian-type rights and duties than on utilitarian principles. In their preambles and also in the way some of the principles and rules or standards are framed, the importance of relationships in social work is often stressed, but this is stated in the form of general prescriptions for action and hence not recognizably reflecting an ethics of care. However, many codes do make some reference to the characteristics or qualities of workers ('virtues' in the ethical terminology). For example, the NASW code (2008, p. 4) states that the principles and standards must be applied by 'individuals of good character', and the Slovakian code mentions 'honesty' as important (Asociácia Sociálnych Pracovníkov na Slovensku, 1997, para. 1.D). The Hong Kong code has one statement referring to the characteristics of workers: 'The social worker should maintain honesty, integrity and responsibility in professional practice' (Hong Kong Social Workers Association, 1998, p. 6). The Russian ethical guidelines speak of the importance of the 'unselfishness' of the social worker (Russian Union of Social Educators and Social Workers, 2003, para. 4.6), while the code for Israel states that social workers should conduct themselves in their work 'with integrity and loyalty' (Association for the Advancement of Social Work, 2007). Many codes list 'integrity' as a core value of social work – a consistent feature of the Australian and US codes from the late 1980s. The code of one of the Swedish unions for social workers (Akademikerförbundet SSR, 2006, p. 11), however, pays much greater attention to the importance of ethical traits of character and gives examples of ethical qualities in social work (as outlined earlier in Table 3.2). In the short set of ethical guidelines, several are framed in terms of attitudes or qualities of character, for example 'show an egalitarian attitude to other citizens and treat clients with respect, empathic attention and amiability', 'be open to cooperation' and 'stand for a democratic social ideal' (p. 13).

Differences and commonalities between codes of ethics

Taken as a whole, the codes of ethics for social work show a great deal of variation in the level of detailed guidance offered and their length. Some codes are quite detailed and contain guidance about how to act in certain types of situation; for example, the Australian Association of Social Workers (2010) code is 33 pages in a 54-page booklet. Others offer general statements of principle with only brief guidance; for example, the code of the Croatia Association of Social Workers (2004) is four pages comprising 34 articles. Some codes go into detail about professional practice issues such as fees and advertising, which are particularly relevant in countries where independent or private practice social work is common, such as in the USA. In terms of subject matter, the code of ethics for the Aotearoa New Zealand Association of Social Workers (2008) is particularly distinctive in that it is framed within the articles of the Treaty of Waitangi (agreed in 1840, it recognizes Māori ownership of their lands and properties) and takes a bicultural perspective, giving equal weight to the values and concepts of Tangata Whenua – the Māori, the indigenous people of New Zealand. Although this first explicitly bicultural code was written in two separate parts in 1993, the 2008 version integrates these into one code. The code includes, for example, 'the right of Tangata Whenua clients to have a Tangata Whenua social worker' (2008, s. 3.3) and recognition of 'the right of the whanāu [tribe] to make its own decisions' (2008, s. 3.8). This is one of the few codes that explicitly locates itself in a national and cultural context and, in so doing, acknowledges the limitations of universalism in practical ethics while also holding on to a universal concept of human dignity and rights as expressed in the UN declarations.

Despite these differences, there are also many similarities between the codes of ethics from different countries, especially in terms of the statements of ethical principles. This is not surprising, given the influence of the International Federation of Social Workers. Indeed, some countries have adopted codes of ethics that are versions of the current or past IFSW statements on ethics, modified slightly to refer to their own countries, or include IFSW principles and standards as part of their own codes. Another reason for the similarities between the codes of ethics is that the professional associations exchange their codes and may adapt or adopt aspects of another code if they are judged to be appropriate. For example, the Russian code (Russian Union of Social Educators and Social Workers, 2003) explicitly acknowledges a debt to the ethical guidelines of associations in Australia, Great Britain, Denmark, Lithuania, Poland, the USA and Finland. The code produced by the National Federation of Social Workers in Romania (2004) draws heavily on the US NASW code, as does that of the Association of Social Workers in Turkey (2003). The Japanese code of ethics, produced jointly by the four major associations for social workers in Japan (JASW et al., 2004), includes five of the six values and principles of the NASW code (dignity, social justice, service, integrity and competence). Differences in the form and content of codes, therefore, do not necessarily reflect current differences in social work practice. Even the code produced by the Bulgarian Association of Social Workers (1999), which explicitly states that it has been 'worked out with a view to the traditional Bulgarian values', follows a fairly standard format covering the various professional responsibilities of the social worker.

As this brief discussion indicates, there are some interesting differences between codes. These may arise for many reasons, including national law, culture and attitudes towards the welfare state and the role of social work, as well as the composition of the committees responsible for drafting the codes. Yet there are also some striking similarities, which reflect the international dimensions of social work and the influence of IFSW and other international associations and networks.

The functions of codes of ethics

The form and content of the codes are linked to the functions they are intended to perform. There are a number of different functions that can be identified for codes of ethics, as outlined in List 4.3.

List 4.3 The functions of codes of ethics

1. *Protection of clients or service users:* through the public pledge to be trustworthy and by explicitly stating what can be expected of a professional practitioner.
2. *Guidance to practitioners:* about how to act and how to make ethical decisions, either through encouraging ethical awareness and reflection or through explicit rules.
3. *Enhancement of professional status:* through the mere existence of a code of ethics, since this is supposed to be one of the hallmarks of a profession.
4 *Creating and maintaining professional identity:* through the explicit statement of the service ideal, key ethical principles, the kinds of qualities expected of people who belong to this profession and the kind of conduct required.
5. *Professional discipline and regulation:* through requiring members of a professional group to adhere to the code and using it for disciplinary purposes in cases of misconduct.

I will briefly consider each of these functions in turn. The two most common reasons given for having a professional code of ethics, as stated in the codes themselves, are to protect service users and to guide social workers. It is partly an acknowledgement of the power that professionals have – particularly related to their possession of specialist knowledge and skills, which may not be fully (or even partially) understood by service users – that professions are said to need codes of ethics. The first code of ethics produced by the British Association of Social Workers (BASW, 1975, para. 1; emphasis added) stated:

> Social work is a professional activity. Implicit in its practice are ethical principles, which prescribe the professional responsibility of the social worker. The primary objective of the Code of Ethics is to make these implicit principles explicit *for the protection of clients* and other members of society.

Protection of service users and guidance to practitioners are clearly interlinked, since if social workers follow the guidance, they should act in ethically acceptable ways in their relationships with service users and hence service users will be protected from malpractice. Equally, of course, if codes explicitly lay out what counts as ethically right conduct on the part of social workers, then service users (or their representatives) can challenge or complain in cases of ethical shortcomings or transgressions.

Two other functions of codes of ethics that are less often stated explicitly in the codes themselves are the enhancement of professional status and the maintenance of professional identity. The point about status, mentioned earlier in this chapter, is still regarded as important, regardless of the critiques of traditional professionalism, as social work struggles to develop and maintain its status alongside other professions. This is exemplified in the foreword to the code of ethics of the Aotearoa New Zealand Association of Social Workers (2008, p. 2), which states, in the context of discussing the significance of the code:

> Organizational theorists have claimed for nearly a hundred years that the adoption of a code of ethics is one essential attribute of a professional, vocational grouping.

Equally important, a code of ethics may help to generate a sense of common identity and shared values among the occupational group. It may be as much about internal recognition as external. Given that social workers are quite fragmented in terms of the variety of types of work they do and the settings in which they operate, and the increasing tendency towards multiprofessional and interprofessional working, the code of ethics and the values upon which it is based may be the one feature that is held in common between social workers. If the codes are discussed in professional education (as they increasingly are), if they are regularly reviewed and consultations are organized to develop new or revised codes, this keeps alive a process of dialogue and debate about the nature of social work, its developing role, new ethical challenges and responses. This is a way of socializing new workers into the profession and building a sense of professional identity.

The final function of codes of ethics, which varies greatly in the extent to which it is used by professional associations, is the role of codes in controlling membership of the profession and enabling professional associations (or in some cases, regulatory bodies) to caution, admonish, suspend or remove people from membership. In some of the countries that do not have statutory regulatory bodies, professional associations are increasingly playing a role in handling complaints about social workers who are members and offer detailed sets of disciplinary rules alongside their codes of ethics. Finally, and importantly, professional associations use their codes of ethics when defending members in disputes with employers – often a more common usage of the professional code than its use in cases where the professional association itself investigates the conduct of its members.

Some limitations and critiques of codes of ethics

As indicated in the preceding discussion, codes fulfil a range of rather different functions and are an essential and useful feature of any profession. Yet they have also been subjected to a range of criticisms, some of which I will now discuss.

Codes are too general and open to interpretation

One of the main criticisms of the early codes of ethics, which equally applies to current shorter codes, is that the ethical principles they contain are very general and open to interpretation. Respecting human dignity, service users' rights to self-determination and confidentiality can be interpreted and applied in numerous ways. The principles are often in conflict and no indication is given as to how to resolve such conflicts. If codes of ethics are really designed to protect service users and guide social workers, should they not contain more detailed rules and prescriptions for action? One response to this criticism is to reply that it is neither possible nor desirable to develop detailed rulebooks, and that the essence of being an educated and reflective professional is the ability to interpret principles in relation to particular cases, recognizing that there may be conflict, but being prepared to seek advice and take responsibility. Another response to this criticism is to develop much longer codes, which actually include more specific guidance on how to act in certain sorts of situation. For example, the 2008 NASW code has 18 subsections in section 1.07 titled 'Privacy and Confidentiality'. These deal with a variety of different circumstances, ranging from confidentiality in relation to deceased clients to seeking agreements about the rights of different parties to confidentiality when counselling families, couples or groups. Specifying what action to take in certain types of circumstance enables social workers to understand much more easily what confidentiality means in practice and what are the limits to its preservation.

Codes are too prescriptive and are 'unethical'

However, the development of these longer, more rule-based codes has led to the opposite criticism – that codes of ethics are too prescriptive, undermining social workers' professional judgement and encouraging a mindless rule-following at the expense of ethical reflection. Dawson (1994, p. 133) even goes so far as to argue that codes are unethical because:

> they minimise the responsibility of the professional for his or her actions ... The professional is liable to follow pre-established rules rather than respond to the individual case and the individual client, and thereby become desensitised to the morally relevant factors in the particular circumstances.

The Australian Association of Social Workers' (2010) code, for example, has a special section called 'Responsibilities in particular contexts' (s. 5.4). One of the five responsibilities listed in subsection 5.5.4 'Remote service delivery' is: 'Social workers will maintain up to date anti-virus, anti-spyware and firewall programs' (p. 39). Other duties include password protection and storage, and backing up computers. This level of detail could be taken to imply that social workers are not to be trusted and need detailed guidance on practical administrative matters. It is also difficult to know where to stop, as rules of this nature relating to specific practice contexts could proliferate from 50-page booklets into multiple volumes or web pages. Arguably, it is the duty of each agency to devise specific codes of practice and guidelines, in line with the principles of the code of ethics, to guide social workers in their specific jobs. In response, the professional associations may refer to instances where the specificity has been helpful in defending a social worker or challenging unethical practice, as well as citing feedback from social workers who welcome the practical detail. Independent or private practice social workers have no employing agencies to provide guidance and many agencies do not have their own codes of practice. The increasing specificity of codes of ethics may also be linked to the role of codes in disciplinary hearings following accusations of misconduct. If codes contain detailed standards or rules, it is easier to point out when a social worker has transgressed these. It is also easier for social workers and professional associations to point out instances where employers are not maintaining the conditions for ethical practice, for example if service users are excluded from case reviews, or if confidential information is routinely passed to other agencies without consent.

Codes of ethics inhibit multiprofessional and interprofessional working

Codes of ethics produced by professional associations are concerned to outline the distinctive missions, loyalties, values and activities of discrete professional groups. They are premised on the idea that professions are distinctive and are concerned to reinforce this distinctiveness. They require that the practitioner adheres to the values and guidelines of their profession in cases of conflict with those of an employer or another profession. They place great store on members not bringing the profession into disrepute and remaining true to their professional values. Yet much practice is in multiprofessional or interprofessional settings and sometimes social workers may need to be flexible and undertake roles that might normally be carried out by other professionals, for example the police or health professionals. Rigidly holding on to the ethical guidelines of the social work profession, say, in relation to confidentiality, may be obstructive and work against the interests of service users and multiprofessional teams. One response to this critique is to suggest that it is often the social worker's unique role and identity that is of value in a multiprofessional context, for example advocating for a particular service user's rights to a service in a context where health professionals are concerned with overall rationing of care. A professional code and clear professional identity can be helpful in such circumstances, and can encourage intelligent debate and discussion in multiprofessional teams about what standards to adopt for the team as a whole.

Codes are professionally defined rather than incorporating service users' values

Another criticism of codes of ethics is that they tend to be developed by professionals, framed in a professional language, outlining the rights and treatment that professionals judge are owed to service users. Beresford (2008, 2011) points out that service users have not tended to be involved in the development of social work values, suggesting that values proposed by service users may be completely different from those defined by professionals. While, in some quarters, there may now be more consultation and involvement of service users in the development of codes of ethics for social work, arguably the very notion of a professional code of ethics is constructed from the perspective of professionals. The incorporation of service user perspectives about what they value might, perhaps, lead to rather different statements that prioritize the ethical qualities of social workers such as trustworthiness and reliability, as well as long-term relationships and the ability to listen (Amy et al., 2010). This critique of codes of ethics is also a critique of the whole project of professionalism, as traditionally conceived, with its tendency towards patronizing and parentalist approaches to service users. It brings us back to some of the issues discussed earlier in the chapter about the extent to which a more democratic form of professionalism is being developed for social work in response to the demands of service users, at the same time as governments are taking more control over professional roles and tasks, and professionals may be unwittingly functioning more as state officials, controllers and surveillance agents, than as allies of service users. These points will be picked up in the next chapter on service users' rights.

Codes are philosophically incoherent and hybrid documents

I have already outlined the range of types of statement and functions of codes of ethics. Among other things, they comprise mixtures of abstract ethical principles, aspirational ideals, descriptions of practice, prescriptions for action and stimuli for reflection and education. Some philosophers have criticized codes for mixing principles from different ethical traditions (Kantian, utilitarian and virtue ethics). Others, assuming codes are about prescriptions for action, have characterized the principles in codes as 'flawed Kantian' principles (Harris, 1994). This kind of criticism is, of course, based on a particular view that statements of ethical principles developed in the context of everyday or professional life (as opposed to those developed by moral philosophers) must fit within, or be derivable from, a single foundational ethical theory. Arguably, this is not necessarily the case and there are moral philosophers who argue for a 'common morality' account of ethics or for the 'fragmentation of value'. These approaches to ethics do not rely on systematic theories that base ethical truth on a single type of moral value (see Beauchamp and Childress, 2009; Nagel, 1979, and the discussions at the ends of Chapters 2 and 3). Furthermore, it could be argued that codes of ethics are not the kinds of documents that aim to be, or should be regarded as, applications of ethical theory or philosophically consistent guides to action. As argued elsewhere (Banks, 2003), codes of ethics should not be taken literally. The statements of principles are as much rhetorical devices to demonstrate professional credibility and/or inspire social workers to aim higher. They are also designed to educate (by highlighting areas of potential ethical conflict or concern) as well as to regulate behaviour by offering rules for action. If they have an essence, it lies in their hybridity.

Codes locate responsibility and blame for public issues with individual social workers

The final criticism that I will mention is arguably the most serious and the most wide-reaching. In one sense, it could apply to the whole enterprise of professional ethics, as traditionally constructed (see Ife, 2008, pp. 122–34). Codes of ethics clearly lay out the duties and responsibilities of social workers, often with a focus on the relationship between the individual worker and a service user. They are framed in such a way as to imply that a large burden of the responsibility for acting ethically lies with the social worker. This serves to individualize social problems as the private troubles of service users, and place responsibility for solutions that respect the dignity, worth, choice and equality of service users on the social worker, rather than on the wider society. The increasing tendency towards disciplining and regulating social workers exemplifies this process of individualization based on conceptions of duty and blame (for a more detailed critique of this version of social work ethics, see Banks, 2011a; Weinberg, 2010).

In countering this critique, it could be pointed out that many of the recent codes of ethics clearly outline the public context within which social work takes places and acknowledge that resource constraints, demands for economy and efficiency and regressive government policies cause ethical challenges for social workers. Many codes stress the importance of employing agencies providing conditions that are conducive to the ethical practice of social work. They also stress the responsibility of social workers to bring to the attention of those in power the ways in which agency practices or government policies may result in discrimination or hardship. This latter point, which is another burden on the individual social worker, is arguably very important if the private troubles of service users and the workers who struggle to help them meet their needs are to be seen as public issues that are the collective responsibility of all social workers, social work agencies, governments and, ultimately, citizens. The idea of moral agency implied in codes of ethics (even those that appear to be about rule-following) is important, as it is this kind of moral agency, commitment and social responsibility that contributes to the broader social justice mission of social work, and can provide the motivation and impetus for political action to challenge the many injustices witnessed by social workers every day. So a conception of moral agency at the level of the individual social worker is important, but not as an isolated individual – rather as a member of a broader community of practitioners and activists who are prepared to take a stand for a set of ideals to which they are committed and who take 'professional pride' in the work they do (Jansen et al., 2010). Codes of ethics and professions are one, albeit fairly traditional, way of doing this. Given their place in occupational life, and the fact that they can have a role in challenging cutbacks in welfare, they may be worth preserving. But we need to be wary of uncritical acceptance of the role of professionalism, codes of ethics and professional regulation, as they have the potential to lean towards self-serving credentialism and to allow state cooption and control of social workers.

Conclusions

This chapter has examined the nature and function of codes of ethics in social work. It was noted that the existence of codes of ethics for social work is intimately related to the notion of professionalism and they can play an important role in maintaining professional status and identity, as well as guiding professionals, protecting service users and professional regulation. In looking at codes of ethics developed by professional associations in different countries, many common features were noted, particularly a congruence around the stated values or principles underpinning social work, including respect for the individual person, promotion of service user self-determination, promotion of social justice, and working for the interests of service users. The codes vary greatly in length and the extent to which they include detailed rules or standards.

The degree to which social workers regard such codes as useful will depend on what they want to use them for. For practical guidance on how to act in certain types of situations and as a means of safeguarding service users' rights, agency codes of practice designed for specific settings may be more useful. However, as a means of defending the profession from outside attack, maintaining professional identity and setting some general benchmarks against which to judge agency policies and practice, they do have a role to play. The codes emphasize that social workers have a responsibility over and above just doing the job and following the agency's rules. This may be useful at a time when resources for social work are being reduced and standards of work and the quality of service to users may be threatened. The codes of ethics remind social workers that because they possess particular knowledge and skills, and work on a daily basis with people living in poverty and suffering crises and problems, they have a duty to inform governments and agencies of inequities, lack of resources or the need for policy changes. Social workers need to be prepared to challenge agency policies and practices and to view themselves as more than just employees doing a job. Professional codes of ethics, along with education and membership of other networks and campaigns, have a role to play in this.

Putting it into practice

Analysing codes of ethics

Aims of the exercise: to encourage reflection on the nature and purpose of codes of ethics and to link this to developing awareness of the nature of professionalism.

1. Consult the website of the International Federation of Social Workers, http://www.ifsw.org.

2. Read the latest version of the IFSW ethical statement and the national codes of ethics from at least three different professional associations.
3. Consider their main similarities and differences.
4. What is the balance between general statements of principle and more practical guidance or rules?
5. What is the balance of emphasis between promoting individual service users' rights, protecting service users and the public, and challenging inequality and promoting social justice? Can you link any of the statements to ethical theories or approaches discussed in Chapters 2 and 3?
6. Are there any references to qualities of character?
7. How useful do you think these codes are in protecting service users and in guiding practitioners?
8. What is said about what happens if social workers breach the principles or rules of the code? How is the disciplinary process linked to the code, if at all?

Practice focus

Case for discussion 4: Maintaining professional secrecy in France[1]

The professional association for social workers in France (Association nationale des assistants de service social, ANAS) represents the profession and promotes social work values at all levels. One of the aims of the association is to clarify the values that underlie the interventions of social workers, in particular to assure service users the guarantee of common values of all social work professionals. ANAS supports all professionals who might have problems with their institution or with police services, which are contrary to the professional ethical code. This case is an example of support given to a professional who was confronted with difficulties with a police service.

---

1. I am grateful to Marie-Geneviève Mounier of the Association nationale des assistants de service social, France, for this case, which was the subject of a presentation at a meeting organized at the DGAS (General Direction of Social Action) on 9 July 2009. I am also grateful to Lauelia Rolland-Fortin for help with translation and Routledge for giving permission to reproduce the case, with revisions, which was originally published in Banks, S. and Nøhr, K. (eds) (2011) *Practising Social Work Ethics Around the World: Cases and Commentaries*, London, Routledge, pp. 236–8.

On 17 July 2007, a social worker, who was a member of the ANAS in Belfort (a town close to the Swiss and German borders), was interrogated by the border police and put in custody. The social worker was based at a refuge for women who have been victims of violence (centre d'hébergement et de réinsertion pour les femmes battues). The social worker was reproached by the police for not having given the address of a particular woman who no longer had a valid residence permit allowing her to stay in France. This woman had stayed in the centre where the professional was working. The woman had been beaten by her male companion and was put in a safe place by the social welfare organization that employed the social worker. The social worker specified that she could not give the woman's address because she (the social worker) was subject to the rules of professional secrecy. In France, professional social workers are subject to a law that requires them not to reveal personal information about their clients. In responding to the request from the police officers, she would have committed an offence.

However, according to the police, this professional was also at risk of being sued for 'aiding illegal residency'. This regulation stipulates that a person who helps someone without official papers (an illegal resident) is committing an offence (a penal infringement).

In the view of ANAS, this situation was an infringement of human rights, as stipulated in international, regional, European and national conventions. Social workers have a function to help people, including adults and minors, French and foreigners, with or without papers. When they protect a beaten woman, allow a pregnant woman to access care, or support a family that needs food, they are not assisting illegal residency, but rather supporting people's rights for a decent life.

ANAS gave its total support to this social worker. Indeed, social workers are required to maintain professional secrecy legally and professionally (as outlined in article L 411 of the Social Action and Families Code, article 226-13 of the Penal Code and Title 1, article 4 of the Code of Ethics). If they have to answer to police inquiries, they also have to keep silent about the private facts they gain knowledge of within the framework of their profession. There is only a duty to speak if the person in question is in danger (article 226-14 of the Penal Code), which was obviously not the case in this situation. In addition, it is worth remembering that illegal residency is not one of the exemptions to professional secrecy contained in article 226-14 of the Penal Code.

ANAS supported this social worker, and the outcome was that the prosecutor of Belfort did not pursue the case further.

Questions for discussion
1. What does this account suggest about the role of professional associations in promoting ethical practice?
2. Can you link differences in approach between the police and social workers to differences in core values, their functions in society or other factors?
3. In cases like this, what role can a code of ethics play? Was it necessary for social work to have a code of ethics in order for the professional association to defend the social worker in this case?
4. Which features, if any, of this case do you think are distinctive to France, and which features are common in many countries?

Further resources

Banks, S. (2004) *Ethics, Accountability and the Social Professions*, Basingstoke, Palgrave Macmillan.
Chapter 4 has a more detailed discussion of codes of ethics, comparing those produced by the South African Black Social Workers Association, the US National Association of Social Workers and the National Youth Agency in the UK.

IFSW website: http://www.ifsw.org.
Has a selection of codes of ethics from different national professional associations that are members of IFSW, plus statements and discussion about the nature of social work and human rights issues in social work.

Sullivan, W. (2005) *Work and Integrity: The Crisis and Promise of Professionalism in America*, 2nd edn, San Francisco, Jossey-Bass.
Covers the evolution of professions, particularly in a US context, with useful chapters on 'reinventing professionalism' (including Sullivan's concept of 'civic professionalism') and some coverage of professional ethics.

CHAPTER 5

Service users' rights: clienthood, citizenship, consumerism and activism

CHAPTER OVERVIEW

In this chapter I will discuss the concepts of 'rights' and 'human rights', including debates about whether the idea of universal and absolute rights makes sense. The concept of 'relational rights' is introduced as a possible conception of rights that goes beyond the focus on the isolated individual. I then explore the concept of rights in relation to service users, considering the difference between regarding the service user as a person, a citizen, consumer or activist and the approaches that need to be adopted by social workers to support, enable and allow service users to exercise their rights. At the end of the chapter, there is an exercise to encourage reflection on rights and a case for discussion about the rights of a pregnant young woman in Turkey.

Introduction

Many of the principles and rules that feature in the codes of ethics discussed in Chapter 4 refer to the rights of service users and the role of social workers in respecting and promoting these rights. Social work has been characterized by some as a 'human rights profession'. This chapter will look at what is meant by the concept of 'rights', with a view to elucidating what it means for service users to have and exercise rights in a social work context.

The idea of rights is generally associated with principle-based ethics or the 'ethics of justice', although rights-based approaches to ethics have also been developed independently of ethical theories based on foundational principles (see Dworkin, 1977; Gewirth, 1996; Rawls, 1973). There are many different political and philosophical theories about rights (see Edmundson, 2004; Jones, 1994), which cover questions concerning:

- What is the nature of rights – for example, are they best understood as claims, benefits, choices or entitlements?
- Where do rights come from – are they derived from God, nature or a social contract, for example?
- What kinds of entities hold rights – is it all or some of: humans, potential humans, future generations, groups of people, animals, plants or other inanimate features of the natural environment?

While these questions are important and do have an impact on social work as part of society, in this chapter I will mainly confine myself to a brief discussion of the nature of the rights of human beings as a precursor to exploring the rights of social work service users.

Rights as valid claims

In this book I am largely concerned with moral rights rather than legal rights. Although the distinction is not hard and fast, legal rights could be regarded as bestowed by virtue of the legal code of a state or customary practice, for example the right to vote, while moral rights are bestowed by a moral code, for example the right to be told the truth. Of course, in social work we are inevitably concerned with both legal and moral rights, and these two categories are not mutually exclusive. Many moral rights are also legal rights, for example in some countries, the right to free speech. However, it is important to bear in mind that a good many rights regarded as moral rights are not legal rights, for example the moral right of asylum seekers in Britain to be free to take paid employment during the many years they wait to have their asylum claims heard.

In an attempt to elucidate the complex and contested nature of rights, it is common in the literature to distinguish four components of rights, following Hohfeld ([1919]1964), the American legal theorist, as outlined in List 5.1. However, it is important to note that Hohfeld was writing about legal rights, not rights in general or moral rights.

List 5.1 Components of rights

1. *Claims:* I have a claim to something or against a person or institution if a person/institution has a duty to me in this respect. For example, a young man in residential care has a claim (against the chair of the review panel) to attend his case review.
2. *Liberties/privileges:* I have a liberty to do something if I do not have a duty not to do it. For example, I have the liberty to pick the vegetables in my garden.
3. *Powers:* I have a power if I have the ability to affect the rights of others within a set of rules. For example, a social worker to whom an allegation of child abuse is reported has the power to investigate.
4. *Immunities:* I have an immunity if I am protected in some way from the actions of others. For example, a child has an immunity from sexual abuse by other people.

Source: Drawing on Hohfeld, [1919]1964

Although these elements are often treated as different types of right in isolation (claim rights, liberty rights and so on), Hohfeld's view was that rights are complex and often comprise a combination of elements (for more details, see Wenar, 2011). Examples of the combinations of elements might include: children's rights not to suffer sexual abuse are claims against others to refrain from abuse and immunities from harmful actions by others; my right to pick vegetables from my garden entails that I have a liberty to pick these vegetables and a claim against other people not to pick them. Hohfeld's view was that all rights are claims, or at least involve claims. This view is commonly held in the literature on rights in moral philosophy.

So what, then, do we mean by 'rights'? When we speak of someone as having a right to something, we generally mean that they have a special claim or entitlement. In the narrow sense of 'rights', a claim is only a right if someone else (or an institution) has a duty to ensure the claim is realized. So, for example, if we say: 'Jufitri (a young man in residential care) has a right to attend his case review', at the very least this means that the chair of the case review panel has a duty to allow him to attend. In a social work context, it will very likely also mean that Jufitri's social worker has a duty to ensure that he is invited, briefed and supported.

One way of describing this kind of special claim that constitutes a right is as a 'valid claim', that is, a claim that is justified according to a system of rules (Feinberg, 1973, p. 64). In the case of Jufitri's right, his claim could be justified with reference to the social work agency's policies and procedures for conducting case reviews. If the agency did not have any procedures, or if they were not publically available, or if they did not mention young people's attendence at case reviews, then Jufitri could assert his more general right as a service user to participate in decision-making about his case (according to the professional code of ethics for social work). The important point, if we follow Feinberg's definition of rights as valid claims, is that in order for the claim that Jufitri be allowed to attend the review to be regarded as a right, it must be socially recognized as a valid claim, with a correlative duty on other people to allow it to be realized.

Human rights

The term 'human rights' features frequently in the social work literature – especially the literature on ethics and values. The IFSW/IASSW (2000, 2004) definition of social work and statement on ethics describe social work as underpinned by principles of human rights and social justice. Ife (2008, p. 1) characterizes social work as a 'human rights profession'. It is important to understand what is meant by 'human rights' in this context.

The term 'human rights' is sometimes used in a broad sense to refer to many kinds of rights that are attributable to human beings (as opposed to, say, the rights of animals or the ecosystem). This might include Jufitri's particular right to attend his case review. However, the term 'human rights' also has a more specialist meaning. In the IFSW/IASSW (2004) statement on ethics, explicit reference is made to various declarations and conventions of the UN, which refer to *universal* rights that are applicable to all people by virtue of their being human. In this sense, human rights are universal, applying to everyone in all places. This is the most common usage of the term 'human rights' and is generally what is meant when we talk of human rights violations, such as torture, slavery or imprisonment without trial.

Human rights are an important part of the modern western liberal tradition in politics and moral philosophy, which developed in importance during the Enlightenment period – as exemplified in the declarations of the rights ('of man') to liberty, property and security, for example, following the revolutions in America (1776) and France (1789) (see Almond, 1993). These rights were regarded as 'natural' and self-evident, existing independently of any particular state or society. Although purporting to be 'universal', they excluded large sections of the population, including women and slaves. Later campaigns against slavery, for women's rights and the rights of black people in the USA extended the coverage of civil and political rights in the nineteenth and twentieth centuries, although the natural rights doctrine lost credibility. For example, according to Kant, the eighteenth-century philosopher, rights were not regarded as 'natural', but rather as derived from our ultimate duty of respect for persons. The nineteenth-century utilitarian philosophers believed rights were created in society, while Marx argued that lists of so-called 'natural' rights (such as rights to own property) were historically developed to justify particular political and economic systems to protect the property of those in power (see Boss, 1998, pp. 341–53). Nevertheless, the notion of *universal* human rights (as standards applicable to all people across the world) was strengthened by UN declarations and conventions following the atrocities of the Second World War, which also extended coverage from civil and political rights to include social, economic and cultural rights, such as the right to work, to adequate standards of living and to participate in the cultural life of the community. More recently, in the later part of the twentieth century, we have seen the emergence of what have been called 'third generation' universal rights that are attributable to collectivities (communities or nations), such as rights to economic development, to clean water and to belong to a stable society. These human rights were developed in response to critiques from more collectivist cultures, for example Asian and African, based on the argument that collective rights are more important in these cultures than the individual rights of the liberal western tradition (Ife, 2008, pp. 44–5).

The so-called second and third generation human rights have been criticized as not meeting the strict definition of rights as valid claims. The Universal Declaration of the Rights of the Child, for example, includes the right of all children to 'adequate nutrition, housing, recreation and medical services' (UN, 1959, principle 4). Feinberg (1973) regards the use of the term 'human rights' in this context as a 'special manifesto sense of right' that identifies basic needs with rights. He argues that such statements should more properly be described as urging on the world community the moral principle that all basic human needs ought to be recognized as 'claims worthy of sympathy and serious consideration now, even though they cannot yet plausibly be treated as valid claims' (Feinberg, 1973, p. 67).

Feinberg may be correct to argue that many of the social and economic rights in the UN declarations and conventions are currently not realizable in many countries of the world. We could also add that they are premised on an assumption of particular types of social and economic system (developed welfare capitalism) – as exemplified in rights such as those to holidays with pay, protection against unemployment and free education. However, although these 'rights' may be aspirational rather than realizable in the present, the whole point of the UN declarations and conventions is that those states that signed up to them are, in fact, taking on a correlative duty to implement the rights outlined. So formally, if not in practice, there is a party that has a duty to implement these rights, namely the states that signed up to them. Whether the usage of the term 'rights' in this context is a stretching of the term, or a misuse of the term, the fact that the term 'rights' is used rather than 'needs' or simply 'claims' gives extra rhetorical weight to demands for improved living and working conditions for all people across the world.

Ife (2008, pp. 47–8) argues that the way the distinction is often made between first, second and third generation human rights is conceptually misleading. It implies that first and second generation rights (political and civil; social, economic and cultural) belong only to individuals, whereas they can, in fact, apply equally to groups, such as indigenous people or people with disabilities. He gives the example of freedom of expression, which might apply to the right of a group of people with disabilities to express themselves collectively. He also argues that third generation rights are often misguidedly seen as less important than those of the first and second generation, and that it is difficult to separate rights meaningfully into these three discrete categories. Ife (2008, p. 49) says that he finds it useful to divide human rights into seven categories, each of which has individual and collective aspects: survival rights; social rights; economic rights; civil and political rights; cultural rights; environmental rights; and spiritual rights. We will return to the issue of collective rights in the later section on relational rights. Other theorists have developed alternative ways of looking at how we frame the requirements for a decent human life that do not rely on concepts of universal rights. For example, the capabilities approach of Nussbaum and Sen focuses on what people are actually able to do and be to live a life that is worthy of the dignity of a human being (Nussbaum, 2000, 2006, pp. 69–81; Sen, 1993).

Universal versus particular and absolute versus conditional rights

We have already noted that the idea of universalism is crucial to the concept of human rights. The language of human rights also suggests that some fundamental rights are also absolute, that is, cannot be qualified. This leads to two further distinctions that are often made between types of right: universal rights (applying to everybody without exception) versus particular rights (applying to a limited class of people); and absolute (or unqualified) rights versus conditional (or qualified) rights. Clark with Asquith (1985, p. 24) drew up a useful table relating to the four possible combinations of rights in these categories, from which List 5.2 is derived.

List 5.2 Universal, particular, absolute and conditional rights

1. *Absolute universal rights:* Apply unconditionally to everybody. Clark with Asquith argue that there is probably only one right in this category and that would be the right to be treated as an end and not simply as a means, which logically follows from the concept of respect for persons. Some people have argued that certain other more specific rights in the UN declaration are absolute universal rights, such as the right not to be tortured.
2. *Qualified universal rights:* Apply to everybody, except they may be withdrawn from anybody on the basis of the application of criteria that apply to all. This category would include those rights that have often been put forward as 'natural rights', that is, rights simply deducible from the nature of humankind, and many of those in the UN declarations on human rights, such as the right to liberty, which can be withheld on certain grounds. For example, the right to liberty is suspended for the imprisoned criminal.
3. *Absolute particular rights:* Apply without qualification to everybody in a certain category. Clark with Asquith (1985, p. 24) give as an example the right of all parents living in Britain to claim

child benefit. However, they acknowledge in an endnote that there are various conditions attaching to eligibility to child benefit, including residence of the parents and age of the children. We might add that there are also qualifications in relation to the immigration status of the parents or carers. Given the number of qualifications involved, arguably this example of the right to child benefit might fit better (or at least equally well) into the category of qualified particular rights. Indeed, it is difficult to think of good examples of what might count as absolute particular rights.

4. *Qualified particular rights:* Apply to certain persons under certain conditions. For example, a British citizen has a right to a state pension if over the prescribed retirement age and having satisfied the necessary contribution conditions.

Source: Drawing on Clark with Asquith, 1985, p. 24

There is an ongoing debate as to whether the concept of universal human rights – based, perhaps, on some basic human needs applying to everyone across the world – makes sense (see Browning, 2006; Doyal and Gough, 1991; Outka and Reeder, 1993; Sullivan and Kymlicka, 2007). This is not just because such rights may not be realizable everywhere, as Feinberg argued, but because the concept of a right in itself assumes a certain kind of individualized world-view. This will be discussed further in the next section on relational rights. Questions have also been raised about the concept of absolute rights – rights that apply unconditionally to everyone. Jones (1994, pp. 192–3) argues that even universal human rights such as the right not to be tortured may come into conflict with other legitimate considerations (he gives the example of torturing a terrorist to find the location of a bomb likely to kill many people). Furthermore, if we view human rights not as 'natural' but as constructed in particular times and places and in a constant state of development, redefinition, change and struggle (Ife, 2008, pp. 151–8), the idea of absolute rights, in the sense of unchanging and unchallengeable, does not make sense.

In relation to social work, the IFSW/IASSW (2004) statement on ethics endorses the UN Universal Declaration of Human Rights (UN, 1948) and other declarations and conventions, including the Declaration of the Rights of the Child (UN, 1959). However, as

Clark with Asquith (1985, p. 27) point out, social workers mainly deal with qualified particular rights on a day-to-day basis and the 'application of universal rights cannot, without absurdity, be essentially different in social work from any other context'. Nevertheless, the statements of values and ethics made by the social work profession invariably focus on what appear to be regarded as either absolute or qualified *universal rights* and social work has been characterized as a 'human rights profession'. What this means is that the rationale for social work as a professional occupation is based on principles of human rights. In other words, social work exists because of a societal commitment to enhancing and protecting the rights of all people to a dignified life, to protecting from discrimination, to providing adequate physical and social resources; and social work is conducted according to human rights principles – treating people with dignity and respect, promoting equality and so on.

Relational rights and responsibilities

The concept of individual rights, when applied to service users, is a useful starting point for social work in individualist cultures. However, it seems less relevant to practice in more collectivist societies or indeed in many of the multicultural contexts where social work is practised in most western countries. Responsibilities and relationships rather than rights may be the primary focus of attention, as described by Graham (2002) in her account of the African-centred worldview, Ejaz's (1991) discussion of social work in India, or Yip's (2004) account of Chinese approaches, for example. If rights are talked about at all, then it may make more sense to talk of the rights of groups of people or collective rights. Certainly, in the context of social work in western countries, this would be the case in relation to indigenous peoples, ethnic and religious groupings. For example, we noted in Chapter 4 when discussing the code of ethics for social work in New Zealand, the rights of Māori people, as Māori.

There remains a question, therefore, as to whether what is essentially a western concept of rights should be imposed on societies where this concept is alien to their ways of thinking and acting (for further discussion, see Banks, 2012; Banks et al., 2008; Healy, 2007; Hugman, 2008, 2010, pp. 121–48; Ife, 2010, pp. 68–88). Arguments for retaining a concept of human rights include the fact that this concept, as used internationally, is deployed in a 'special manifesto sense' and should not be equated with western concepts of individual-focused rights.

Some commentators have suggested that the concept of 'relational rights' might be a more useful way of looking at rights in this context. Boss (1998, p. 341), for example, argues that even where rights have not been explicitly discussed in traditional writings, such as Buddhist philosophy, 'the assumption of rights is embedded in the concepts of duty and respect for the dignity of people'. Buddhist ethics, for example (see de Silva, 1993; Keown, 2005; McFarlane, 1994; Øvrelid, 2008), is based on the notion of human interdependence and can be interpreted as both affirming the worth of the individual being, and regarding the individual as subservient to the good of many. A similar interpretation could be made of Confucian ethics, African ethics or Graham's (2002) African-centred worldview. Whether we wish to interpret Buddhism or other religious or cultural worldviews as having a concept of relational rights embedded within them, or as placing a primary focus on responsibility and the interconnectedness of all things (humans and the whole of the natural world), may seem like an academic question. What is important is the use of the term 'relational', which stresses the importance of people and things in connection, rather than 'individual', which implies abstraction and isolation.

The individualistic conception of rights in use in western society at present is also questioned by Marxist and neo-Marxist philosophers and thinkers, the care ethicists discussed in Chapter 3 and by communitarian philosophers, from a variety of perspectives, which can be viewed as both progressive and reactionary (see Etzioni, 1995, 1997; MacIntyre, 1985; Sandel, 1998; Taylor, C., 1989). Etzioni (1995) argues that a rights-focused culture is developing in the western world (he focuses particularly on the USA), which generates individual demands without balancing these with a more developed commitment to responsibilities to other individuals, groups and communities. Not only needs, but desires and wants may be given the status of rights. He calls for a moratorium on the creation of rights, alongside the development of communal responsibility, with a focus on family and community life. However, his particular brand of communitarianism could be regarded as authoritarian and dangerous. If communities police themselves, for example, how do we guard against the exclusion of minority interests, racism, sexism and so on?

As was pointed out in the discussion of the concept of international human rights, so in a national context, rights have been important in the struggles of oppressed groups for recognition and redistribution of power and resources. The social rights of parents to state support for childcare in many western countries, for example, have been a vital element in helping women to shake off some of their traditional responsibilities for home and family caring roles in their fight for equality and justice. There is no doubt that it is important to guard against the excessive 'manufacture' of social rights, as this undervalues important and fundamental human rights to life and freedom of expression, as well as creating a culture of complaint and unfulfilled expectations. However, in social work, we are often working with people whose voices are not heard, whose basic needs are not being met and who are being treated with disrespect – so a concept of individual and group rights is important, alongside a balancing of rights with responsibilities. In this context, 'relational rights' is a useful concept.

Internationally, through the United Nations, the concept of human rights as including the rights of peoples, that is, territorial, ethnic and religious groups, to self-determination has been an important way of attempting to protect minority groups from persecution, ethnic cleansing and other forms of oppression and abuse. The concept of human rights as belonging to individuals has also been important as part of a worldwide movement (exemplified through organizations such as Amnesty International) to challenge oppressive regimes and individual cases of unjust treatment, torture, imprisonment and murder. Such abuses are frequently perpetrated upon individuals because of their membership of particular religious or ethnic groupings, but equally they may be perpetrated on people for other reasons. Hence a concept of human rights attributed to individuals (presented as absolute and universal) is an important one to draw upon to mobilize support to challenge such treatment as inhuman and degrading.

Service users as persons (in a relationship of clienthood)

The lists of Kantian principles discussed in Chapter 2 focus on individual rights, with more emphasis on the universal rights that should apply to all people than on the particular rights applying to service users qua service users. The emphasis on the social work service user as a *person* with the basic moral rights derived from the principle of respect for persons was the dominant one in western social work literature until perhaps the 1980s, although the term 'client' (rather than 'service user') was used to refer to the person in a relationship with a social worker. This meant that the kinds of moral principles stated for social work were no different to the kinds of moral principles that would be stated for morality in general, although the context in which they were applied (social worker–client relationship) obviously presented specific issues and difficulties for workers. This type of view, based on Kantian philosophy and Biestek's list of casework principles, has already been discussed in the section on the principles of the social worker–service user relationship in Chapter 2.

However, the traditional notion of 'personhood' presented problems for social work, in that it entailed a focus on the abstract individual in isolation and a particular view of persons as rational individuals with a capacity for self-determined choice and action. This seemed to downplay features of the social context in which any relationship took place and to legitimate parentalist ('paternalistic') treatment of those judged to be less than fully rational, for example children, people with mental health problems or learning disabilities, who did not have the status of 'full personhood'. So although 'respect for persons' might appear to entail an equal relationship between social worker and service user, the narrow and undifferentiated view of 'personhood', which took no account of relationships of power and control, the differentiated and diverse cultural and religious identities or the contextual features of the professional relationship with 'clients', also contained within it the seeds of parentalism and professional control.

Service users as fellow citizens and active citizens

In the late 1970s and early 1980s, the notion of 'clients as fellow citizens' began to be stressed (BASW, 1980; Jordan, 1975) as part of the reaction against the view of the social worker as expert giving psychological explanations of service users' problems, and as a move towards regarding social workers as allies of service users (Payne, 1989, p. 121). In the UK, for example, studies had been published (see Mayer and Timms, 1970) relating to service users' views of social work, which contributed to the pressure to alter the power balance between service users and social workers. As Phelan commented: 'As social workers we have a responsibility to bear constantly in mind that our clients are equal with us. They have complete citizenship' (BASW, 1980). This led to a redefinition of professionalism, often termed the 'new' or 'democratic' professionalism, concerned with shifting the balance of power between workers and service users (BASW, 1989).

This kind of view entailed that the rights of service users should be seen as rights of citizens not to be treated arbitrarily by state officials and therefore as having rights of access to information about the purpose of social work, to see personal information held on file by social work agencies and to participate in planning and decision-making, for example. The principle of respecting service users as a fellow citizens could be regarded as a development of the idea of respect for persons. However, the term 'citizen' is narrower than 'person', in that it focuses on the rights of the person in the role of citizen, rather than respect for the person as a person. Citizenship entails more specific rights, including social rights to state-provided welfare benefits and services, as well as political and civil rights. It also entails responsibilities. The 'service users as fellow citizens' approach therefore increases the accountability of social workers, although it is reductive in its view of the service user.

The term 'citizen' is as contested as many of the others we have been using. The notion of the service user as a fellow citizen will be interpreted differently depending on how citizenship is construed – whether in terms of the liberal tradition of individual rights, or social citizenship with a stress on reciprocity and common interests (communitarianism or civic republicanism) or citizenship based on meeting people's needs. The idea of service users as fellow citizens suggests that both social workers and service users are members of a common community or society and, as such, possess certain rights and responsibilities. According to Marshall (1963, p. 87), citizenship is:

> a status bestowed on those who are full members of a community. All those who possess the status are equal with respect to the rights and duties with which the status is endowed.

This implies that these rights and duties apply equally to everyone. Yet, as D. Taylor (1989) has argued, citizenship, with its notions of membership of a community (particularly a nation), is based on a set of practices that excludes certain people from full membership. One example is the way asylum seekers and refugees are currently treated in Britain and many countries around the world. Hayes (2009) graphically describes the separate and inferior welfare benefits, housing and dispersal schemes operating in the UK for asylum seekers, which social workers are involved in implementing (see also Hayes and Humphries, 2004; Humphries, 2004).

Case example 5.1 offers a perspective from an asylum seeker from the Cameroon, who was getting support and advice from a church-based project in a British city on her asylum application, which had been refused four times.

Practice focus

Case example 5.1: An asylum seeker's story[1]

There are a lot of difficulties when you are an asylum seeker. It's a very, very difficult situation. People who haven't experienced it could never really understand. Sometimes you need to go to Immigration to report. I have to report once a month and when I go there I don't know what will happen. Anything can happen there: they can arrest me. Sometimes it's difficult when I go to collect my benefit at the Post Office. There are a lot of English people in the queue. They are not happy at all. Sometimes it's not nice to see the way they are looking at you. Sometimes they insult you. One day I went there and someone said to me: 'Go back to your country.' Again, when you live as an asylum seeker, like me, I don't feel right. I'm always scared because anything can happen any time. I could be at home with my baby and Immigration can come and arrest me at any time. You don't know what might happen to you. You're not living a normal life. You're in prison because there are a lot of things you can't do in this country if you're an asylum seeker. You're just living a scared life. It's not easy at all.

If I could get status in this country, I would begin to feel free because I would be able to do things that I want to do – like a training course or get a job. At the moment there is no choice. I'm forced to get benefit from the Post Office and some people make it clear that they are not happy about it. I would like to be able to get my money by working for it. It's horrible because you are not in prison but you feel that you are in prison. You're not free. I think it's very, very horrible when people don't have freedom.

The account given by this woman of her daily life in Britain as 'in prison' highlights her feeling not just of exclusion from 'normal life', but also the commonly expressed feelings of humiliation and

---

1. I am grateful to the person whose story this is, and to Chris Carroll for giving permission to use this extract from an interview.

lack of dignity experienced by people seeking asylum in another country. It is also an exemplification of what O'Neill (2010, p. xiv) refers to as 'the withdrawal of humanising practices' that is happening in social welfare services as much as in agencies concerned with immigration and border control.

There are many other ways in which some people are denied full citizenship rights, particularly women, people from minority ethnic groups, people with disabilities, people who are lesbian, gay or bisexual and children. It is likely that a significant number of the people who become users of social work services may not have or may not be able to exercise full citizenship rights. While social workers may believe that everyone in society ought to have equal status, and it may be a good principle for the social worker to regard service users as fellow citizens, we cannot pretend that this is the case in our present society. Service users are often people who have been excluded from the political process (for example, with no address they cannot vote) and who do not share in the rights and benefits associated with employment. Social workers alone do not have the power to make people fellow citizens, but it is important that they are not complicit in implementing inhumane and degrading systems of welfare and control, that they do advocate on behalf of people who are denied basic citizenship rights and that they engage in campaigns to change practices and policies that they regard as unjust, for example in the case of asylum seekers and refugees. Furthermore, at the micro-level, the services and contact offered by social workers can be delivered in a way that treats people as fellow citizens ought to be treated, that is, service users should not be stigmatized, humiliated or treated as undeserving. One of the ways in which service users' rights as citizens can be made more real is if they are given more information about the service offered and the right to appeal and treated more as equals and partners than as needy recipients of welfare handouts and social work advice. As Marshall (1963, p. 89) said: 'the right of appeal helps keep alive the idea that the granting of assistance is not a fact of grace, but the satisfaction of a right'.

It should also be noted that there was a growing trend towards the end of the twentieth century to emphasize not just citizenship rights, but also the duties and responsibilities of citizens to each other. As Lund (1999, p. 447) comments in relation to the welfare reforms of 'New Labour' in Britain, there was a 'fastening of duties to rights' and a stress on the importance of mutual obligations. These kinds of ideas are part of the 'new communitarian' thinking, mentioned earlier in the section on relational rights, and also link to ideas of active citizenship, democratic renewal and citizenship as a practice (Banks, 2004a, pp. 87–9; Shaw and Martin, 2000). The concept of active citizenship is a more recent development of the idea of service users as fellow citizens, with a particular focus not just on the right to participate in the life of society, but on people's responsibilities to contribute to the production of their own welfare and the welfare of others. This move towards active citizenship is not just based on egalitarian and participatory ideals, but is also linked with repositioning the role of the state in welfare provision and shifting the emphasis and responsibility for the production of welfare onto individuals and communities (Johansson and Hvinden, 2005; Newman, 2005). Van Ewijk (2009, p. 174) suggests a redefinition of the international statement on social work to stress the notions of social citizenship:

> Citizenship-based social work, as a field of action, knowledge and research, aims at integration of all citizens and supports and encourages self responsibility, social responsibility and the implementation of social rights.

Service users as consumers and customers

The notion of service users as 'consumers' possessing quite specific rights to be treated in a certain kind of way and to receive a certain standard of service is an even further narrowing down, or arguably a move away from, the concept of a person with universal rights. This developed in the 1980s and 90s as part of the growth of uniform standards and quality assurance indicators as well as the development of markets, private provision and business principles associated with new managerialist practices and the privatization of public services (see Harris, 2003, 2009). One of the aims of adopting the terminology of consumers (sometimes used interchangeably with 'customers') was to emphasize the notion of *choice*. Although customers are people who receive services, they are able to choose between the services on offer. If they do not like a particular service, they are free to go elsewhere (the power of 'exit'). They exert some power in exercising this choice and are therefore not merely passive recipients. This model is obviously based on the traditional idea of the marketplace, with sellers of goods and services competing with each other to find buyers. The buyers will be looking for services that meet their particular needs or demands, offering the level of quality desired, at the right price. Such a notion was not traditionally applied to the services provided by the welfare state, largely because there was often a monopoly supplier, the state, and although it would make sense to say that people's welfare rights entitled them to a certain standard of service, it was usually difficult for them to 'take their custom elsewhere'. Choice for many social work service users may, in fact, mean the right of exit from declining services that have been starved of resources. This is probably why the term 'consumer' is more commonly used than 'customer' in a social work context.

However, from the late 1990s, the concept of consumerism was taken a step further towards a more developed notion of service users as 'customer-consumers' by the introduction of 'personalized' or 'cash for care' schemes in many developed welfare states. These schemes give certain types of service user, especially adults with disabilities and older people, the possibility of choosing, purchasing and managing the specific services they require. The rationale for the development of 'personalization' is varied, including increasing demand on welfare services from ageing populations (resulting in a shifting of responsibilities from the state to the private sector and families) and demands from the disability rights and other service user organizations for more choice and control over whether or not to use increasingly poor and fragmented public services (Lloyd, 2010; Rummery, 2011).

Rummery (2011) outlines schemes for personalized care in a number of countries in Europe and the USA. These vary in the way they are organized, but generally entail the state either paying service users cash benefits (direct payments) to enable them to purchase services directly from formal providers or informal carers, or giving them control over individual budgets within which they can choose their own combinations of care and support, but without having to manage budgets or employ carers themselves. 'Personalization' or 'cash for care' has been welcomed in some quarters as offering greater power and control for service users and enabling them to tailor services to their particular needs and requirements. These approaches have also been subject to intense criticism for placing large burdens of responsibility on service users, who may already be experiencing high levels of stress in their lives, to take on the role of entrepreneurs, managers and employers. Examples have been given of carers employed on low wages and sometimes exploited. Above all, such schemes, based on the idea of service user as purchaser in a marketplace, undermine the very essence of collective welfare provision, which is a public good, not a commodity to be purchased by individual consumers (Barnes, 2011; Ferguson, 2007; Lloyd, 2010; Scourfield, 2007).

In spite of the rhetoric of personalization and consumer choice, the majority of users of social work services cannot be regarded as consumers or customers in the sense we have discussed above. People on a compulsory court order or a parent whose child is suspected of having been abused do not have rights to choose or even to exit from welfare services, or if they do exit, their choice may be imprisonment, a fine, or removal of a child. This does not mean that many of the service users' rights promoted under the auspices of consumerism do not apply in the case of compulsory statutory social work involvement, such as rights to access to files or to information about legal rights. However, the idea of consumer *choice* makes even less sense in this context. This is why Hugman (1998a, p. 149) prefers to use the term 'quasi-consumer'. Others have used the term 'citizen-consumer' (Clarke et al., 2007) or 'customer-citizen' (Harris, 2009). These terms imply a limitation on consumer choice, as the consumers of welfare are also citizens in receipt of publicly funded services, with responsibilities as well as freedoms.

Calling service users 'consumers' or 'customers' also serves to hide the fact of social workers as controllers. It implies an active role for service users and the possibility to exercise choice. It plays down the role of social workers or other welfare workers as rationers of scarce resources, who have to make an assessment of the services or finances to be allocated to each individual based on their specific needs and the overall welfare budgets available for all potential service users. It also covers up the role of welfare as control, what Foucault (1999, p. 93) called 'surveillance-correction' and others have termed the 'new authoritarianism', which is based on the notion of the service user as dangerous, as a risk to be assessed, as deviant and as an outsider (Jeffs and Smith, 1994; Parton, 1999, 2006; Webb, 2006). This is another feature that can be identified in the policies and ideologies of many political parties and regimes, whether of the right, centre or left, contrary to the traditional social work values of respect for persons. It marks the re-emergence of the distinction between the deserving and undeserving poor and a determination to punish and control those on the margins of society – the 'outcasts' or the 'underclass'.

While aspects of these consumerist policies could be regarded as progressive in the promotion, for example, of children's rights and service user participation in or control over service delivery, other aspects are about treatment and control of service users – seeing the service user as a problem to be technically assessed, clinically managed and processed through a proceduralized system. Many policies and procedures relating to child protection, community care and criminal justice in Britain and other countries are now based much more explicitly than in the past on the utilitarian values of procedural justice and the promotion of public welfare.

Nevertheless, it could be argued that the notion of service users as consumers is helpful, in some ways, provided it is not linked with the idea of consumer choice. It is more honest about the nature of the social work relationship, which often is not a relationship between two free individual persons, or even two fellow citizens, but between representatives of an agency that provides services or purchases services on behalf of the state and someone who enters into a relationship with that agency or its representatives for a specific purpose. While this may not be how social workers wish to see the relationship, this is, in effect, an important aspect of how it is, especially in the context of state-sponsored social work.

Service users as activists, experts and allies

As indicated in the previous discussion of service users as consumers, some of the rights obtained for service users have come about through the campaigning work of service user groups and other social movements. In this context, the service user is seen neither as a passive recipient nor simply as an individual consumer of welfare services, but rather as an active member of a group or movement that is resisting identification with victimhood, resisting having needs defined solely by professionals or the state and asserting demands for better and different kinds of services, relationships and treatment. This is essentially a collective identity. Clearly, many service users do not and cannot take on roles as activists, but it is important to recognize this as a potential alternative role to that of consumer, and as a development of the notion of service users as active citizens. However, on this model of activist citizens, they define their own agendas rather than fulfilling a predetermined role as part of engineered or managed participation.

From the 1980s, there has been a growing emergence of service user organizations run by and for people who have been long-term users of welfare services (Beresford, 2011; Campbell and Oliver, 1996; Charlton, 1998; Wallcraft and Bryant, 2003). Service user groups, organizations and movements overlap with, but nevertheless should be distinguished from, broader campaigning and self-help organizations that are not necessarily focused around issues relating to use of welfare services per se and may be run by professionals who are not service users. Strong and influential service user organizations have emerged in many countries at the local and national levels, some of which are also active internationally. The disability rights movement is particularly vocal, as are many other organizations run by and for older people, mental health service users and young people looked after in state care.

In Britain, for example, there is a national organization called Shaping Our Lives, which was founded in 2002 as a national network of service users and disabled people. It describes itself as 'an independent user-controlled organisation, think tank and network' (www.shapingourlives.org.uk). Members of Shaping Our Lives undertake research, training, campaigning and contribute to social work education. A National Voice (www.anationalvoice.org) is an organization run for and by young people who are or have been in care in England, with the aim of helping young people change the care system for the better, helping them speak up and have an effect on decisions about the care system. The requirements in Britain for the involvement of service users in policy-making, the design and delivery of services, and the professional education of social work students has stimulated the growth of service user groups, including many linked to universities. The University of Bedfordshire in the UK, for example, supports a group called eXperts by eXperience (see www.beds.ac.uk/xbx), comprising people with experience of either social care or mental health services as users or carers, who are involved in interviewing prospective students, giving talks to students and assessing their work.

The concept of 'expertise by experience' is increasingly being used to characterize the knowledge that users of services bring to social work education, policy-making, service delivery and the encounter with the professional practitioner. This expertise is not just the insights, skills and knowledge of consumers, who know what they want. Rather, it is an expertise that is developed and shared with, and valued by, other service users, students, academics, social workers and other practitioners, managers, policy-makers and politicians. This is a more radical version of the co-production of knowledge and welfare services, which tends more towards the service user-led end of the spectrum than co-production. There is a danger, of course, of tokenism and of the inappropriate cooption of service users under the banner of 'expertise by experience' to carry out the state's agenda (see Scourfield, 2010 for a critical discussion of the involvement of 'experts by experience' in social care inspections). There are issues about who represents service users and whether some of the policy imperatives have resulted in the creation of an 'elite' and trained group of people who know how to participate in ways that do not present radical challenges (Carey, 2009). This does not devalue the concept of expertise by experience, but it does suggest the exercise of caution in uncritical acceptance of such concepts.

So far, discussion has focused on service user movements. The concept of 'service user' is useful in that it identifies those with experience of using services and hence with important insights into how services could be changed. Yet it is also quite narrow in that it excludes people who may have been refused services (but who might be regarded as having legitimate demands) and people who might be potential service users in the future. For those social workers who do community work, community organizing or community development work, the term 'service user' is not one that is often used. Social workers or other professionals in those contexts work with residents, community activists, volunteers and campaigners. They usually focus on collective issues relevant to people experiencing poverty, unemployment, discrimination, lack of voice, or living in neighbourhoods and communities with inadequate facilities and services. They may work by helping create alliances and coalitions between groups with different goals and rationales – ranging from trade unions and churches to groups campaigning against domestic violence or for action on climate change (Butcher et al, 2007; Hardcastle et al., 2011; Pyles, 2009).

In exploring the connection between radical social work and service users, Beresford (2008, p. 92) calls for new alliances, particularly between service users and face-to-face practitioners. This was a key element of radical social work in the 1970s and 80s (although user movements per se were less well developed at that time) and is echoed in some recent literature on radical social work (see Ferguson, 2008, pp. 81–7). Ferguson and Woodward (2009, pp. 134–9) advocate the adoption of community development approaches, which, while not necessarily radical in themselves (see Banks, 2011b), nevertheless start with the articulation of collective problems and are based on principles of solidarity. Beresford (2011, p. 104) draws attention to the Social Work

Action Network (SWAN), which began in Britain in 2004 and is now developing an international presence as a:

> radical, campaigning organisation of social work and social care practitioners, students, service users, carers and academics, united by our concern that social work practice is being undermined by managerialism and marketisation, by the stigmatisation of service users and by welfare cuts and restrictions. (SWAN, 2009)

Democratic professionalism, consumerism or radicalism?

The increasing concern with service users' rights can be regarded as a move towards a 'democratic' professionalism, consumerism and/or a new radicalism in social work. Democratic professionalism entails giving more power to service users in the context of the professional relationship (see Dzur, 2008). However, the focus is still on the professional as the one giving the power. So although the service user may be given more rights and be referred to as a 'partner' or even a 'co-producer', it could be argued that it is still the professional that is in control. A consumerist approach, by way of contrast, moves away from the idea of the social worker as a professional who exercises professional judgement on the basis of expertise towards the idea of social workers as officials – distributors of resources according to certain prescribed standards and procedures. On this model, the social worker is merely the intermediary between the state and the citizen-consumer. As McDonald (2006, pp. 120-1) comments: 'The consumer-citizen is largely constructed within his or her relationship with the state as opposed to a professional.' Consumerism has strong strands of anti-professionalism embedded in it, exemplifying a desire on the part of governments as well as consumer rights movements to challenge the power and exclusiveness of professional groups, in medicine, law and education, as well as social work. Radical social work has traditionally also been suspicious of the notion of professionalism and called for alliances between social workers and organizations representing the interests of people experiencing poverty and oppression. On this model, service users are seen as allies in a struggle, as co-activists and campaigners.

The concept of democratic professionalism may be about trying to retain some of the status and power, or at least the identity, of professionals, while also becoming more responsive to service users' rights – developing a model of professionalism that does not have to be elitist and exclusive. Democratic professionalism retains the notion of the social worker as a professional requiring special education and adhering to a professional code of ethics, while also trying to regard the service user as more of an active participant. It entails extending the traditional value of self-determination to include meaningful service user participation in decision-making. In practice, it is sometimes difficult to distinguish democratic professionalism from a consumerist approach. Developments that began as part of the so-called 'new professionalism', for example complaints procedures, advocacy and contracts between worker and service user, have become absorbed into the broader changes brought about by government legislation and a focus on consumerism. Ideas that at first seemed radical – the involvement of service users in social work education and anti-oppressive practice – are now mainstream in Britain and some other countries.

Yet in spite of the rhetoric of policy documents, in a time of economic recession and neoliberal government policies (particularly in the global North) and continuing poverty, famine, war and natural disasters in many parts of the world, the resources for welfare are increasingly limited and may often be of poor quality. In many countries, especially the USA and parts of Europe, the economic crisis that began in 2008 has led to cuts in welfare services, reductions in benefits, tightening of eligibility criteria, closure of residential homes and an increasing tendency to shift responsibility for care onto individuals, families and communities. Building on the strengths of the anti-capitalist movement (Callincos, 2003), new and stronger coalitions of people and organizations are developing to protest against particular welfare cuts, but also to challenge the whole basis of a flawed neoliberal agenda based on global capitalism (Lavalette and Ferguson, 2007).

The next part of this chapter will explore various ways of working alongside service users at a micro-level positively to enhance their ability to recognize and exercise their rights, including the promotion of participation in decision-making and empowerment to take action for change at the micro-, mezzo- and macro-level. The re-emergence of radical social work and the development of concepts such as 'green social work' or 'ecospiritual social work' (Dominelli, 2010, Ferreira, 2010) concerned with environmental sustainability are ways of looking at service users and social workers in a broad global political and environmental context in which the practice of social work is located in a much more holistic and challenging way.

There is a danger that these ideas are seen as only applying to macro-level policy and politics, but they can also be translated into everyday practice at the micro-level.

Involvement and participation of service users in decision-making

The degree of service users' involvement or participation in decisions about their own cases obviously varies not just according to the policies of particular agencies and the commitment of individual social workers, but also according to social workers' judgements regarding service users' capacities to understand the situation and make an informed statement of their own needs and choice of services or courses of action. However, as Lansdown (1995, p. 29) points out, it is important to distinguish between service users' rights to self-determination (the right to make their own decisions), which will be limited by judgements of their competence and their need for protection, and their rights to participate in the process of making decisions about their case. In the context of work with children, he argues that the right to participate and have their views listened to is not contingent on adults' judgements about children's competence or their best interests. However, this depends on what we mean by 'participation'. The term can be used in a number of senses, and is often regarded as a continuum or 'ladder' (Arnstein, 1969) or more usefully a sphere, suggesting a circular process (see Abrioux, 1998), which may include:

1. Informing, listening to or consulting service users
2. Giving service users some involvement in decision-making
3. Joint decision-making with professionals, or service users having full decision-making powers (see Øvretveit, 1997, pp. 85–8).

The terms 'consultation', 'involvement' and 'participation' are often used rather loosely and interchangeably. While the consultation (1) and involvement (2) of service users should no doubt be an unconditional right, 'participation' in the strong sense of joint or full decision-making powers (3) will usually depend on the capacity of the service user to make a decision.

There is then a question of how to judge whether someone is capable of understanding what is going on and making a decision. According to Wicclair (1991), writing in a healthcare context, decision-making capacity is judged according to whether people have a capacity to understand and communicate, to reason and deliberate, and whether they possess a set of values and goals. Some

might argue that the requirement for reasoning capacity and possession of goals is too demanding, especially in a social work context.
In Britain, for example, the Mental Capacity Act 2005 (Ch. 9, s. 3(1))
states that a person is unable to make their own decision if they
cannot do one or more of the following:

- Understand information given to them
- Retain that information long enough to be able to make the
decision
- Weigh up the information available to make the decision
- Communicate their decision – this could be by talking, using
sign language or even simple muscle movements such as
blinking an eye or squeezing a hand.

Not surprisingly, there is no single, universally accepted standard of
decision-making capacity. This is not only because health and social
care professionals' judgements about what constitutes a capacity to
understand and reason will vary, but also because the levels of competence required will vary according to what type of decision is being
made. Buchanan and Brock (1989) suggest that the relevant criteria
should vary according to the risk to the person's wellbeing. If the treatment is relatively low risk, then a weaker standard of decision-making
capacity is appropriate. These are debated issues (see Brock, 1991;
Veatch, 1999; Wicclair, 1991), but are of relevance to the issue of
service user choice in social work, particularly in relation to work with
children, people with learning disabilities or mental health problems.
As the Social Care Institute for Excellence (www.scie.org.uk/publica-
tions/mca/what.asp) states, in relation to mental capacity:

> because someone lacks capacity to make major decisions, this
> does not mean they are unable to make minor decisions. For
> example, an individual with a learning disability whilst unable to
> make a decision about where to live, is able to make other smaller
> decisions, such as what to eat, wear or do each day.

This is why it may be appropriate for some service users to have independent advocates to support them in speaking for themselves or to
speak on their behalf. This is especially important where the social
worker's role is to act on behalf of the agency in distributing resources
or exercising control. In relation to community-based care for older
people, for example, the social worker (or care manager) who assesses
the service user and prepares a budget or purchases and manages the
care package will generally be separate from the person or organization
that provides the care. It might therefore be assumed that the care

manager would advocate on behalf of the service user to gain the best possible budget or care package. However, since resources are limited, and the social work agency may have set some limits on certain types of services and prioritized the meeting of certain kinds of needs, the care manager will be constrained. The care manager may be working on behalf of the service user, but he or she is also working for an agency. The rights and needs of the individual service user will often conflict with agency policies for distributing available resources between service users; and needs that cannot be met may not be taken into account. Laws, policies and procedures can lay the ground rules for service users' rights, but are meaningless if not developed alongside the commitment of agencies and workers to respect people's own considered (if risky) choices and provide resources for service users to exercise their rights.

Case example 5.2 illustrates the barriers many older service users and people with disabilities experience in exercising their rights to make their own considered choices when faced with opposition not only from professionals, but also family members.

Practice focus

Case example 5.2: An older woman's rights versus the care business[2]

Ava was a woman in her seventies and, until recently, she had lived alone in her own home in a small town in Australia. About a month ago, she had a fall at home in her kitchen, and she had lain there, conscious but incapacitated, for almost 24 hours before her neighbours found her. Ava was hospitalized for a few days, and then spent several weeks in a respite room at a privately owned residential care home. Ava was keen to return home as soon as possible. She had lived in the same house for 40 years and wanted to stay there until she died. She told this to the occupational therapist who came to assess her. The occupational therapist (a new employee at the care home) did an assessment of global functioning and noted Ava's wishes. Although she judged Ava's situation was borderline, she wanted to respect Ava's own self-assessment and so she proposed a support plan to enable Ava to return home. The support plan involved daily meals on wheels, a nurse checking three times a week and various home aids and alarms. However, the team manager was sceptical whether the community health team would provide three visits a week.

---

2. I am grateful to Donna McAuliffe and Matthew Armstrong for allowing me to use and adapt this example.

The owner of the home then called a meeting with the occupational therapist, a private practice psychologist she had hired and Ava's son. The psychologist reported that in his professional judgement, Ava was not able to make an informed choice about her future care arrangements. When challenged by the occupational therapist, he admitted that Ava had no specific mental impairments, but said she was not making decisions in her own best interests. Ava's son said he was extremely concerned for his mother's safety in her own home and wanted her to stay in the residential care home. He indicated his support for the residential home, and offered to join the board of directors and bring significant cash investment into the facility. The occupational therapist was asked to reconsider her report.

The big question in this case is how someone like Ava, who can clearly express her preferences, can find a way to have them heard and taken seriously and get them put into practice. The occupational therapist is one potential advocate or ally. Although she is an employee of the residential care home and may have conflicting loyalties, ultimately, if she views herself first and foremost as a professional practitioner, she should put the choices and interests of the service user first. Although the other stakeholders have different judgements about Ava's capacity to make choices and about what is 'really' in her interests, unless the occupational therapist judges their arguments to be valid, then she should maintain her position and support Ava in her right to participate actively in decisions affecting her life. While a cash investment in the home may benefit a large number of other residents, this is not an argument for changing her assessment and recommended plan. If the occupational therapist judges Ava to be competent to make her own choices, then she should insist that Ava should also participate in any further meetings to discuss plans for her future.

Empowerment of service users: individual and collective

I will now briefly discuss the concept of 'empowerment' as going a stage beyond 'participation'. 'Empowerment' is also a contested concept. Rather like 'participation', it has a range of meanings from giving service users some limited choices (the consumerist approach) to power-sharing (the citizenship approach) to supporting and encouraging people or groups to realize their own power and take action for themselves (a 'radical' approach). A 'radical' approach is often advocated through linking empowerment to oppression and seeing empowerment as part of anti-oppressive practice (see, for example, Ahmad, 1990; Mullender and Ward, 1991; Thompson, 2006). Thompson (2006, p. 40) defines oppression as:

> Inhuman or degrading treatment of individuals or groups; hardship and injustice brought about by the dominance of one group over another; the negative and demeaning exercise of power. It [oppression] often involves disregarding the rights of an individual or group and thus is a denial of citizenship.

Discussion of anti-oppressive practice is often couched in terms of challenging structural oppression, that is, challenging the systems of beliefs, policies, institutions and culture that systematically discriminate against and demean women, people from minority ethnic groups, people with disabilities, lesbian, gay and bisexual people, working-class people and other oppressed groups (Clifford and Burke, 2009; Dalrymple and Burke, 2006: Dominelli, 2002). Yet as this rhetoric has been incorporated into mainstream practice, it is questionable sometimes whether 'empowerment' and 'anti-oppressive practice' consist of anything more than enabling individual service users to gain confidence and offering 'individually sensitive practice' that takes account of, for example, a service user's dietary and religious needs and their personal experience of oppression. This is not to undermine some of the radical and challenging social work that has happened and is taking place, but rather to suggest that this still does not necessarily represent the mainstream of social work practice.

In social work generally, the emphasis is more often on individual service users becoming more confident and personally powerful than on achieving societal change. Thompson's definition tends to reflect this when he states that empowerment 'involves seeking to maximize the power of clients and to give them as much control as possible over their circumstances. It is the opposite of creating dependency and subjecting clients to agency power' (Thompson, 2006, p. 95). In talking of service users gaining control over rather than changing their circumstances, this suggests that the aim is to empower people to live a better quality of life in the world as it is. Of course, other parts of Thompson's book on anti-discriminatory practice do embrace societal change, but if the focus of social work is on the individual service user or family, as it currently is in Britain, then inevitably the stress is on personal change, even if the broader societal context is acknowledged.

The idea of social workers working alongside service users in taking collective action for social change is a more radical version of empowerment. Here, concepts of solidarity, collectivity, community and relational rights are important. In many parts of the world, community organization or community development work is regarded as part of social work and social workers conceive of their work in relation to communities of place, interest and identity. This involves working alongside service users to identify collective needs and demands, to articulate these and challenge existing regimes of power and control. Case example 5.3 is an example of a campaign against cutbacks in public sector services in Britain, which comprised a coalition of service user groups, trade unions, social workers and other groups and individuals.

Practice focus

Case example 5.3: Hands off our services: disabled people, carers and social workers fight back[3]

Following central government reductions in funding to English local authorities, an annoucement was made by a city council that it was going to cut £33.2 million from its budget, including £107 million from adult care services. The council was proposing to increase the eligibility thresholds for adult care and to outsource all its adult social workers to a social enterprise. It was estimated that 5,000 disabled and older people would lose vital services, six residential homes for older people would be closed, charges for personal care would be increased and care workers made redundant. A High Court judge subsequently ruled as unlawful the proposal to raise thresholds for adult social care so that only personal care needs categorized as 'critical' would be eligible for support – meaning that 'substantial' personal care needs and other nonpersonal needs would not be eligible. The ruling stated that the council had failed to pay due regard to the impact on people with disabilities and had contravened the Disability Discrimination Act. However, the council's plans for cuts in adult services still remained and a campaign was launched comprising Disabled People Against Cuts, local branches of the

---

3. Further details of this campaign can be found on the Social Work Action Network website: www.socialworkfuture.org/index.php/the-news/103-handsoffbrum, and details of the legal ruling at: www.communitycare.co.uk/Articles/2011/04/21/116716/judge-overturns-council-plan-to-raise-eligibility-to-critical.htm, accessed August 2011.

public service workers' trade unions, the regional Social Work Action Network group, a City Against the Cuts group and the Right to Work campaign. A month of action was planned to coincide with the first UK monitoring of the 2008 UN Convention on the Rights of Persons with Disabilities.

Conclusions

This chapter has examined the gradual shift from seeing service users as persons in a relationship of clienthood to seeing service users as a fellow citizens, consumers/customers and/or activists. In one sense, the move towards a consumer rights approach can be regarded as a development of the principle of respect for persons, in that it is actualizing the rights of a person in the specific situation of being a social work service user – in particular, rights to information, certain standards of service and to choice. We noted the development of policies and procedures for gaining access to records, shared record-making, shared decision-making, making complaints, personalization and direct control over budgets for care. Within the predefined boundaries of the social work relationship and the agency context, these procedures aim to give service users more power. But the procedures in themselves do not guarantee respect for service users as equal citizens or consumers with real choice. Social workers inevitably tend to be more powerful and articulate than service users and there may be constraints in terms of agency resources. Procedures need to be developed alongside a systematic and long-term approach that promotes the participation of service users in service delivery, works towards individual and collective empowerment and offers advocacy for those service users who find it difficult to articulate their needs and rights.

This is not an easy task, as it is time-consuming and involves social workers and agencies being prepared to give up some of their power and change their ways of working. It also brings into focus the contradictions between individual and structural approaches to change. While social workers may work towards empowering individuals to take control over parts of their personal lives, unless the policies and practices in the state welfare system and in society generally that oppress certain individuals and groups are changed, then social work can only go so far towards putting these principles into action. This requires a more radical and community-oriented practice based on a commitment to the articulation of collective demands and the realization of relational rights.

Putting it into practice

Reflecting on rights in practice

Aims of the exercise: to encourage the reader to think practically about what rights are possible and desirable in relation to a context of which he/she has experience.

1. Think of an agency that you are currently working for/have worked for.
2. Draw up a list of what you think should be the service users' rights in relation to their contact with this agency.
3. Why do you think these particular rights are important?
4. How would you ensure that they are put into practice?

Practice focus

Case for discussion 5: Working with a pregnant girl in Turkey

A 16-year-old girl who had been feeling unwell came into a hospital in a Turkish city with her mother. As a result of a medical examination, it became clear that she was pregnant and the medical staff then referred her to the hospital social worker. In Turkey, for single women and their families, virginity is regarded as important. If a single woman has sexual intercourse and gets pregnant, this is a very negative situation in terms of their traditional cultural gender roles. Women in these situations are subject to different sanctions in different regions of the country. In order to have an abortion legally in Turkey, pregnancy must not be more than 10 weeks. Another issue to take into account in terms of the legal process is whether a child younger than 18 years old has been subject to sexual abuse or not, as an abortion is allowable in such cases up until 20 weeks.

Due to the young age of the girl, the social worker investigated whether she had realized that she was pregnant and whether she had been abused or not. After detailed interviews with the girl, it was understood that the young girl had a lover, and she had only just learned that she was pregnant. The pregnancy was over 17 weeks, so legally there was no possibility of an abortion. In the interview with the mother, it appeared that she had accepted her daughter's situation and was prepared to support her daughter to give birth. The social worker felt this was a favourable situation. However, the mother also said she wanted to place the child for adoption after the birth, whereas her daughter indicated that she wanted to raise the child herself.

The hospital social worker contacted his colleague in City Social Services Directorate and referred the case to her, because this agency offers support for pregnant women and handles adoption processes after birth. The situation of the child was evaluated and information was given about the resources available to support her (economic assistance, assistance about nursing during pregnancy and so on). However, the social worker in the City Social Services Directorate had a difficult ethical dilemma in relation to her professional intervention. Should the social worker respect the girl as an individual and support her to keep the baby by providing moral and material support? Or should she consider the 16-year-old girl as a child according to the Turkish Penal Code (Article 6, Clause 1.b), which states: 'Child means a person who is not over 18 years of age'? The social worker was also mindful of Article 12(1) of the UN Convention on the Rights of the Child, which states that the views of the child should be given due weight 'in accordance with the age and maturity of the child'. This entails that when some kind of intervention is proposed, it is especially important to take both the cognitive and emotional development of the child into account.

In this case, the social worker had to make a difficult decision, bearing in mind the conditions in Turkey. Having evaluated the development and maturity of the girl, should the social worker respect the decisions of the girl, who was classified according to age as a 'minor', and support her and the baby with assistance and counselling after the birth? Alternatively, thinking about the difficulties that the child of a young single mother would face in the cultural and social environment in Turkey, should the social worker proceed with the adoption option?

Questions for discussion

1. What do you think are the rights of the different parties in this case and how would you prioritize them?
2. How would you assess whether the pregnant girl is capable of making a decision about whether to keep the baby?
3. The writer of the case presents the situation as a dilemma for the social worker: either support the young women in looking after the baby after the birth, or proceed with the adoption option. Would you see the situation in this way, at this point in the story, before the birth of the baby?
4. How important do you think the cultural and social environment in Turkey might be in influencing this social worker's decisions and actions?

Further resources

Edmundson, W. (2004) *An Introduction to Rights*, Cambridge,
Cambridge University Press.
Clearly written introduction to the subject, offering a historical
overview of the development of the idea of rights and discussion of
the nature and future of rights.

Ife, J. (2008) *Human Rights and Social Work: Towards Rights-based
Practice*, revised edition, Cambridge, Cambridge University Press.
Offers a well-developed rights-based framework for social work
practice.

International Federation of Social Workers, human rights website,
http://www.ifsw.org/p38001792.html.
This excellent website outlines the nature and importance of human
rights in social work, some of the dilemmas faced by social workers
across the world in relation to human rights abuse and case
examples and other resources for use in teaching.

Reamer, F. (2006) *Social Work Values and Ethics*, 3rd edn, New York,
Columbia University Press.
Takes a rights-based approach to social work ethics, covering a range
of ethical dilemmas and professional misconduct issues in a North
American context.

Social Work Action Network website, www.socialworkfuture.org.
This is the website for SWAN, a radical, campaigning organization
of social work and social care practitioners, students, service users
and carers. It has the text of the SWAN manifesto, a discussion
forum, links to publications and information about current
campaigns and actions.

CHAPTER 6

Social workers' responsibilities: policies, procedures and managerialism

CHAPTER OVERVIEW

In this chapter I will explore the nature of social workers' duties to service users in relation to their other duties and broader responsibilities, including those to employing agencies, the profession and society. Professional codes of ethics say more about duties to service users and to the profession and tend to argue that these have primacy. Employing agencies, on the other hand, tend to require that employees put agency policies and procedures first. This chapter will explore the conflicts that arise between different sets of duties and responsibilities, particularly in the context of the increasing proceduralization and bureaucratization of social work (managerialism) and privatization of welfare services. At the end of the chapter, there is an exercise to encourage reflection on personal, agency and societal values, and a case for discussion about social workers acting as informants during the last military dictatorship in Argentina.

Introduction

Chapter 5 focused on service users' rights. According to the narrow definition of a right (as a valid claim belonging to an individual or group of individuals), if service users have certain rights, then some person or some institution has a corresponding duty to fulfil those rights. In many cases, it may be the social worker directly that has a duty, for example the duty to treat the service user with respect, or it may be the social worker indirectly acting on behalf of an agency (the duty to provide services for children in need). The direct duties could be said to be inherent in the role of professional social worker, and the indirect ones inherent in the particular job the social worker has. If we take a broader conception of rights – what we called the 'manifesto' sense of rights or relational rights, which might include the fulfilment of certain basic human needs across the world – this may require a more expansive kind of duty, what has been characterized as 'relational responsibility'. The term 'responsibility' is broader than 'duty' and has been used in the chapter heading to encompass abstract duties in a Kantian sense and specific procedural duties defined by the employing agency, as well as the more situated relational responsibilities that are prominent in care ethics.

Duties

The concept of 'duty' is central to Kantian ethics, which has often been categorized as 'duty ethics' or deontology. Many of the religious ethical systems also have 'duty' as a central concept, although focused around duty to a god. In the context of professional ethics, the types of duties we tend to talk about are those owed to service users, the profession and to the employing agency; those duties to which people commit themselves when they take on the job of social worker. In this sense, a duty is a consequence of a contract or undertaking, either implicit or explicit. As Whitley (1969, p. 54) states:

> My duty is that which I am engaged or committed to do, and which other people can therefore expect and require me to do. I have a duty to keep a promise, because I have bound myself thereto.

However, we may have conflicting duties because different commitments may have been undertaken that are incompatible with each other in a particular situation. We may therefore have to choose between duties. For example, I have a duty to keep the information service users give me confidential, but I also have a duty to protect service users from serious danger. Therefore I might decide to break the confidence of a young person who has said she is planning to commit suicide. The duty of confidentiality may be said to be a prima facie duty, that is, it is what I ought to do, other things being equal. This notion of duty is also connected to accountability. If I have made a contract or undertaking to do something (duty), then I am also expected to be able to explain or justify my performance or nonperformance of that duty (accountability). In social work, this latter aspect of a duty is regarded as important, as social workers must be publicly accountable for what they do (see Banks, 2009b).

It is important to distinguish this sense of duty – an obligation or commitment as a consequence of a contract or undertaking – from how the term is sometimes used, particularly in moral philosophy, to mean 'the right action': 'what I ought to do'. We might say in relation to the case of the girl threatening to commit suicide that I decided it was my duty to tell her parents. 'Duty' in this sense is a definitive recommendation regarding what ought to be done, taking all the circumstances into account. 'Duty' here means *the* right action, and there is only one action. Therefore it would not make sense to talk of a conflict of duties. I am going to use the term 'duty' in the first sense, where duties are regarded as commitments or obligations that may be in conflict with each other. So a duty is what I am committed to do, other things being equal. Very often, other things are not equal. It may be morally right for me to neglect one particular duty in favour of another. When talking about duty in the sense of the right action, or what I ought to do having taken all circumstances into account, I will use terms like 'making a moral judgement about how to act' or 'deciding on the morally right course of action'.

'Relational duties' or responsibilities

The concept of duty as proposed in Kantian ethics, some forms of religious ethics (but by no means all) and professional ethics is often associated with a set of commitments that have been externally defined by, for example, the moral law, God, a set of socially given norms or a professional association. Nevertheless, it is the moral agent who has the task of interpreting and carrying out these duties and deciding how to act in cases of conflict. The notion of 'responsibility' encapsulates this sense of engagement by moral agents with their commitments or obligations.

The term 'responsibility' is frequently found in codes of ethics and literature on professional ethics, and encompasses both the rather narrowly conceived professional duties, such as obligations to respect confidentiality or to protect children, and a broader sense of a network of commitments and ties that are created together and shared with service users, other professionals, other people and groups. The term 'responsibility' is rooted in the notion of 'response', that is, responding to the perceived needs of other people, to demands or calls from others. As discussed in Chapter 3, this is a central focus of what has been called 'the ethics of proximity' found in the philosophical work of Buber (1937) and Levinas (1989, 1997), for example, and drawn upon by Bauman (1993), where ethics arises in response to the call of the other person. The starting point is not abstract principles outlining duties leading to a process of moral reasoning, but a pre-rational face-to-face encounter with another person who evokes my response.

Responsibility is also one of the concepts at the heart of the ethics of care, as discussed in Chapter 3, based around the relationship of caring for others, and is the focus of much attention in feminist ethics (Noddings, 2002; Tronto, 1993). It is also at the heart of many non-western ethical traditions that take a holistic starting point to ethics based on interconnections and interrelatedness, such as the African-centred worldview articulated by Graham (1999, 2002), also mentioned in Chapter 3.

This links with the discussion of 'relational rights' in Chapter 5. In broadening the concept of duty from an individualistic to a relational focus, this brings it closer to the notion of responsibility. We discussed a similar refocusing of the concept of rights, which also leads us towards responsibility. Some theorists have developed the notion of 'relational responsibility' (McNamee et al., 1999), which may seem somewhat superfluous (if we see responsibility as centred around response to another/others), but it does serve to emphasize the dialogical and dynamic nature of responsibility and shifts the centre of concern from the individual. The starting point of the philosophy of Levinas and Buber, for example, is the I–Thou relation – the dyad, or twosome. For Gergen and colleagues, writing from a (social) constructionist perspective, the starting point is the social. As Burkitt (1999, p. 79) comments:

> To supplement Levinas's (1989) notion of responsibility located in the recognition of the other's face, we can say that this is not just the bare face of human physiognomy but a face superimposed with social identity taken from the way the person to whom it belongs is situated in social relations.

Although the terms 'duties' and 'responsibilities' are often used interchangeably, strictly speaking, the term 'responsibilities' is broader than 'duties'. It encompasses 'duties' that may be quite specific and definable, as well as 'responses' that may be owed to others simply as fellow human beings. In codes of ethics, the term 'responsibilities' is often used in this broad sense.

Social work as a 'role-job' with specific duties

Social work takes place within an institutional framework of rights and duties defined by the law, employing agencies and the professional code. Chapter 4 discussed the specific duties and broader responsibilities of the social worker as laid down in professional codes of ethics and practice. There are other rights and duties that make up the job in particular countries, such as the legal right (or power) and/or the duty to intervene in people's lives in cases where a child is thought to be at risk, or the procedural duty to follow agency guidelines in assessing risk in child protection cases. For this reason, Downie and Loudfoot (1978) describe social work as a 'role-job' – meaning that the job of social work is defined by a set of institutional rights and duties. They argue that it is important for social work to have an institutional framework because social workers intervene in the lives of others and it is in the interests of service users that they have a right to intervene. Second, social workers discover many intimate details of people's lives and it is important that there are rules, such as confidentiality, which provide security for the service user. Third, social workers themselves can find security from working in an institutional framework, for example they can fall back on their official position to give guidance on proper procedures with a service user in case of legal action.

Downie and Loudfoot (1978) list four different types of rights and duties that attach to the role of social worker, to which I have added a fifth, as outlined in List 6.1. Although they use the term 'duties' throughout, I have indicated occasions when a broader concept of responsibility may also be relevant.

List 6.1 Types of rights and duties attaching to the role of social worker

1. *Legal rights and duties* to service users, employers and others.
2. *Professional rights and duties* (and responsibilities) arising from membership of a profession with its own standards of conduct.
3. *Moral duties* (and responsibilities) arising from the fact that the social worker is dealing with specific individuals in specific situations.
4. *Social duties* (and responsibilities) arising from the fact that the social worker is also a citizen who has the opportunity to do

more civil good than many, for example through working towards
reforming or changing social policies.
5. *Procedural rights and duties* arising from the fact that the social
worker may be employed by an agency that has its own rules
concerning how the work should be done and how social workers
should behave or be bound by a contract with a service user or
purchaser of social work services.

Source: Drawing on Downie and Loudfoot, 1978

When someone takes on the role of a social worker, they are in
effect agreeing to work within this framework of rights, duties,
broader responsibilities and rules. In particular, the employing
agency will expect them to work within its rules and procedures,
since it is this agency that is paying their wages. Usually, an
employing agency will also expect the worker to work within the
framework of the law and indeed, if it is a statutory agency, many
of its policies and procedures will be based on interpretations of
laws and statutory guidance.

Conflicting responsibilities

In an ideal world, it might be assumed that legal, professional,
social, moral and procedural rights, duties and broader responsibilities would complement or coincide with each other. However,
this is not always the case. A social worker may judge, for example,
that the employing agency's procedures regarding confidentiality
are too lax compared with the standards laid down in the professional code, or that the methods in common usage entail treating
service users as objects rather than respecting them as persons.
The professional associations usually state that it is the principles
laid down in the professional codes that should come first, as these
codes are designed with the protection of service users in mind,
whereas the law or agency rules may be designed for the conven-
ience of the majority.

In taking on the role of social worker, a person takes on several
different layers of responsibilities that may conflict with each
other. These are often laid out in codes of ethics, as discussed in

Chapter 4. List 6.2 summarizes these responsibilities and the main sources of documented external guidance, that is, guidance stemming from outside authorities as opposed to the social worker's personal moral code.

List 6.2 Responsibilities of social workers to different parties

1. *Responsibilities to service users:* for example, to respect service users' rights to make their own decisions, to respect their rights to confidentiality, to safeguard and promote the welfare of children (acting on behalf of the local authority). Sources of guidance include professional codes of ethics, codes of practice published by national regulatory bodies, national government guidance, agency policies and codes of practice, the law, public opinion and charters for service users' rights.
2. *Responsibilities to the profession:* for example, to uphold the good name of social work by maintaining effective and ethical practice. Sources of guidance include professional codes of ethics and the professional association and/or regulatory body.
3. *Responsibilities to the employing agency:* for example, following the prescribed rules and procedures and safeguarding the reputation of the agency. Sources of guidance include the worker's job description and contract and agency policies and procedures.
4. *Responsibilities to society:* for example, maintaining social order, executing the responsibilities of state social work agencies as laid down by statute and challenging inhumane practices. Sources of guidance include the law, government guidance, public opinion and codes of ethics.

How does the social worker judge between these different responsibilities when they conflict? It might be with reference to the values and principles outlined in professional codes or professional literature. But what if professional codes are not explicit enough, or if there is a conflict between the principles of the code and what seems to be required by the agency or the law? There is an ongoing debate about whether it makes sense to distinguish values that social workers hold or should hold as professionals from the prevailing values of their employing agencies, the wider society in which they live and personal values to which a social worker has a commitment as a private individual. This may include secular or religious values about what is morally good/bad, right/ wrong and political beliefs or commitments about how these values should be implemented in society. We will now consider some of these debates briefly (for more detailed discussion of the relationship between professional ethics and the ethics of everyday life, see Banks, 2004a, Ch. 2).

The professional is personal: vocation and commitment in social work

There is a school of thought in social work (and other caring professions) that maintains that social work is a vocation, which suggests a blurring of the distinction between personal and professional life, values and responsibilities (see LeCroy, 2002). This may be argued from a number of perspectives, including religious. Eastham (2002, p. 71) claims that the term 'vocation' is Jewish in origin, meaning, in this context, a direct invitation from God to lead a certain kind of life. On this view, becoming a social worker might be akin to someone taking on a religious calling to become a priest, whose whole life should be lived according to the moral duties of the religion, not just parts of it when he or she is performing the role of a priest. The idea of vocation has resonances with the origins of social work in the global North and West in the religious movements of the mid- to late nineteenth century. Here, the early inhabitants of the settlement houses and 'friendly visitors' were committed to their work as part of a religious calling, whether to convert or educate people or simply to alleviate poverty and suffering (Banks, 2004a, pp. 26–35; Younghusband, 1981). They did not regard their personal and professional lives as separate. As Picht (1914, p. 2) comments in relation to the early settlers in Toynbee Hall (established in 1884) in East London: 'not as an official but as a friend does he approach the poor'.

Although the origins of the term 'profession' come from the declaration or vow made by someone entering a religious order and one meaning of the term 'profession' is 'a vocation or calling', as social work 'professionalized' and secularized, that is, became a recognized occupation, it developed sets of principles and rules designed to protect clients from exploitation, patronizing treatment and variations in practice. Yet, as discussed in Chapter 4, there is a continuing debate about the extent to which such principles and rules are desirable or necessary. Some have argued that the very essence of social work is the personal commitment that practitioners have to working alongside people experiencing difficulties in life and to working to change society.

Ronnby (1993) notes the tendency for the welfare state (of which social work is a part) to reinforce existing inequalities in society and to treat those who are the poorest and least powerful as objects to be pitied or changed. His solution is for social workers to adhere to their personal 'humanistic ethics' and to come closer to their service users as fellow human beings. He notes that 'techniques and routines as well as professional self-interest can prevent the social worker from acting humanely' (pp. 5–6). This has resonances with the references to 'love' in the 1997 version of the Swedish code of ethics (Akademikerförbundet SSR, 1997) and to the 'ethics of proximity' of Levinas (1989) and some Nordic ethicists such as Løgstrup (1997), as discussed in Chapter 3. Bauman (1993), in his discussion of postmodern ethics, is also influenced by Levinas, talking of the 'moral impulse' – a personal capacity to act morally, which is the property of an individual as opposed to external ethical frameworks, such as professional ethics. Bauman (1993, p. 19) emphasizes the moral responsibility of the individual over and above the various roles people play (one of which might be 'social worker'), each with their ethical rules. Husband (1995, p. 99) applies this to social work, arguing that the moral impulse is a necessary basis for responsible social work intervention: 'By its untrammelled innocence and generosity it is the creative core of caring.' This view seems to entail that the relationship between social worker and service user might be one of unconditional caring, in the same way as a mother cares for her child, for example. It would involve removing the distinction between private and public morality. It has resonances with, although it is distinct from, the ethics of care discussed in Chapter 3, which is based on relationships of caring between connected individuals as opposed to the externally imposed ethics of justice based on duty, universal principles and the notion of separate individuals.

However, the view that the social worker should genuinely care about service users and treat them as she would friends or strangers in her ordinary life seems problematic in the context of much current social work practice, especially in the state sector. While an ethics of proximity based on the responsibility I feel in the face-to-face encounter between myself and the 'other' may be a foundation, a precondition or starting point of ethics, there is a need, as Bauman (1997, p. 222) acknowledges, to go beyond 'the moral party of two' to reach justice – 'the realm of choice, proportion, judgement – and comparison'.

Bringing the discussion back to concrete realities, when out shopping on a Saturday, I might give some cash to a man in the street who asked for some money for food and take him home for a cup of coffee. But surely, while at work as a social worker on Monday, I should not give money out of my own pocket to a service user in the social work office who asked for money for food and take him home for a cup of coffee? First, this might leave me open to accusations of favouritism, as I cannot do this with all service users. Second, if I did give this level of personal care to all service users, I would be impoverished and exhausted. Third, this would involve developing a personal relationship with a service user, which might leave him and me open to abuse. These reasons echo those given by Downie and Loudfoot (1978) as to why it is important that social work operates within an institutional framework of rights and duties, to protect both the social worker and the service user.

It is doubtful if Ronnby (1993) or Husband (1995) are actually arguing that social workers should treat service users as friends. Rather, the implication is that social workers should treat service users as fellow human beings for whom they feel empathy and respect; and that social workers should regard themselves as people first and foremost, applying the same fundamental ethical principles to the situations they encounter in social work as they would to other situations in other parts of their lives. A more moderate version of this view would be to acknowledge that social workers are employed by organizations that operate by certain rules and procedures and are constrained by professional norms, societal mores and the legal system. Within this framework, they should treat service users with as much honesty and respect as possible, but it is not usually regarded as part of the job to care for service users unconditionally. It is arguably more important that social workers hold on to their own personal values not in order to give unconditional love to service users, but in order to challenge laws, policies and practices regarded as unjust and oppressive, including 'blowing the whistle' on institutionalized malpractice. This requires not just a commitment to a set of ethical principles, but also characteristics of moral perception, sensitivity and courage – qualities discussed in Chapter 3 in relation to virtue ethics.

The professional is political: challenging injustices and 'blowing the whistle'

One of the responsibilities of professionals is to be independent and critical of their employers, colleagues, funders and government agencies in cases where they judge poor, unethical and dangerous practice is occurring. Generally, the term 'whistleblowing' is used to refer to cases when employees go outside the normal internal channels for reporting and tackling complaints. Martin (2000, p. 139) distinguishes internal whistleblowing, which involves informing people further up the internal hierarchy than might normally be expected, and external whistleblowing, which involves taking the issue outside the organization – perhaps to the press or politicians. He also distinguishes between open whistleblowing, where the identity of the whistleblower is openly given, and anonymous whistleblowing, where identity is withheld. Many organizations now have whistleblowing policies, which support legitimate whistleblowing – recognizing that it is in their interests that employees report dangerous or unethical behaviour or unsafe practices. However, they usually require that the normal channels of complaint have been exhausted first and that the whistleblower acts in good faith and in the public interest – not for personal gain, or with malicious intent. In spite of laws and policies supporting whistleblowing, many staff are reluctant to take action and those who do, even if their actions are proved to be based on serious and legitimate concerns, may ultimately find themselves ostracized or without a job. It requires a great deal of moral courage to blow the whistle and is more effective and safer for the individual concerned if support from other colleagues, trade unions, professional associations or other bodies is available. In his overview of 'administrative evil-doing' in social work, Preston-Shoot (2011) notes how infrequently social workers take action to challenge their organizations and suggests that there is a serious disjuncture between espoused professional ethics and ethics in practice.

Machin (1998) gives an account of her experience as a social worker in a secure hospital for mentally disordered offenders in Britain, her decision to give evidence to a public inquiry investigating allegations of patient abuse and her subsequent dismissal from her job. She speaks of her own beliefs as being important:

> My social work practice was born within the radical model. My formal training confirmed my belief that the traditional social

work models need to be challenged in the light of human exper- ience and emotion, and that workers need to get alongside their clients in order to foster empowerment and counteract the effects of their disabling conditions of life. My efforts to under- stand the context of the social and economic conditions in which my clients existed did not distance me from feelings of warmth and compassion, or from painful emotions born from understanding the effects of poverty and deprivation. (Machin, 1998, p. 118)

Machin specifically locates herself within the 'radical model' – working for change in social conditions – while also retaining compassion for the people she is working with. One of the slogans of the early feminist movement was: 'the personal is political'. Machin's comments are a reminder that the professional is also political, that is, as a person in a professional role, a social worker has a responsi- bility publicly to challenge inhuman, degrading, unjust and oppres- sive practices committed by fellow professionals.

Briskman (2005), writing from an Australian perspective on the abusive and inhumane treatment of indigenous people and asylum seekers by services that are delivered by social workers, exempli- fies a similar commitment to expose and challenge unjust policies and practices with which social workers are often complicit. This was achieved through undertaking research, writing newspaper articles and campaigning with others within and outside the university where she worked. Many of the social workers, who later gave evidence to the People's Inquiry into Detention initiated by Briskman and fellow Australian academics (Briskman et al., 2008), did not give their names and had not found other channels to challenge their employers or government policies on detention. 'Jennifer' was one of the social workers who gave evidence. Her story is outlined in Banks and Nøhr (2012, pp. 195–7), including her struggle to find ways of meeting the needs of asylum seekers who were not entitled to services at that time and over 'whether to speak publicly about damaging policies and practices when a culture of organisational silence pervades' (p. 195). She felt unable 'to challenge or subvert the workplace policies as the organisation was dependent on government funding' (p. 197). Instead, she undertook voluntary work outside her professional job, offering advice to refugees, advocates and volunteers in a refugee advocacy group. She also wrote a confidential submission to the People's Inquiry into Detention. In deciding to give evidence:

she gave priority to her belief that social workers had a professional and moral obligation to ensure that all people had access
to services. She also stressed that the wider community needed
to be informed of the existing injustices. In deciding to take
action, she came to the view that acting to restore justice over-
rode obligations to her employing organisation. (Banks and
Nøhr, 2012, p. 197)

There are many similar cases of social workers speaking out. Yet
there are also even more cases where systematic abuse and deception
has been uncovered where social workers were complicit. Cases may
range from social workers' involvement in and observation of the
abuse of young people in residential care homes to their active
involvement in the torture of political prisoners or the seizure of children in political regimes of military dictatorship. It is easy to condemn
inaction from the sidelines. Yet it is also important that social work
as a profession and individual social workers work together to make
it possible to take a stance to resist involvement or complicity with
any form of exploitation and human rights abuses. The case for
discussion at the end of this chapter is taken from a recent judgement
made by the professional associations in Argentina and Latin America
regarding to the involvement of social workers as informants during
the last military dictatorship in Argentina.

Case example 6.1 is an account from a social worker in Britain
about aspects of her everyday practice that made her feel deeply
uncomfortable. In the end, she left her job.

Practice focus

Case example 6.1: 'Please tell me you don't need any services from
us': screening older people for personalized care

I was working for an adult social services team in a local authority in a
large British city. We introduced a new way of working called
'personalization'. This was supposed to eliminate some of the
problems with care management that had led to social workers
spending 80–90% of our time in the office, working with the 'system'
rather than with people and spending a lot of time trying to meet
targets and deadlines. However, since the introduction of the new
system we had much higher workloads and stricter targets, with far
fewer staff.

One day I was working on the phone, screening the needs of people who call social services. I was not supposed to be doing this work, but I had been asked to help the screening team as there were some staff off sick that day. At the time, I was also under huge pressure to complete a number of other tasks from my own workload within a short period of time, including gathering information for a 'safeguarding' case where a service user was thought to be suffering from or at risk of harm. When doing the screening work that day, if anyone I spoke to 'passed' our screening test and went through to the next stage, I would then have to complete a number of tasks, including gathering large amounts of their personal information to supply sufficient 'evidence' to convince the duty manager why I felt this person was entitled to be assessed by us. In reality, for this person, all this would mean would be that they were entitled to receive a self-assessment questionnaire in post.

At that time, I was talking to a male service user in his eighties, who had just come out of a local hospital. He was struggling with his daily living. During my conversation with him, somewhere in my mind I was desperately praying: 'please tell me you don't need any services from us'. I was so relieved when he said he was just managing to cope with his personal care. This meant he was not entitled to be assessed by the local authority. If he had been in need of some form of personal care assistance, my tasks would have involved at least a 20-minute telephone conversation with him to gather much more information and then fill in several forms with numerous pages and complete comprehensive reports to the manager and service provider. It would have taken at least two hours (unless interrupted by other work) and I would not have been able to leave the office until late.

At the same time, I would have 'failed' to meet my targets for my own safeguarding case. We were under warning of dismissal if unable to meet targets, so I would have been in an extremely difficult position if he was in need of care. So in my mind I was praying that he did not need care. But I should not have been having these thoughts. Although I was under huge pressure, I was very scared of myself: 'why was my mind screaming?' I had always put my service users first, but I somewhat lost myself at that moment. I felt I could not continue to do the kind of social work practice in which I believe under this target-driven environment. There is a huge danger in this new system. Previously we were allowed to install services for service users in any emergencies. This could be a one-night sitting service or 'checking call' for a week until a person settled. However, the new system no longer allowed us to protect vulnerable people, so people at risk might be left in a dangerous situation for days or weeks until the person's lengthy paperwork passed a series of managers' checks to approve funding for a particular service. If this 80-year-old man on the phone had been in urgent need of services, he might have waited for weeks to get the funding approval and any social workers in my shoes would have had sleepless nights worrying about him. So my mind was praying for his sake also. Could this be forgiven?

This social worker's story is typical of many working in similar circumstances. Her feeling of despair at the system and concern about her own response come over very clearly. This could be categorized as a story of moral distress, where the professional knows what is the right course of action but is unable to carry it out. 'Moral distress' is a much discussed topic in nursing, but not in social work (see, for example, Ohnishi et al., 2010 for an empirical study of Japanese psychiatric nurses). Jameton (1994, p. 6), who is credited with first introducing the concept, defines moral distress as arising when 'one knows the right thing to do but institutional constraints make it nearly impossible to pursue the right course of action'.

The separation of personal, professional and agency values and life

The possibility of and moral imperative for whistleblowing is based on the assumption that, at a personal level, individuals have a conscience and a set of values that they can and should apply to the values and norms in operation at their workplaces or prevailing in society at the time. They also can and should make critical recourse to the espoused values of the profession to which they belong. For if we do not have this view, then there is a danger of colluding with inhumane and unethical practice. Yet there is also a need for 'professional distance' – a separation between personal and work life – not just to protect the service user, but also the social worker and society. Social workers are encouraged to be aware of and maintain appropriate boundaries between their personal and professional lives. Many of the cases of professional misconduct dealt with by regulatory bodies and professional associations relate to 'boundary issues', particularly friendships and sexual relationships between social workers and current or former service users (Doel et al., 2009; GSCC, 2008). The issue of 'dual relationships' is often referred to in the social work literature, for example cases where a social worker relates to someone as both a friend and a service user. Emphasis is placed in the professional guidelines on either avoiding dual relationships, which may be difficult in small communities and remote rural areas, or being clear about the boundaries between the two (Halverson and Brownlee, 2010).

One fairly extreme view on the separation of personal, professional and agency values is expressed by Leighton (1985). This is worth examining as it puts the argument clearly and argues for quite rigid boundaries in a way that more recent literature does not. Leighton suggests that social work aims to manipulate and change people; social workers act not as ordinary human beings as they would in their personal lives, but take on a separate role, which requires them to appear to care, but not in the genuine way in which one would care for a friend. He gives the example of a social worker who needs to get certain intimate information from a young person in residential care (presumably for a report):

> The social worker is therefore obliged to try to draw the child into a relationship for no other purpose than to satisfy the social worker's job requirements. It is exceptional if the worker offers important parts of himself or herself to the child's personal social world. The relationship is part of a statutory and financial transaction from which only the social worker benefits financially.
> (Leighton, 1985, p. 78)

He argues that we must separate the personal and the professional, so that we do not feel guilty about manipulating people and using relationships as we would if we treated someone in the same way in ordinary life. According to Leighton (1985, p. 79), the social worker is required to:

> manipulate people and their relationships, and must learn the art of appearing to care when his natural feeling is not to care. To survive as a private person and to do his work well he must sometimes operate within a mode of 'bad faith', a lack of absolute honesty in the relationship

We may all recognize elements of truth in this depiction of the social work role, which we can connect with more recent work on the 'emotional labour' that those in the service and caring professions have to undertake to do their work (Hochschild, 1983; Leeson, 2010). However, Leighton's view seems rather extreme. It could ultimately lead to the social worker simply taking on a job and following all the norms, procedures and practices required by the agency, regardless of whether they appeared to be morally wrong or to be allowing morally wrong actions to occur, according to the ethical principles of the profession or her own personal moral code. Taken to its limit, such a view could imply that a social worker working in a secure hospital where systematic abuse of residents is taking place (as described by Machin, 1998) could justify her actions by saying 'I was only doing my duty in accordance with the agency procedures', as if it was nothing to do with her if the agency norms were immoral or cruel. It would leave little room for whistle-blowing as a moral duty in cases of institutionalized malpractice.

This type of view seems to entail that there is no person over and above a series of social roles of which the private/personal is just one. Leighton gives an example of a social worker, Mr Anthony, and argues that certain values from his personal life, such as converting people to Catholicism and believing abortion to be morally wrong, conflict with professional values such as service user self-determination and nonjudgementalism, both of which conflict with the employer's values such as assisting with birth control techniques and encouraging conformity to social norms. His conclusion seems to be that being a social worker is a totally different and separate thing from being a private individual. But is it? Surely the private individual or person decided to accept the job of social worker with its particular values and duties. If Mr Anthony was the kind of person who was such a strong Catholic that he went around trying to convert neighbours, friends and people in the street and he strongly opposed birth control, then arguably he would not have chosen to become a social worker with this particular agency. Most Catholics do not try to convert people in the street or to dissuade strangers from having abortions. Surely moral standards similar to those Mr Anthony has for relating in his private life to strangers and acquaintances may apply also in social work. When Mr Anthony goes to a concert or visits the bank, certain rules of behaviour apply, which do not usually involve trying to convert the bank clerk or handing out anti-abortion leaflets in the concert hall. Similarly, social work may be regarded as a particular setting in which certain ways of behaving are appropriate and to which particular duties apply. As Koehn (1994, p. 153) argues, professionals do have special duties towards their clients and service users, but these are based on ordinary morality and represent an intensification of the relationship of trust in everyday life.

Most people would probably agree with Leighton that, as a general rule, social workers should refrain from trying to persuade service users not to have abortions and that social workers do not and cannot treat service users as friends. However, it does not follow that personal, professional and agency values should be treated as totally separate. Where they conflict, the social worker as a person has a moral responsibility to decide which have primacy and to justify this decision. Mr Anthony may decide that he cannot work in an agency that involves so much work promoting birth control or that he will request not to deal with certain cases where he would feel compromised. Indeed, someone who has a strong commitment to the Catholic faith may actively choose to work for a Catholic charity that provides support to pregnant young women.

Case example 6.2 is about a Christian social worker practising in an East Asian country, who finds herself facing a dilemma when her agency takes on a new area of work.

Practice focus

Case example 6.2: Dilemmas for a Christian social worker

Linda is a licensed social worker employed by a non-profit, faith-based organization (FBO) located in a rural area of Taiwan. This organization is run by a local Christian church and provides social services for children and youths. Since this agency is one of the few social service agencies that employs professional social workers in that area, the local government approached this organization to take on a contract to provide services for low-income women. The services included financial assistance, legal advice services, employment referrals and psychological support. The director of the agency, who is a priest, decided to cooperate with the government because he saw it as an opportunity for evangelism and for the organization to develop its work in this area.

One year later, the FBO started to provide social services for the women in the community. As an experienced social worker, Linda was asked to be the supervisor of this new programme. A small but significant number of women using the service are single women who are pregnant. Usually, women in this situation tend to have an abortion due to the low toleration of unmarried mothers in society, particularly in rural areas. This is challenging for Linda. On the one hand, Linda's own Christian beliefs and the mission of the FBO would entail taking an active pro-life stance (anti-abortion). On the other hand, the government requires the agency to implement the principle of separation of church and state in the work it does. Hence, the staff of the organization should not persuade an adult woman to keep her baby and look after it herself or let someone adopt the baby. Linda is also aware of two important professional principles in social work: value neutrality – meaning social workers should not impose their own personal values on clients – and self-determination – social workers should respect clients' own decisions. She feels she is facing conflicts between her personal beliefs, professional standards, the agency's goals and government policy as well as societal pressure. Linda spends some time considering what she should do.

Linda, the social worker in this case example, is clearly more troubled than Mr Anthony about how to reconcile her religious beliefs and various aspects of her work. Without knowing the background, it is difficult to surmise what her options might be. But clearly this is an issue as much for the director and the agency as a whole as it is for Linda. This case neatly exemplifies the tensions between different moral codes and hence responsibilities attaching to different roles. Figure 6.1 illustrates the cumulative layering of personal, agency, professional and societal moral codes.

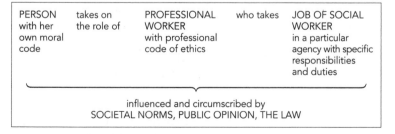

Figure 6.1 Relationship between the personal, agency, professional and societal moral codes

Committed/radical, professional, technical-bureaucratic and quasi-business models of practice

The two positions outlined above, that there should be no separation between personal and professional values and that they should be kept completely separate, represent divergent views at a theoretical level. In practice, individual social workers may give more priority to personal, professional or agency values, depending upon what kind of work they do, how they view their jobs and lives, the conflicts and pressures arising in their work at particular times, and the professional and societal norms operating in the country where they work. Table 6.1 outlines four ideal typical models of social work practice that I have called the committed/radical, professional, technical-bureaucratic and quasi-business models. These are 'ideal types' as they are artificial categories and it would not be expected to find the practice of workers and agencies conforming neatly to these models. However, they are presented to help us explore the different emphases that social workers may adopt in their practice according to their ethical stance and their particular work settings.

1. The *committed/radical practitioner* model sees the social worker as a person who has chosen to take on the job out of a personal or ideological commitment to work for change and who puts this first. This model encompasses many different types of approach ranging from the individual 'ministration in love' model to the more collectivist approaches espoused by Marxists, feminists and anti-racists. Although the same heading has been used to encompass all these approaches, there are obvious differences in focus ranging from the empowerment of individual service users to societal change.

2. The *professional* model focuses on the social worker as an autonomous professional with expertise gained through education and guidance coming from the professional code of ethics. Her first priority would be the rights and interests of service users; her identity as a social worker would be as a member of the profession first, and as a private individual or worker in an agency second.

3. The *technical-bureaucratic* model regards the social worker first and foremost as a worker in an agency with a duty to carry out the prescribed tasks and roles of that agency. Guidance comes from agency rules and procedures.

Table 6.1 Models of social work practice

	Committed/radical	Professional	Technical-bureaucratic	Quasi-business
Social work as	Vocation/social movement	Profession	Job	Business
Social worker as	Equal/ally	Professional	Technician/official	Producer/provider
Power from	Competence to deal with situation	Professional expertise	Organizational role	Competence in the market
Service user as	Equal/ally	Client	Consumer	Customer
Focus on	Individual or group empowerment/societal change	Individual worker–service user relationship	Service provision	Customer satisfaction/profit
Guidance from	Personal commitment/ideology	Professional code of ethics	Agency rules and procedures	Market norms, customer preferences, contracts
Key principles	Empathy, genuineness, raising consciousness, collective action	Users' rights to self-determination, acceptance, confidentiality, etc	Agency duties to distribute resources fairly and to promote public good	Customer choice and independence
Organizational setting that would best facilitate this	Independent voluntary agency or campaigning group	Private practice or large degree of autonomy in agency	Bureaucratic agency in voluntary, statutory or private sector	Private agency

4. The *quasi-business* model focuses on the social worker's role in providing competitive services to customers in a marketplace. Guidance comes from customer choice and norms of the market (including profit).

All four models are evident in the social work literature and social work practice, although the fourth is the most recent and challenging. The professional codes tend to contain elements of the first three, with emphasis more on the professional model, tempered with duties to the employing agency (technical-bureaucratic) and personal commitment to work for societal change (committed/ radical). Social workers have never comfortably fitted into the role of 'professional experts' because of the ideological tendency to identify with oppressed service users and the fact that social work is frequently located in state-sponsored or state-funded agencies.

The technical-bureaucratic model is, arguably, becoming more dominant, at least in the state sector and large not-for-profit organizations. Many commentators have expressed concern about the 'deprofessionalization' of social work, which relates to the increasing specification of tasks and procedures (as described in Case example 6.1), attempts to reduce indeterminacy in decision-making and reduce reliance on or trust in autonomous professional judgement, and the adoption of competency-based approaches to education and training (Dominelli, 1996; Hugman, 1998b). The growth of interest in 'evidence-based practice' could be seen to be part of this trend. Although a focus on evidence-based practice is relatively recent in social work (see Gibbs and Gambrill, 2002; Smith, 2004), in medicine it is already well developed and has been described as a 'process of systematically finding, appraising and using contemporaneous research findings as a basis for clinical decisions' (Long and Harrison, 1996, p. 11, quoted in Malin, 2000, p. 21). In a social work context, the concept of evidence-based practice has been criticized for focusing on measurable interventions within a managerial and social control framework, while neglecting reflexivity, flexibility and creativity in the social work role (for a useful summary of arguments for and against, see Payne, 2005, p. 64; also Gibbs and Gambrill, 2002; Webb, 2001, 2002). Other commentators have argued that the evidence-based approach offers opportunities for greater professionalization and is a way of advancing claims to professionalism (Malin, 2000, p. 21). The reasons for this, of course, are that it is an approach based on scientific rationality that appears to give more credibility to the effectiveness of professional interventions, hence enhancing the notion of professional expertise in dealing with increasingly technical and complex tasks.

The quasi-business model as applied in social work does not simply apply to social workers in private practice or private sector care organizations. For the whole idea of being a professional is that professional workers retain their approach and values in whatever setting they work – whether as a lawyer, doctor or social worker in private practice or a for-profit organization. The quasi-business model applies to social work in all settings and refers to an orientation of social workers (and the agency for which they work) towards defining the services they provide, and those who use them, in terms more commonly associated with market transactions (see Harris 2003, 2009). The critiques of this model, with its focus on the service user as a consumer-customer, were discussed in Chapter 5. What this means for the social worker is that the relationship with the service user becomes more one of brokerage (if the worker is a care manager) or customer care and service (if the worker is a direct service provider).

With the increasing fragmentation of social work in many countries, and with services previously provided by the local state being shifted to the private and not-for-profit sector, there is also an increasing opportunity in some areas of work for workers to operate within more traditional professional or committed/radical models of practice. For example, specialist advocacy or counselling projects can be established with an unequivocal focus on the individual service user–worker relationship, where it is clear that the advocate or counsellor is primarily concerned with the rights or interests of the service user. As it is increasingly recognized that people in powerless positions or who find it difficult to speak for themselves should have independent advocates to support them, this results in the separation of the advocacy role from the general social work role. This means that the state-sponsored social worker may be concerned with allocating and rationing resources between many service users, whereas the advocate will push for the wishes, needs and rights of this particular service user.

Similarly, there is a growth of a range of 'detached', outreach or street-work posts with specific service user groups, often defined as 'hard to reach', which recognize the importance of workers having personal and life experiences close to the experiences of those with whom they are working. Deverell's research in the UK with HIV prevention outreach workers demonstrates that many workers do the job because, as gay men, they have 'a keen interest in seeing HIV prevention done amongst gay men ... and because politically I wanted to be involved in a job that had something to say to me personally' (worker quoted in Deverell and Sharma, 2000, p. 29). Deverell found that at times the workers felt 'more like a peer than a professional' (p. 30), with workers using the terms 'vocation' (p. 35) and 'way of life' (p. 31). Yet while recounting many instances of when they were 'off duty' but still responded to requests for advice, many workers were also aware of the importance of setting certain professional boundaries and standards in the work, which could otherwise be fluid and open-ended, with the potential for exploitation (of service users by workers and vice versa). Some community and social development work may also have this character, particularly in countries where social work is less organized as a profession. For example, Herscovitch (in Healy, 2001, pp. 174–5) describes the practice of a social worker, herself a Cambodian refugee, working on mental health issues in a large refugee camp in Thailand through training 'natural helpers' (Buddhist nuns). Many faith-based organizations have explicit religious values as part of their mission, and social workers employed in those organizations may join them in order to live out these values in their working practice, as demonstrated in Case example 6.2.

A social worker may often find herself working within several or all four models, and hence experience conflicting responsibilities. The emphasis of the work will vary not only according to the individual worker's view of her role, but also according to the particular piece of work being undertaken and the type of work setting. A social worker employed as a counsellor by an independent voluntary organization to work in complete confidence with people with HIV/AIDS will find the organizational and work setting much more conducive to operating within a professional model of practice than a practitioner employed by the local state, working in team, a large part of whose job is to assess and plan care packages for older service users. A community development worker employed by a neighbourhood residents' association with a campaigning brief will find it easier to work within a radical model. A youth development worker, herself a committed Muslim employed by a local mosque to undertake informal educational work with Muslim young people, will readily be able to see her work in promoting young people's spiritual development in terms of her own faith commitment. Exactly how these practitioners work and put these values, principles and commitments into practice will also depend upon their personal qualities, levels of confidence, knowledge and skill and the broader cultural and national frameworks of values, policies and laws. For example, an HIV/AIDS counsellor working in India or Zimbabwe would have a different role from one working in Britain or Finland. The implications of a white counsellor meeting a black service user, or vice versa, will be different depending on the context. A Muslim youth development worker working in Australia, Canada, the Netherlands or Britain will face a different set of dilemmas and problems than she would in India or Malaysia.

If we look briefly at some of the key ethical principles for social work, we can see how the organizational and work setting changes the interpretation and implementation of these principles. Here, I take the principles of confidentiality, the primacy of service users' choices and interests, and distributive justice and outline how these might apply to social workers in four different work settings and employed as: an HIV/AIDS counsellor; a care manager for older people; a community development worker; and a youth development worker.

1. Confidentiality

- *HIV/AIDS counsellor:* confidentiality is a key focus of the counselling relationship and it is important that the counsellor can assure complete confidentiality (privacy) between herself and the service user, except in circumstances where it is legally permitted or required that the counsellor disclose information, for example where another person is likely to be seriously harmed or where a court requires information. There is nevertheless potential for tensions and dilemmas in this role, precisely around when, if ever, it is judged right to breach confidentiality, for example if the service user refuses to disclose their HIV status to a sexual partner. In Chapter 4's Case for discussion 4, the social worker working in a women's refuge is not a counsellor as such, but similar strict requirements regarding confidentiality apply in such settings.
- *Social worker/care manager for the elderly:* the limits of confidentiality are much broader and may include other members of the team and other healthcare professionals and service providers. If a particular social worker is unavailable or sick, it would be expected that another social worker would consult the service user's file and continue with the work. The relationship between service user and worker is not a private one. This kind of relationship would apply in Case example 6.1 about the social worker working in the adult social care field.

- *Community development worker:* while acknowledging the need to respect the confidentiality of certain personal information relating to individual residents, confidentiality might be regarded as relatively unimportant in the context of residents working together collectively to achieve change, as might apply in Case example 0.2 about the community and youth worker responding to local riots.

- *Youth development worker:* this worker will take account of the importance of family and community in the context of the Muslim faith and culture. While recognizing confidentiality as important as part of the relationship of trust with particular young people, this will be balanced with a concern for the young people's welfare and safety and the needs of the wider group/community. There is potential for generational and cultural tensions, especially if the young people have grown up in a western country, straddling the different value systems, as exemplified in Case example 1.3 about the young Bangladeshi men in Wales.

2. The primacy of service user self-determination and the service user's interests

- *HIV/AIDS counsellor:* while the counsellor may need to ration time between one service user and another and, in exceptional cases, consider the interests of others (for example if a service user has not disclosed their HIV status to a partner)s within these limits, the counsellor can focus on the needs and interests of the service user. It will depend on the style of the particular counsellor and the nature of the service user's needs as to whether the counsellor respects the service user's own choices and decisions or adopts a more parentalist or directive style.

- *Social worker/care manager for the elderly:* this worker will need to keep in mind the needs and interests of other people as well as the service user, for example any family carers, neighbours, service providers and other current and potential service users who will need resources. While the service user's own choices and interests may be respected as far as possible, there are many limitations on this.

- *Community development worker:* this worker would see the promotion of individual self-determination or empowerment as part of the process of collective empowerment to achieve change. However, there may be conflicts between individual, group and community development, including subgroups within the neighbourhood.

- *Youth development worker:* this worker may be concerned to facilitate the spiritual development of each young person in the context of the teachings of Islam, focusing on a concern for the self-determination of young people as Muslim young people. However, there may be conflicts between young people's decisions and choices and those of the wider Muslim community.

3. Distributive justice

- *HIV/AIDS counsellor:* except for the rationing of time between service users, this worker does not have a direct role in distributing resources between individual service users. However, the worker may choose to campaign and draw to the attention of service providers and policy-makers the inadequacy of resources for this service user group in particular and the discrimination they face in society; indeed, the social work codes of ethics include this as a principle.
- *Social worker/care manager for the elderly:* this worker does have a duty to distribute the resources of the agency fairly between individual service users and to manage them efficiently. In making a decision about what course of action to take, resourcing issues will be as important as an individual service user's choices and needs.
- *Community development worker:* this worker will be concerned to achieve redistribution of resources (power, wealth, good housing) to residents as a group according to need, linked to a striving for equality of result, and may use campaigning and community action approaches.
- *Youth development worker:* this worker may be concerned to get young people's voices heard in the organizational structures of the mosque, the wider Muslim community and in the neighbourhood more generally – challenging religious discrimination, racism and ageism as part of a broader movement for social change. The youth development worker may be able to see herself clearly as an advocate for Muslim young people, although there is a lot of potential for tensions between young people, adults and the wider community.

These simplified examples do not explore the details of the potential tensions and dilemmas within each role – handling ethical conflicts and dilemmas is the subject of the next chapter. But the examples above do indicate how the work setting, the type of agency and the role defined for the social worker influence the extent to which a social worker may work more within one model than another. In Britain and many other countries, there has been an increasing shift towards the technical-bureaucratic model within statutory social work, alongside tendencies towards a 'quasi-business' approach. In Japan, for example, these trends have been particularly strong (see Ando, 2010; Ito, 2010; Kosaka, 2010).

The growth of managerialism, authoritarianism and marketization: the case of Britain

Since the late 1980s in Britain, and many other countries in the global North, there has been a growth in the production of quality standards, procedural manuals and assessment schedules in state-sponsored social work. This is particularly noticeable in the field of child protection, although these trends are evident throughout social work and the public, independent and private sectors generally. There has also been a growing trend to set targets for both services and individual workers and to measure performance in terms of outcomes. These developments are often discussed under the label of the 'new public management' (NPM) in the context of the growth of neoliberal policies and programmes (Clarke, 2000; Dunleavy and Hood, 1994). While some have argued that we are now entering a 'post-NPM' or 'digital governance' era (Dunleavy, 2006; Pollitt, 2010), the economic constraints on public spending in Britain and many parts of the world mean that concerns with measurement of performance, particularly linked to cost-effectiveness and value for money, are a continuing feature of welfare services. There are a number of interrelated features of these trends, including:

- *Marketization:* a concern to offer 'customer choice', alongside increasing efficiency and competitiveness in service delivery
- *Consumerism:* a concern to offer a consistent standard of service, linked to service users' rights and quality assurance
- *Managerialism:* which seeks greater control over the work of employees
- *Authoritarianism:* which emphasizes the social control function of practitioners

- *Deprofessionalization:* a process that entails characterizing social workers as officials carrying out agency policy and/or as sales brokers.

If we take the example of child protection social work, these trends were given added impetus by a series of public inquiries into child abuse cases where either children died in their homes or they were taken away from home unnecessarily and it was said that social workers should have acted differently. This led to a vast quantity of guidance and advice from central government about how to assess children thought to be at risk, how to monitor them and their families, how to conduct interagency case reviews, how to investigate suspected cases of child abuse and how to prepare evidence for court. In the context of child protection work, Howe (1992, p. 496) argued in the early 1990s that a new perspective was emerging based on a view that:

> Injury and neglect suffered by some children results in the demand that children should be protected; that protection is achieved by improving, standardising and prescribing full and proper methods of investigation and assessment; and that bureaucratic forms of organization appear to be the best way of handling the ever more detailed and complex requirements of this new perspective.

Yet, despite a proliferation of policies, procedures, assessment schedules and the development of vast national computerized systems for monitoring and recording interventions in the late 2000s, further child protection scandals occurred. Social workers became increasingly demoralized at the impact on their work, in particular the depersonalizing effect of the nationally defined systems, which required a vast input of time entering information into computers (White et al., 2010). Finally, there is evidence of a turn against excessively procedure-driven practice in public welfare services, partly fuelled by the economic recession and a desire to drive down welfare costs by cutting down on bureaucracy. A major review of child protection was conducted by Munro, an academic from the London School of Economics and Political Science. At the start of her first report, Munro (2011) comments:

> A dominant theme in the criticisms of current practice is the skew in priorities that has developed between the demands of the management and inspection processes and professionals' ability to exercise their professional judgment and act in the best interests of the child. This has led to an over-standardised system that cannot respond adequately to the varied range of children's needs. (p. 5)

188 Ethics and values in social work

> For some, following rules and being compliant can appear less risky than carrying the personal responsibility for exercising judgment. (p. 6)

To regard child welfare and protection purely as a technical exercise ignores the ethical questions about how much 'abuse' society is prepared to tolerate, balanced against how much interference in family life is thought to be justified. As was argued in Chapter 1, social workers are faced with trying to balance these contradictory, ambivalent and changing societal values. If their major role becomes one of surveillance and collecting evidence, rather than close supportive work and/or therapy with the families, this leads, at best, to bureaucratic practice, which focuses primarily on issues of needs or risk assessment and resource allocation as determined by agency rules and procedures. At worst, it leads to defensive practice, such as going by the book and denying personal responsibility (see Harris, 1987).

The growth of customer-oriented and business-like models, as discussed in Chapter 5, is most prominent in the adult social care field. Here, a toxic mix of market principles, cost-saving measures and a target culture has created a confusing and ethically challenging environment for social workers. Baldwin (2011, p. 188) characterizes this as the 'EasyCare' model of social work – inviting comparison with 'low-cost airlines that reduce services to the minimum and charge for extras'. A social worker working in adult social care made this comment (personal communication) about her work:

> Practice is strictly monitored by managers for its quantity, efficiency and contribution to meeting 'targets' and deadlines. For instance, we have to 'sell' a piece of equipment [one of several kinds of home alarm systems for use in an emergency] to service users at least once a month and our performance is often evaluated by quantitative measures – who sells well and who does not. When we questioned this, the management told us that selling this equipment promotes service users' independence. But most of the frontline practitioners didn't feel that was true, as we had to remove the home care service [visits from a carer] at the same time and a number of service users wished to keep the carers' visits instead of having a machine. As the target was really strict, we were sometimes begging service users to buy one (or at least try the service for a few months) to meet the target.

Clearly, there is a cost-saving imperative at work here, as well as 'management by results' and an approach that depersonalizes and privatizes services offered to older and disabled people. Such approaches to practice can be distinguished from the 'professional' model, which focuses more on the individual worker–service user relationship with guidance from the code of ethics, and the 'committed/radical' model, which stresses individual or societal change and does not separate out the personal from the professional or agency values (see Table 6.1). While there is an increasing emphasis on the 'technical-bureaucratic' and quasi-business models, there are constant tensions between all four and this is part of the reason why ethical challenges are endemic in social work, because of the many layers of responsibilities involved.

Ethics in bureaucratic and quasi-business settings: defensive, reflective and reflexive practice

Rhodes (1986, p. 137) notes the contradictions between the individualized, caring concerns of social workers and the impersonal requirements of bureaucracies and argues that 'being a good worker may mean acting unethically'. However, working in a bureaucracy arguably does not inevitably mean acting 'unethically'. Indeed, as du Gay (2000) argues in defence of bureaucracy, the impartial rules that are the hallmark of a bureaucracy play an important role in professional life. Such rules could be seen to be derived from utilitarian approaches to ethics that focus on the fair distribution of resources. In fact, it is vital to see such work as very much in the sphere of the ethical, rather than the purely technical. This enables us to debate the fairness of the bureaucratic rules and principles and to question the value of the assumptions on which they are based and in whose interests they have been devised. Otherwise there is a danger that we become 'defensive' practitioners. The ethical decisions regarding resource allocation or what is to count as child abuse may have been made elsewhere (by central government or agency managers), but that does not absolve the social worker of the responsibility to challenge these decisions if necessary. For example, we need to guard against the preoccupation with the distribution of existing resources that the bureaucratic approach encourages and think about arguing for more resources for social work service users.

There is a tendency to assume that questions about the distribution of resources, efficiency and cost are not ethical ones. They are, and it is dangerous not to regard them as such. Seeking the cheapest service may not be an unethical decision, if it can be argued that this results in more people getting some level of service, rather than a few people getting good quality service. This may be based on utilitarian ethical principles about promoting the greatest good for the greatest number of people. What is unethical, of course, is simply to accept inadequate levels of resources without questioning or pressing for better provision.

The social worker in an organization where bureaucratic and/or business-oriented approaches frame the work can and should still be both a 'reflective' and 'reflexive' practitioner. In summary, we may distinguish between defensive, reflective and reflexive practitioners as follows:

- *Defensive practitioners:* If we extend Harris's (1987) notion of defensive practice to the field of professional ethics, then defensive practitioners 'go by the book' and fulfil duties/responsibilities defined by the agency and the law. There is no need to take the blame if the prescribed rules and procedures have been followed. Social workers are 'officials' or 'technicians'. Doing 'my duty' means fulfilling my obligations to the agency, rather than doing what I know to be the morally right action; personal and agency values tend to be separated, and the latter tend to be adopted while in the role of social worker.
- *Reflective practitioners:* Building on Schön's (1983, 1987) notions of 'reflection-on-action' (after the event) and 'reflection-in-action' (while doing), there has been an increasing recognition of the importance of reflective practice in social work (see Banks, 2003; Gould and Taylor, 1996; Martyn, 2000). Reflective practitioners are able to recognize and analyse ethical dilemmas and conflicts in their practice and consider how and why they arise, for example through unequal power relationships with service users, contradictions within the welfare system and society's ambivalence towards state welfare and social workers in particular. They are more confident about their own values and how to put them into practice; integrate knowledge, values and skills; learn from experience; and are prepared to take risks and moral blame. There is a recognition that personal and agency values may conflict and that the worker as a person has a moral responsibility to make decisions

about these conflicts. *Critical reflection*, as defined by Fook (2002, p. 43) involves a focus on issues of power and a redevelopment of practice and theory in relation to changing power structures to become more emancipatory.

• *Reflexive practitioners:* Often the terms 'reflective' and 'reflexive' are used interchangeably. However, as Fook (2002, p. 43) points out, 'reflexive' is also used to refer to a stance taken (it has often been used in relation to practitioners undertaking research) whereby the practitioner is able to locate herself in the picture and recognize how she both influences and is influenced by the people and events she is observing. Reflexivity may embrace reflection, but is a more complex process, as Taylor and White (2000, pp. 6, 34–5) outline in their exploration of how knowledge is made and used in professional encounters. Reflexive practitioners are aware of the dominant professional constructions influencing their practice and subject their own knowledge and value claims to critical analysis. This may involve questioning received ideas and professional practices, analysing how truth claims are made, how professionals and service users perform as credible, reliable or morally adequate people or how form-filling prescribes action. *Critical reflexivity* would focus on how dominant discourses construct knowledge and values, on the potential for challenging and changing existing power relations and on the role of social work in changing welfare systems (see Kessl, 2009). Critical practice, as Adams et al. (2002, p. 309) stress, is transformational.

Conclusions

This chapter has discussed the many layers of often conflicting duties and broader responsibilities that social workers have to balance and choose between. It has been argued that the critically reflective and reflexive practitioner needs to be aware of how these conflicts arise, to make informed ethical judgements about which responsibilities have priority, while recognizing how the ethical frameworks she is using are themselves constructed and contested. She may have to operate within several contradictory models of social work practice and be able to recognize and hold the tensions between them. If the social worker takes on one model to the exclusion of others, then important aspects of social work practice will be ignored. If the social worker regards herself exclusively as a 'professional', ignoring the constraints imposed by the employing agency, then she may become narrow and elitist. If she wholeheartedly takes on board the technical-bureaucratic model, she may become a defensive practitioner, mindlessly following agency rules. If she sees service users as customers choosing care in a market, she may lose her sense of collective and professional responsibility for tackling social evils and promoting social justice. If she sees her own personal religious or political beliefs as paramount, then she may become unaccountable to her agency or to service users. To recognize and balance these layers of responsibilities is part of what it means to be a competent, committed and ethically reflexive practitioner. We need to recognize that personal, professional, agency and societal values are interlocking, yet in tension.

Putting it into practice

Reflecting on personal, agency and societal values

Aims of the exercise: to show how the values of the individual, the agency and society may be similar and/or conflicting.

1. Think of the job that you are currently doing or one that you have done in the past:
   - What are your main *aims* in the job?
   - What *roles* do you play?
   - Describe your major *achievements* in this job.
   - What *values* do you think underpin your work in this job? (What you regard as your major achievements may help you think through what your values are)
2. Now imagine looking at your job from the point of view of the agency you are working for or used to work for:
   - What do you think the agency's *aims* are?
   - What do you think is the agency view of the *role* you are playing?
   - What pieces of work do you think would be highly *valued* by the agency?
   - What *values* do you think underpin the agency's work?
3. Now imagine looking at your job from the point of view of society as a whole, or 'the public':
   - What do you think are the public perceptions of the *aims* of the job?

- What *role* do you think the public regards you as playing?
- What pieces of work do you think would be highly *valued* by the public?
- What *values* do you think underpin public perceptions of your job?
4. Are there differences between your values and those of the agency and/or society? If so, why do you think this is the case?

Practice focus

Case for discussion 6: Social workers as informants in Argentina[1]

A recent tribunal conducted by a professional association for social workers in Argentina involved a retired male social worker, who had worked for many years at a local hospital. Records were published, giving the names of those who served as civilian intelligence agents during the last military dictatorship. These records showed that this particular social worker had been involved as an informant as a civilian member of an intelligence detachment between 1976 and 1983. The principal function of informants was to infiltrate organizations, unions and universities and provide information to the armed forces. During this time, many people disappeared, including many social workers and social work students, as a result of the work of the informants. These informants were also responsible for the abduction of many children. This involved denouncing their mothers, taking them to clandestine maternity clinics and keeping them alive until the moment of childbirth. After the birth of their children, the mothers would 'disappear'. The abducted children were categorized as 'spoils of war' and registered as their own by members of the armed forces or their relatives and acquaintances. In other cases, the children were sold or abandoned in nameless institutions.

---

1. I am grateful to Laura Acotto, vice president of the Latin America and the Caribbean region of the IFSW, for permission to use this case. The information is taken from the tribunal records of the Colegio Profesional de Servicio Social del Neuquén (23 April 2010) and the statement of the Latin America and the Caribbean region of the IFSW: 'Disclaimer statement of ethical civilians who served as "informants" to the military dictatorship (1976–1983) and were accomplices in the genocide and disappearance of 30,000 Argentines among whom were abducted children who currently remain unfound.' The original documents can be found at www.cpss.org.ar.

The professional association for social work (Colegio Profesional de Servicio Social del Neuquén) held an ethical tribunal in the town where the retired hospital social worker had practised. This led to the cancellation of his licence to practise and a denunciation of his role as an informant. Local social workers were shocked, including a former colleague in the provincial hospital who instigated the complaint. She commented that when her colleague's name appeared in the list, his former co-workers were very affected 'by having shared many years of work with someone who has known all the intimacies that this profession has'.

The Argentinian Association of Social Workers and the Latin America and the Caribbean region of the International Federation of Social Workers issued a repudiation of the social workers involved as informants in Argentina. The statement published by the Latin America and Caribbean region of the IFSW included the following declaration:

> We call this ethical declaration of repudiation for each professional or social work student who has been involved in such violations of the ethical principles of provincial, national and international Social Work. Also to put the validity of these acts in value, so long as the action carried out by people who participated as informants, not expired 30 years ago, and that crimes (complicity in the kidnapping, disappearance, murder and appropriation of people) remain in force through the concealment of information that would enable the location of the dead and 300 adults who now know their true identity.

In an article on the website (www.cpss.org.ar), Norberto Alayón, a social worker and lecturer, makes the following comment in relation to professional ethics:

> Cases such as these are also crucial for keeping the memory, because dictators do not emerge just because of the terrible action of the military, but also and perhaps primarily, by the management and support of certain civilians, many of them recognized professionals.

Questions for discussion[2]
1. What do you think were the main reasons that the professional association for social work of Neuquén decided to remove the licence and condemn the actions of a retired social worker for crimes commited 30 years ago?

2. I am grateful to Maria Moritz for suggesting some of these questions.

2. At the present time, in countries with liberal democratic regimes, professional associations and individual social workers would not hesitate to condemn social workers who were complicit in human rights abuses. But how many do you think would do this if there was a military dictatorship ruling their country?

3. This case is an extreme example of crimes against humanity committed by social workers, in a very specific context. How similar do you think some of the ethical and political issues are in this case to those raised by the complicity of social workers in inhumane treatment of asylum seekers and refugees in the case from Australia in the earlier section on whistleblowing?

4. What measures do you think professional associations and other networks of social workers, social work academics and students can and should take to ensure that social workers do not abuse their professional positions and are not silent observers of abuses committed by others?

Further resources

Banks, S. (2004) *Ethics, Accountability and the Social Professions*, Basingstoke, Palgrave Macmillan.
Chapter 2 discusses the relationship between the ethics of everyday life and professional ethics, while Chapter 6 explores aspects of the new managerialism in the light of interviews with professional practitioners.

Fook, J. (2002) *Social Work: Critical Theory and Practice*, London, Sage.
Useful outline of a critically reflective and reflexive approach to social work practice, based within a clear theoretical framework with a focus on strategies for practice. Covers issues of power, diversity, discourse, deconstruction, reconstruction and narrative approaches.

Harris, J. (2003) *The Social Work Business*, London, Routledge.
Examines the introduction of business thinking into social work and how this is impacting on the profession and service users. Largely based on the UK experience, but the trends have wider relevance.

CHAPTER 7

Ethical problems and dilemmas in practice

CHAPTER OVERVIEW

This chapter will explore some of the ethical problems and dilemmas that arise in everyday social work practice in contexts where social workers have to make judgements and decisions. First, I will briefly outline a particular view of the nature of ethical judgements in professional practice. I will then explore, in the light of the discussion in the previous chapters, examples of problems and dilemmas that have been collected from both trainee and experienced social workers. The chapter ends with an exercise to encourage reflection on readers' own dilemmas and a case for discussion from a social worker in Japan about how best to support a woman and her family.

Introduction

In this chapter I will take a closer look at the different types of situation that social workers experience as causing them ethical difficulties. These may be situations where it is difficult to make an ethical judgement about what is right and wrong, good or bad; or where it is clear what ought to happen but this is not implemented in practice. An ethical judgement is an evaluation of a situation or person(s); for example: 'The right course of action is to denounce the social worker who was an informant' or 'This social worker is morally blameworthy.' Sometimes, this process of ethical evaluation is referred to as 'ethical decision-making', in that making an ethical judgement could be regarded as deciding what is right or wrong, good or bad. But usually a decision involves making a commitment to taking action; for example: 'We decided to denounce the social worker.' This decision about what to do is based on one or more ethical judgements, but it takes the judgements one step further. Although a judgement such as 'the right course of action is to denounce the social worker' implies action (it is prescriptive), this does not necessarily mean that the person making the judgement or anyone else will decide to take the action prescribed – it may not be in their power, they may be weak-willed and so on.

Ethical judgements

In order to examine the nature of ethical judgements in a little more detail, it may be helpful to use a case example for illustrative purposes.

Practice focus

Case example 7.1: An older woman suffering from confusion

Carla Jones is an 87-year-old woman of African Caribbean origin. She lives alone in a quiet street near the centre of a small town in southern Scotland. She is the only black person living in the street. She has support from a home care worker and daily visits from her only daughter, who has a full-time job and four young children. She has been diagnosed as having Alzheimer's disease and is becoming increasingly confused about times and dates, forgets to take her medication and has left her cooker turned on and wandered out of the house wearing only her night clothes several times. Recently, she became violent when her daughter tried to take her home on one of these occasions, causing her daughter to be admitted to hospital with severe cuts and bruises. The daughter and neighbours are increasingly concerned and have asked for an assessment by the social worker, demanding that Ms Jones be admitted immediately to a psychiatric hospital. Ms Jones has hitherto refused to go to hospital for an assessment of her condition and believes that her daughter should spend more time with her.

The social worker, along with a medical practitioner and the others involved in this case, will have to make a decision about what to do. One element of the decision-making process may be the social worker's ethical judgement, having assessed Ms Jones, that: 'It would be morally wrong to commit this woman to hospital against her will.'

As is apparent from the discussion in Chapters 2 and 3, there is considerable disagreement among ethical theorists not only about the nature of ethics, but also about how judgements are arrived at and justified, and, indeed, whether ethical judgements are more akin to expressions of taste or feeling than rational prescriptions for action. Nevertheless, in the context of professional ethics – where professionals have defined roles and responsibilities and deal with the distribution of public resources – notions of accountability, rationality and fairness are regarded as important aspects of making ethical judgements and decisions. A view about the nature of ethical judgements that I think fits with the general context of the work of the welfare professions is now summarized (List 7.1). It articulates many of the preconditions for principle-based ethics, with an emphasis on rational justification with reference to principles (as articulated in Chapter 2). However, the importance of the particularity of situations, attitudes and emotions is also included, building on the discussions in Chapter 3.

List 7.1 The nature of ethical judgements

1. *Welfare:* Ethical judgements are about the welfare of living beings. If we focus on human beings, the subject matter might, for example, be about the promotion of human happiness or the satisfaction of human needs (Norman, 1998, pp. 218–20; Warnock, 1967, pp. 48–72). What counts as a 'human need' will be relative to a particular society or belief system and will change over time. This does not necessarily mean that there are no universal values, but how they are implemented may vary according to time, place and circumstances (Ife, 1999, pp. 218–19). Arguably, the wellbeing of non-human animals is also part of the subject matter of ethical judgements, although in social work it is usually human welfare that is at stake.

2. *Prescription:* Ethical judgements take the form of prescriptions for action (Hare, 1952, 1963). If a social worker makes the moral judgement that Ms Jones, the woman suffering from confusion, ought not to be committed to hospital against her will, then the worker should be prepared to act on this or recommend that others do so. This might include making plans for Ms Jones to be supported to stay at home and being prepared to argue the case to her family, neighbours and to professional colleagues.

3. *Context:* Ethical judgements about particular cases take into account the context of the situation, including the particular relationships and responsibilities of the people involved. The relationship between mother and daughter will be a crucial one in the case of Ms Jones. The fact that Ms Jones is of African Caribbean origin may be important in appreciating her expectations of her daughter and in considering whether the white neighbours may be less tolerant of her behaviour because she is black. The relationship between the social worker and Ms Jones is also important, including the responsibilities inherent in the social worker's role, her specific responsibilities deriving from her understanding of Ms Jones's situation and the degree of empathy she feels with her.

4. *Consistency:* Nevertheless, an ethical judgement should exhibit consistency with previous and future judgements in the sense that it should apply to other people in similar circumstances. We would expect that the social worker would make the same judgement about another confused woman, unless it could be demonstrated that the situation was significantly different. We would not expect the social worker to champion Ms Jones's cause just because she has known her for a long time, although this makes it easier to do so.

5. *Justification:* It makes sense to ask people to justify their ethical judgements. They may do so with reference to some general principles within their particular system of morality or with reference to particular relationships and responsibilities. In the case of Ms Jones, the social worker might refer to a belief that 'all individuals have a right to decide for themselves what they want to do, unless they are at serious risk of harming themselves or others' (the principle of self-determination). This in turn might be justified with reference to the principle that 'the dignity and worth of all persons should be respected'. Ultimately, a stage is reached where no further justification can be given and certain beliefs about the nature of human welfare and needs have to be taken as given. Alternatively, or in addition, the social worker might justify her judgement with reference to her particular relationship with Ms Jones, her understanding of Ms Jones's feelings or her responsibilities as a social worker. In coming to a judgement about what is the right course of action and making a decision to put this into practice, the social worker may also have had a dialogue with Ms Jones and her daughter, with the doctor and

perhaps the neighbours. Part of this dialogue may have been about listening to the stories and views of these people, questioning racist attitudes, family relationships and expectations and seeking consensus about a course of action. This is an important process of justification in action, achieved through dialogue with others.

Ethical judgements in context

In considering how practitioners respond when faced with situations that raise ethical issues, problems and dilemmas, there is a tendency to focus on the process of making a moral judgement and to see this primarily in terms of moral reasoning. However, as James Rest (1994, p. 22) comments, in the context of his study of moral psychology:

> There is widespread agreement that there are more components to morality than just moral judgement. The trick, however, is to identify more precisely what else there is in morality, and how all these pieces fit together.

Rest (1994, pp. 22–6) identifies four components of moral behaviour, of which moral judgement is just one. I will summarize and elaborate upon these below (List 7.2). Since Rest uses the terms 'morality' and 'moral' rather than 'ethics' and 'ethical', I will continue with his use of terminology, bearing in mind that in this book I am using the terms interchangeably.

List 7.2 Four components of moral behaviour

1. *Moral sensitivity*: awareness of how our actions affect others. One of the most important moral qualities of a professional practitioner is that of empathy and the ability to perceive a situation as one of moral significance. This can be linked to what Blum (1994, pp. 30–61) calls 'moral perception' (see also Vetlesen, 1994, p. 6), which involves the use of the faculty of empathy (a disposition to develop concern for others) to see the morally relevant features of a situation – 'the features that carry importance for the weal and

woe of human beings involved'. For example, Vetlesen (1994, pp. 85–125) regards Eichmann's failure to see himself as responsible for following orders to kill Jews in Nazi Germany as a failure of moral perception (an emotional failure). In the case of Ms Jones, the social worker has to see the situation as not simply a case of implementing the law as contained in the mental health legislation or following a mental health assessment schedule, but as involving Ms Jones's freedom to remain in her home, her feelings of dismay, discomfort and disruption.

2. *Moral reasoning or judgement:* the ability to make critical judgements regarding moral values and various courses of action – to judge which action is morally justifiable. The traditional view of moral reasoning would be the application of general moral principles by individual moral agents to particular cases through a rational, deductive process (Kohlberg, 1981, 1984). There are other versions of moral reasoning, however, which work from particular cases ('casuistry') or start from the practical idea of 'reasonableness' (Toulmin, 2001), based on dialogue with others. I have already outlined some of the elements of this process in the previous section.

3. *Moral motivation:* placing moral values above competing non-moral values. Rest (1994, p. 24) gives the examples of Hitler and Stalin whose moral failures are less to do with deficiencies in awareness or reasoning, but rather because they set aside moral values in pursuit of other values. In a professional context, this might include values such as self-actualization or protecting the employing organization.

4. *Moral character:* having certain moral dispositions or 'virtues', such as moral courage and trustworthiness, or personality traits, such as perseverance and high self-esteem, that predispose us to act morally. Rest (1994, p. 24) comments that someone may be morally sensitive, make good moral judgements and put a high priority on moral values, but 'if the person wilts under pressure, is easily distracted or discouraged, is a wimp and weak-willed', then moral failure occurs because of weak character. In the case of Ms Jones, the social worker may need to persevere quite strongly to persuade the daughter to accept that her mother can still be cared for at home and then have to make extensive and time-consuming preparations to provide adequate support.

Source: Adapted and developed from Rest, 1994, pp. 22–6

All these components are vital when considering how social workers and other professionals develop into ethically sensitive and competent practitioners. While ethical reasoning or judgement is important, the other components are equally so, although we often do not regard them as being part of the domain of ethics. Sensitivity, motive and character inform our judgements – we require sensitivity to see a moral problem in the first place.

Ethical sensitivity, motivation and character are less easily abstractable, observable or teachable than ethical reasoning based on ethical principles. We often used decontextualized cases in teaching professional ethics (Banks, 2010; Banks and Nyboe, 2003; Chambers, 1997) that focus more on the action taking place than on the motivations of the people concerned, their complex webs of prior relationships and the emotions generated. Situated ethics, ethics in practice, is deeply contextualized. Distinctions are often made between the ethical, practical, technical and political; between the personal, professional, societal and religious; or between the emotional, rational and affective dimensions of our lives, judgements and decisions. These are artificial, although useful conceptual distinctions. So in the discussions of what we have already identified as the ethical dimensions of situations, we can further abstract from the situations and focus on the principles at stake and the processes of ethical reasoning that might be undertaken to make judgements, or be used to justify actions, by the key moral agents involved. This does not mean that issues of sensitivity, motives and character are less important, just that they may not always feature highly in the accounts that people give.

Ethical decision-making and 'ethics work'

Making decisions about what to do in cases that feature ethical problems and dilemmas incorporates our ethical judgements or evaluations of what is right/wrong, good/bad in a particular situation. But what we decide to do may also depend upon our motivations and character, non-moral factors (such as practicality and available resources) and the influence of other stakeholders. In Case example 7.1, if the social worker's manager refused to authorize further support for Ms Jones at home, then a decision might be made to commit Ms Jones to hospital. Numerous interrelated factors – ethical, psychological, emotional, practical, technical and legal – come into the decision-making process. Various models of ethical decision-making have been developed, which aim to encapsulate as many features (or steps) of the decision-making process as possible. These models can be useful in helping social workers or students to analyse cases in a classroom setting, supervision session or case review meeting, but they are of limited use in day-to-day social work practice. McAuliffe and Chenoweth (2007, pp. 40–1) offer a useful review and classification of such models, which include 'process' models (often following rational, linear steps), 'reflective' models (also taking account of emotional dimensions) and 'cultural' models (taking account of cultural values and worldviews). Instead, they propose an 'inclusive model' that takes account of core social work values, includes four interlinked 'platforms' for good decision-making (accountability, consultation, cultural sensitivity and critical reflection) and follows a circular process based on the following steps:

- defining the ethical dilemma
- mapping legitimacy (who has a legitimate stake in the decision-making process)
- gathering information
- assessing alternative approaches and actions
- critical analysis and evaluation.

McAuliffe and Chenoweth focus on making decisions in cases involving ethical dilemmas. But their model could also be used in other types of difficult situation, where the issue is not so much the making of a judgement about what is right, but deciding how to put this judgement into practice.

Other simpler, linear models can also be used to analyse ethical problems and dilemmas, such as that proposed by Goovaerts (2003), which focuses very much on the practical dimensions of making a decision:

1. What are the facts?
2. Whose interests are at stake?
3. What is the dilemma about?
4. What are the alternatives?
5. What is the conclusion?
6. How to carry out the decision?
7. Evaluation and reflection.

There are numerous other similar models, including Gallagher's ETHICS framework, which includes the identification of (ethical) principles at the fourth stage:

1. Enquire about facts

2. Think through options
3. Hear views
4. Identify principles
5. Clarify meaning
6. Select action (Gallagher and Sykes, 2008).

Congress (1999) developed a model using a similar acronym – ETHIC:

1. Examine personal, cultural, societal, client, agency and professional values
2. Think about the various UN declarations on rights and related covenants, codes of ethics, laws and agency regulations
3. Hypothesize different courses of action based on varied decisions
4. Identify who is most vulnerable, who will be harmed or helped
5. Consult with supervisors and colleagues.

These are all ways of encouraging systematic, comprehensive and analytical thinking about the range of factors to be taken into consideration in making difficult ethical decisions and can be helpful in teaching and learning about ethical reasoning.

In everyday practice, the many moment-to-moment small 'decisions' that are made about how to proceed may be quite intuitive and hardly recognized as decisions unless a social worker is asked to justify or explain afterwards what she did and why she did it. A lot of the time social workers are doing what I have called elsewhere 'ethics work' (Banks, 2009a). This involves practitioners being constantly alert about their roles in a situation and critically aware of the political context in which they are working; attending to the particular needs, desires, emotions, rights and responsibilities of the people involved and the ethically salient features of the situation; and being caring, compassionate, reliable and trustworthy. This idea of 'ethics work' sees ethics as deeply embedded in professional (and personal) life. It takes account of qualities of character, emotions, relationships – drawing on the ethics of care, virtue and proximity discussed in Chapter 3 and the situated ethics of social justice elaborated at the end of that chapter. It includes ethical reasoning, rationality, logic, principles and rights, but places these in a broader context that highlights other relevant factors, as outlined in List 7.3.

List 7.3 Some components of 'ethics work'

1. Moral perception or attentiveness to the salient moral features of situations.
2. Recognition of the political context of practice and the practitioner's own professional power (reflexivity).
3. The moral struggle to be a good practitioner – maintaining personal and professional integrity while carrying out the requirements of the agency role. This would include handling and acting on the moral distress that comes from seeing what ought to be done but not being able to do it. It involves developing the moral qualities of courage and professional wisdom to make difficult judgements and decisions and carry them out. It entails being caring, compassionate and fair in situations where this is not easy.
4. Ethical reasoning, including analysis of relevant factors at stake, weighing of principles, rights, consequences, decision-making, justification and professional accountability.

Source: Developed from Banks, 2009a

In the short case examples, such as Case example 7.1 about Carla Jones presented earlier, many of these features of the 'ethics work' undertaken by the social worker are not present in the account. It is hard to encapsulate these in short ethics cases. But they can be extrapolated by using our moral imagination or by undertaking role-plays (as outlined in the Putting it into practice exercise at the end of Chapter 3). The cases for discussion at the end of each chapter, including the one at the end of this chapter about a Japanese social worker in a difficult situation, illustrate some of the features of 'ethics work' and can be used to explore aspects of emotion, character, care and relationships embedded within the everyday 'ethics work' of social work practitioners.

Practitioners' accounts of ethical difficulties

In talking to social workers about their ethical difficulties in practice, it is noticeable that they tell different kinds of stories about their own roles in the situations they outline. In some accounts, the social workers feature as moral agents, responsible for making judgements and decisions. These accounts may be framed as *ethical problems* – when it is clear what is the right course of action but nevertheless it is not easy to implement, as perhaps somebody's rights are infringed or interests harmed – or *ethical dilemmas* – when it is not clear which course of action is the right one. In other cases, the stories feature the social workers in a more passive role as observers or bystanders, sometimes as powerless and without agency. These latter kinds of stories are accounts that highlight ethical issues, that is, matters of rights, responsibilities, harms or benefits are present in the case, but the social worker telling the story does not position herself as an active moral agent or decision-maker.

The distinction between ethical issues, problems and dilemmas was outlined in Chapter 1 and is discussed in more detail in Banks and Williams (2006). In this chapter, I am concerned with the making of ethical judgements and decisions in cases identified as ethical problems and dilemmas. However, it is important to note that a large part of everyday social work practice does not involve the conscious and considered making of judgements and decisions in difficult cases. Rather, it comprises routine actions, attitudes, approaches and orientations towards the work (Banks, 2009a). Difficult judgements and decisions, especially those involving dilemmas, are given more attention in ethics textbooks because it is these that social workers agonize over, seek help about and remember long after the event. However, it is equally important that social workers regard the whole of their practice as having an ethical dimension, and see ethical issues about human welfare, social control, inequality, responsibility, care and control in all aspects of the work they do and as embedded in the context in which their work takes place.

Some of the cases from trainee social workers in this chapter might be regarded as stories that point to the ethical issues in social work, rather than accounts of situations requiring complex judgements and decision-making. Yet for students, many matters taken for granted by experienced practitioners are seen as problematic and challenging. The students' accounts highlight issues of institutional culture that may be taken for granted or accepted as the norm by experienced practitioners. They also raise questions of power and powerlessness and illustrate the moral distress felt by practitioners who know the right thing to do but are unable to do it due to institutional constraints (Jameton, 1984).

All the case examples in this chapter are based on real accounts given by practitioners, either as written cases or in the course of interviews when they were specifically asked to recount examples of ethical problems and dilemmas. The accounts they gave me were already highly selective, and were inevitably constructed around what they thought would be relevant to exemplify ethical problems and dilemmas. They feature action, judgements and decisions more than character and situations. In turning these accounts into shorter 'cases' suitable for discussion in an ethics text, I have inevitably created stories that highlight the ethical dimensions I think are important and relevant. However, I have tried to stay as close as possible to the language of the practitioners. All examples are from Britain, unless otherwise stated, and some details have been changed in order to preserve anonymity.

Developing the reflective and reflexive practitioner: case examples from trainee social workers

> Ethical dilemmas come up all the time and the smallest incidents sometimes spark the hardest ethical problems because you don't get time to think about them or go to a manager. A response is required straightaway and then it's your intuition that guides you, and unless you are well versed in thinking about ethics and your own value system, this can be affected by what's easiest, least embarrassing or causes the least discomfort, rather than what is right. Herein lies the road to regret. *(Trainee social worker)*

In discussing ethical difficulties with trainee social workers, there is often an acute sense of confusion, anxiety, guilt and regret about the judgements and decisions social workers have to make and the roles they play. This may arise from limited understanding of the nature of the social worker's role (that it is complex and contradictory), idealism, a lack of information about policies and procedures or simply an absence of opportunity to rehearse situations and learn from experience. An important part, therefore, of the education and training of social workers is to facilitate the development of skills in critical reflection.

Developing a capacity for critical reflection and reflexivity is much more than simply learning procedures or achieving particular 'competences'. As noted in Chapter 6, the notion of the helping professional as a reflective practitioner was developed particularly

by Schön (1983, 1987) and is now an influential strand in the literature of the caring professions (see Askeland and Fook, 2009; Brookfield, 2009; Gould and Taylor, 1996; Smith, 1994; White et al.,
2006; Yelloly and Henkel, 1995). It is based on the notion of the
practitioner reflecting on what is happening while in action and
reflecting on what happened afterwards ('reflection-in-action' and
'reflection-on-action'). According to Brookfield (1987, p. 156):
'Practitioners develop strategies, techniques, and habitual responses
to deal with different kinds of situations, drawing chiefly on their
acquired experience and intuitive understanding.'

Part of the process of becoming a reflective and reflexive practitioner is the adoption of a critical and informed stance towards
practice. This can only come about through doing the practice,
reflecting on it through dialogue and questioning and changing the
practice in the light of the reflection. It also involves being aware of
the contradictory position of social work in society, practitioners'
own positions of power and how dominant discourses in the profession and society construct the knowledge and values social workers
use in their work. This links to the concept of 'praxis' and the
inseparability of theory and practice. Arguably, the social worker
should be not only a reflective practitioner, but also a committed
practitioner, working for change in society through her action. This
fusion of reflection and action has been called *praxis* – a concept
found in Aristotle and developed in Marxist thinking and in the
works of Paulo Freire, the Brazilian educator and activist, and many
other thinkers. This moves beyond simply stating that values, knowledge and skill are inseparable to a normative statement about what
the role of the social worker ought to be. If the social worker
compartmentalizes reflection (values and knowledge) from action
(use of skill), she is, in fact, deceiving herself. She is in 'bad faith', as
Sartre (1969, pp. 47–70) would say, because she is pretending that
her action can be value-free and purely 'technical'. She is denying
her own responsibility as a moral agent for that action. For Freire
(1972), reflection without action results in 'mentalism' and action
without reflection results in 'activism' – and both are empty.

'Beginning' practitioners, or those with little experience, have
obviously had less opportunity to gain experience and develop
strategies and responses – what Schön calls 'theories in use'. What a
beginning practitioner may regard as an ethical dilemma – a choice
between two equally unwelcome alternatives involving a conflict
between ethical values (principles, relationships or qualities of character) – an experienced practitioner may not. For the experienced

practitioner, it may be obvious that one alternative is less unwelcome than the other or that one value has priority over another, so she does not even conceptualize the decision as involving an ethical dilemma. This does not mean there are no ethical dimensions to the situation or that the situation should not be seen as involving an ethical problem or issue, just that, strictly speaking, a dilemma is what confronts the worker before a judgement is made. If the situation is familiar or the worker has a clear sense of which ethical principles, relationships or qualities of character have priority in this type of situation, then the situation will not be experienced as a dilemma, but simply a case of having to make a moral choice.

Thompson et al. (2000, pp. 6–9) distinguish between ethical problems and ethical dilemmas, arguing that an ethical problem usually has a solution or a possible solution. This seems to imply that a dilemma does not. However, I would argue that most of the time social workers do have to resolve dilemmas, in that they do have to take some action, even if this is deciding not to act, in which case they make a choice between the alternatives. This may be done either by making a random choice or, more usually, after a process of reflection and research that eventually leads the worker to judge that one course of action may be better than another and therefore is the right action.

Some of the anxieties around the ethical difficulties experienced by trainee social workers seem to be based on the following:

1. low levels of confidence in their own status/position, especially in relation to other professionals
2. lack of power in relation to the supervisor/practice teacher during a fieldwork placement
3. lack of clarity about the role of social worker, for example carer or controller, and rules attached to the role such as confidentiality
4. limited experience and knowledge in a new situation
5. narrow focus on the needs or rights of one individual service user, or on one issue, without seeing the complexity of the case
6. the complexity of the situation is seen, but found to be overwhelming.

The following short case examples from trainee social workers illustrate the above points. These are all examples of ethical difficulties experienced by trainee social workers either while undertaking fieldwork practice or before they joined a social work training programme (that is, when they were unqualified workers or volunteers). It is important to remind readers that I am using the term 'value' in the context of discussions about ethics (as described in Chapter 1) to cover ethical principles, virtues, commitments to particular others, to projects and to political and/or religious beliefs and ideals.

Low levels of confidence in status/position

The following example was given by a student, reflecting on her previous work experience in a residential home.

Practice focus

Case example 7.2: Poor treatment of a resident in an institution

Susan was a 22-year-old woman living in a residential care home for people with cerebral palsy and related disabilities. She was prone to spells of depression, which resulted in her crying a lot, or refusing to communicate or eat. She communicated by means of a communication board attached to her wheelchair. The trainee social worker, who had worked in the home as an unqualified care worker for four months, was told by the other staff that Susan's behaviour was due to homesickness, a 'crush' on (an infatuation with) a member of staff and a 'predisposition towards attention-seeking behaviour'. When Susan became upset, the policy was to take her to her room, shut the door and leave her there to calm down. When the care worker talked to her, Susan said she would like to get out of the home more often, meet more people and take a course at a local college. She asked the care worker to pass this information on at the next staff meeting. When the care worker did this, Susan's request was dismissed as 'playing up' and 'nagging susceptible new members of staff'. The care worker felt that there was a culture of running the home to suit the staff, who spent a large part of their time smoking and drinking coffee, while residents watched TV or sat motionless in the corridors. The care worker commented afterwards:

> I was worried that I was rocking the boat too much, that I asked too many questions and that I refused to fit into the team and their way of doing things … Nothing happened and shortly afterwards I left.

This case is typical of many recounted by inexperienced workers who give accounts of feeling powerless to challenge or change what they consider to be bad practice in not meeting the needs or respecting the rights and dignity of individual service users. In this case, it is a question of not fitting in with the team norms. In other cases (as in Case example 7.3), it may be fear of reprisals or of the power of the practice teacher or fieldwork supervisor to fail a student's placement. In the way the case is written, it is not explicitly framed as a dilemma or a problem, with the care worker facing a choice. It can be seen as a story about an ethical issue, a story of moral distress – the worker knows what is right, but cannot put this into action – or an 'atrocity story' – an account of the bad practice of others. Yet it implicitly raises questions about what the worker could or should have decided to do to take her concerns further.

This case raises the question of how to challenge practice within a staff team, which may lead to making a complaint or even whistle-blowing. For inexperienced workers who are not confident of the expected 'standards' or how a complaints procedure may work and may be worried about reprisals, it is often difficult to take any action at all. They are left feeling that they ought to have acted, yet failed to do so. Seeking alliances with other workers and trainees and talking to college tutors may help in rehearsing the arguments and testing others' understandings of what counts as bad practice and how it can be challenged.

The care worker's comments that she 'did not fit in' and was 'rocking the boat' are ways of presenting herself as different from the rest of the staff. In her account, she is performing the role of the 'good and sensitive worker' in contrast to the other staff. This worker's own words indicate how practitioners construct accounts of themselves as morally good and sensitive.

Lack of power in relation to the supervisor/practice teacher during a fieldwork placement

The next case is drawn from an account of ethical difficulties faced by a social work student while undertaking his fieldwork practice placement.

Practice focus

Case example 7.3: Issues for a black male student in an agency working mainly with women

Jim was a male student undertaking a fieldwork placement in an independent sector agency working with the families of children who have been placed in care. Jim sometimes described himself as 'black' (his father was originally from Kenya and his mother was English), and he said that this was one of the reasons the agency was keen to have him on placement, as there were no other black staff working there. He recounted how he had immediately been assigned the case of a man from Botswana as it was thought the two men would 'have something in common'.

He found the placement difficult since the majority of the people he worked with were women, whom he described as often vulnerable single parents. He felt it was potentially easy for them to get attached to him as a supportive young man. So he refused to do home visits on his own with 'vulnerable women'. However, his practice teacher (who was also male) would make visits on his own, and expected Jim to do the same. Jim felt quite uncomfortable about this and other aspects of his practice teacher's work. In particular, he noticed that the practice teacher often made what Jim thought were inappropriate comments to female service users. Jim considered whether he should challenge his practice teacher and/or share his observations with the agency coordinator. He explained that he felt unable to do this for a number of reasons. The agency was small and a complaint might have a bad effect on the organization and the delivery of much needed services. The smallness of the agency meant that the practice teacher was the only staff member who could assess Jim's practice. He also knew that when students had made complaints in the past, the issues had not been dealt with. Jim commented:

> I think it's also hard for a student to challenge a professional who's been in the job for a long time, because the student always feels 'what do I know?', or they feel like the professional is going to say 'what the hell do you know, you're a student?'

In this case, a male student is giving an account of his attitudes and actions that suggests he is very aware of his gender and his own potential position of power in relation to female service users. This is placed in the context of an agency where the prevalent culture seems to condone what the student considers to be not only poor practice, but potentially dangerous and oppressive behaviour. However, because of his position as an inexperienced student, who is also black (although Jim did not mention this in the context of discussing his relationship with his supervisor), he felt unable to do anything. The quotation above from Jim shows him presenting himself as a person of inexperience and vulnerable to challenge. He adds strength to this characterization by speaking in the voice of 'a student' (implying it is not just him that feels like this) and a supervisor, to whom he refers as 'a professional' (which emphasizes the contrast with the unqualified student).

The issues in this case have some similarities with Case example 7.2, but with the added dimensions of race and gender. Jim was not only inexperienced but also a black student undergoing assessment in a predominantly white agency that had already demonstrated a simplistic understanding of issues of ethnicity and an institutional blindness to sexist attitudes and behaviour. The feeling of powerlessness as a student is a common one. It is not always clear what the standard of acceptable practice should be, and sometimes students have a tendency to be idealistic. Yet they also see things with fresh eyes and can disturb a cosy complacency or, even worse, a seriously neglectful or abusive situation. It is important that students feel able to raise issues such as those experienced by Jim, particularly with their college tutors, if not directly to the agency concerned. Structures for doing this in a confidential and supportive manner should be in place, otherwise poor and oppressive practice will remain unchallenged.

Lack of clarity about role

The next case comes from a student who was working in a family centre, which provided support to parents and children. She was acting as the key worker for a number of families.

Practice focus

Case example 7.4: A young mother who was working and claiming benefit

A young mother was referred to a family centre because of feelings of social isolation. During a counselling session between the woman and the student (as her key worker), they discussed budgeting and the problems caused by spending time away from her daughter. The woman revealed that she was claiming income support (a state benefit for people on low incomes) and working nights as a cleaner. Her hours of work were over the limit allowed in order to be eligible to claim income support. The student posed the following questions:

Should I ignore it? By discussing it with her, am I legally condoning it? Should the matter be reported to the relevant government agency that deals with income support? Should the principle of confidentiality be upheld? Is the social worker an agent of the state?

This trainee worker, having outlined the details of the case (which I have summarized) asks several questions. These questions indicate that she is constructing this example as a dilemma, or at least a difficult choice where she feels there is no one right answer. She presents herself as thoughtful, raising ethical issues and particularly as wondering about the extent to which she is 'an agent of social control'.

It appears that the worker is assuming that her responsibilities to the state extend more widely than, in fact, they do. She does not realize that if a service user has done or is doing something illegal, the social worker does not automatically have to report this to the appropriate authority. Usually, a social worker would only break confidentiality in these circumstances if a very serious crime was being committed or a life was in danger. While the social worker should not aid and abet a service user in an illegal pursuit, discussing the matter does not necessarily entail condoning it. In fact, the social worker can make it clear that what the service user is doing is illegal and cannot be condoned. Not only would the experienced practitioner be clearer about the law but she would also probably have had time to reflect on the complex and contradictory nature of the social worker's role and know when it was appropriate to adopt a social control role, an enabling role or a caring role. She might also ask the question 'whose dilemma is it anyway?' (Bond, 2010, p. 228) and realize that whether to tell the authorities about the cleaning job is, in fact, the service user's own ethical dilemma, not the social worker's.

Limited experience and knowledge in a new situation

This case was given by a social work student, relating to her experience as a volunteer before she started her studies.

Practice focus

Case example 7.5: Child abuse disclosure to a volunteer

A volunteer working in a day centre was approached by a nine-year-old girl with whom she had a good relationship, saying that her father had been hitting her and she was upset. The girl asked if the volunteer would sit in on a meeting between the girl and her parents. The centre manager encouraged the volunteer to go ahead and provided a room. The volunteer was given no guidance on procedure. She was asked to swear confidentiality by the father at the outset of the meeting. She commented afterwards: 'in my naivety I agreed, which I later found out was a mistake'. She was told about a variety of sexual and physical abuse and then faced a dilemma regarding what to do about this.

This trainee social worker presents herself as a naive volunteer. She gives an account of a situation where she made a mistake. The dilemma here for the volunteer could be construed as a choice between respecting the confidence and keeping her promise to the girl (this could be linked to a Kantian approach) or breaking the confidence and discussing the matter with her line manager because of the serious harm that is being done to the girl (a utilitarian approach). A decision may be made by balancing the importance of respecting the confidence against what is in the girl's best interests – weighing up the immediate danger to the girl and the likelihood of the volunteer being able to persuade the girl to tell someone else. Alternatively, the volunteer may realize or discover that the agency she works for has a policy that all suspicions about child abuse must be reported to the line manager. She may decide that agency rules should always be followed or that this particular rule is an important one and it is in the interests of all that it is followed. Therefore the dilemma is resolved and she should tell her line manager.

For the experienced practitioner, this case may not present a dilemma at all. First, the experienced practitioner would probably have said at the start that she could not promise confidentiality. However, assuming she had promised confidentiality because she knew the girl had something important to say and would not be able to say it otherwise, the experienced social worker would usually be much more aware of herself as an employee of an agency and would be familiar with agency rules and procedures and have worked out which ones it was important to follow. She may have worked out from past experience that confidentiality can never be absolute and, in her view, the best interests of the service user always come first.

The learning from this experience for the volunteer is that, in similar circumstances, next time she might simply refer the matter to her manager and ask the manager to deal with it, or she might insist that the manager should sit in on the meeting as well. If she did attend such a meeting on her own, she would start the meeting by explaining that any information she was given might be shared with the line manager. This might not stop her feeling anxious about sharing the information she was given, but she might perhaps feel less guilty about breaking a confidence.

Narrow focus on individual service user/one issue

This case was given by a social work student who had been working in a local authority social work team with a focus on older people.

Practice focus

Case example 7.6: An elderly couple and residential care

Mr and Mrs Finch, aged 91 and 86, were admitted to residential care by the social work night duty team, following a call from the warden of the sheltered accommodation where they lived. They were reported as being unable to cope with everyday domestic functions and Mrs Finch had had a fall in the night. There was pressure from the family, the warden and senior social work colleagues for them to be admitted permanently to residential care. The trainee social worker stated that when she visited them: 'Mr and Mrs Finch were suffering from impaired memory function. They could not comprehend why they had been admitted to residential accommodation, but were categoric that they wanted to return home.' She felt that 'the couple should be allowed to return home on the basis of their individual right to choose'.

The trainee social worker in this case expresses her ethical judgement using the language of social work ethics: 'their individual right to choose'. This case is presented as quite clear and unequivocal and the use of the word 'categoric' emphasizes the strong voice of the service users. The trainee social worker may well be right in this case – that the couple should be allowed to return home – but focusing on their right to choose (which links to Kantian ethical principles) is only one way of looking at the issue. She might consider the extent to which they are capable of making an informed choice, as well as taking into account the rights and needs of the warden and the family. It seems as though she sees herself principally in the role of advocate for the service users, whereas it is often the social worker's job to assess the whole situation and work for a solution in the best interests of all concerned (a more utilitarian approach). In stressing the principle of service user self-determination, there appears to be no dilemma here for the trainee social worker. Since she knows what is the morally right course of action, what she feels she is facing is a moral problem – how to achieve this in the face of opposition. Others might see it as a dilemma – to be resolved by taking various other factors into account, such as whether the service users understand the risks attached to returning home and what level of support and responsibility it is fair to place on the warden.

The complexity of the situation is seen, but found to be overwhelming

This case was given by a social work student and related to a time when he was working as a care worker in a residential unit for drug users, before he joined a social work qualifying programme.

Practice focus

Case example 7.7: Banning a particular newspaper in a residential home

At a staff meeting at a residential unit for drug users, it was decided that the unit should stop buying newspapers published by News International, a large multinational company owned by the Murdoch family. The reason for this was the dispute at the time between the printers' trade unions and this publisher. The union for public sector employees, to which the staff of the unit belonged, was supporting a boycott of these papers. The initial ban was just on newspapers bought with the unit's funds, but subsequently the ban was extended to residents themselves buying *The Sun*, a British newspaper owned by News International, on the grounds not only of the union dispute but also its sexist, homophobic and racist stance and its distortions on the subject of AIDS. The trainee social worker reported that 'what initially appeared to be a straightforward dilemma when the ban was introduced as a union issue soon became a complex and deeply disturbing problem for all concerned'. He said it raised questions for him about 'whether social workers are agents of change, and if so, where the limits of their responsibility to bring about change lie?'

The trainee social worker, in talking about this case, identifies it as 'complex and disturbing'. He raises a series of questions at the end of his account about the role of social workers in society. He is presenting the case as one where complex ethical issues arise and he has been troubled by these. If *The Sun* is banned, what about TV programmes and pornographic magazines? Have workers the right to impose their own values on residents? It was only after much reflection and discussion afterwards that this worker reported that he came to the view that *The Sun* should not be banned, but rather the issues regarding the dispute with the unions and the prejudiced and offensive nature of much of the material in the newspaper should be discussed with residents. This would entail treating the residents as capable of making their own choices and encouraging them to participate in decision-making. This case illustrates the dangers of taking an unquestioning 'radical' stance, treating service users in a parentalist fashion (making judgements about what is best for them) and using them as part of social workers' own political campaign. This worker engaged in a process of dialogue with colleagues and quiet reflection in order to work out a course of action he felt was ethically justified in order to resolve the dilemma. In effect, his conclusion was that the role of the workers should be to engage in political education, which would include working with residents themselves to engage in critical questioning about the power of multinational companies and the role of the media in perpetuating stereotypes and discrimination.

When is blame and guilt justified? Case examples from experienced practitioners

In experienced practitioners, we would generally expect some clarity about their roles as social workers, a certain confidence in acting in accordance with their own values and principles and an ability to hold complexity and contradiction in the work. Indeed, when senior social work practitioners were interviewed about ethical difficulties in their work, their responses frequently referred to difficult cases involving ethical issues and problems, particularly around a lack of suitable resources or threats to service users' wellbeing, rather than ethical dilemmas as such. A team manager in a childcare team told me of several difficult cases where other agencies had recommended courses of action with which she disagreed. Although she frequently used the term 'ethical dilemma', it was clear that she knew the right course of action and was prepared to act on this. One of her examples (Case for discussion 7) is given at the end of this chapter, which highlights some of the value conflicts in multiprofessional work in the field of health and social care.

Nevertheless, even the most experienced practitioners find themselves facing ethical dilemmas and have feelings of guilt about the choices and actions they take. Some of this guilt and blame is necessary – if we do what we know to be morally wrong, or retreat into defensive practice or take a decision that turns out to have a bad outcome that we could have predicted if we had thought about it more deeply. Yet some of the guilt and blame is unnecessary and unproductive, as was discussed in Chapter 1. It is easy to see how it comes about, for the nature of a dilemma is that, whatever course of action is taken, there will be some unwelcome outcomes. Usually, there is a choice between two or more conflicting values or ethical principles, all of which we believe are important. If we can understand that this is the nature of the job and that, for example, in a particular case, we chose to break confidentiality because another overriding value relating to the welfare of the service user was more important, then we should not regard ourselves as having acted immorally. Rather, we have faced up to a difficult ethical choice.

The following four case examples relate to two situations where social workers said they felt bad about the judgements and decisions they had made and wondered if they should have acted differently and two situations where the workers knew they had made hard or uncomfortable judgements and decisions, but still felt confident that they had made the right choice. In the two cases where the workers reported feeling confident about their judgements and decisions (one of which also resulted in a bad outcome), both workers felt clear about where they stood on a particular issue – they had thought through their positions and accepted what the consequences of their actions might be. The four case examples can be categorized as follows (names and some details have been changed to preserve anonymity):

1. The worker felt guilty because a bad outcome occurred and he was aware of the dangers and wondered if he should have done more to prevent this.
2. The worker felt her actions were morally right, despite a bad outcome, because she stuck to a deeply held principle.
3. The worker felt guilty because he had to compromise an ethical principle to which he was committed.
4. The worker felt her actions were morally right, despite having to compromise one of her values, because another value had priority.

Worker felt guilty about a bad outcome

The following example was given to me by an approved psychiatric social worker and is a case where the social worker felt he did not act in the service user's best interests and felt guilty about this. The fact that there was a bad outcome to the case (the person died) no doubt exacerbated the feelings of guilt.

Practice focus

Case example 7.8: The service user's interests versus the constraints of the agency role

The social worker described a case where he felt that the drugs administered by a psychiatrist had caused the physical health of a hospital patient, Mrs Baldwin, to deteriorate, culminating in death by pneumonia. Mrs Baldwin's family were concerned about whether she had been given the right treatment and whether the pneumonia had been picked up soon enough. The social worker commented: 'I thought it was the drugs that had caused her death. I didn't say it to the family. In the end, you're working so much with other health professionals. I colluded.'

The social worker clearly felt quite bad about this case. He had been involved with admitting this woman to hospital originally for 28 days under the mental health legislation. The social worker felt this was the right decision. On going to hospital, Mrs Baldwin became calmer, accepted her fate and agreed to take medication. But it soon became obvious to the social worker that the medication was affecting her physically. The social worker said he felt responsible for her, as he watched her condition deteriorate as she was shipped backwards and forwards between the psychiatric and general hospitals. He did not seem sure what he could or should have done: 'It is difficult to question hospital consultants. You can only question whether hospital is the best place, not the diagnosis and treatment.'

With hindsight, he suggested that the point at which he could have done something was after the original 28-day period of detention in hospital ran out and was then renewed for six months. He did have a choice at this stage regarding whether to sign the documents as an approved social worker. However, he did feel Mrs Baldwin needed to be in hospital, and trusted the hospital to pick up on any serious physical problems.

This case seems to have three stages. The first stage was the initial committal to hospital, which the social worker felt was legally and morally justified. The second stage was the time during the treatment, including the time when the application for compulsory detention in hospital had to be renewed, when he knew Mrs Baldwin was deteriorating physically, but did not do anything about it. The third stage was after her death when he had to decide whether or not to tell the relatives the truth about his own feelings relating to the cause of death. He commented that with hindsight perhaps he could have acted differently at the second stage, but it would have been difficult. Did he retreat into a kind of defensive practice? He acted within the law and according to agency rules, but was he denying some moral responsibility for the situation when he said that it was not his role to question the diagnosis? It is always difficult to go beyond the agency-defined role – to risk going out on a limb, to challenge another professional when it is not one's role to do so.

This is a good example of the type of tough dilemma often faced by social workers, when no course of action has a good outcome. The worker has to try to weigh up how much risk or harm to a service user should be allowed before some action is taken. We can understand the social worker's inaction in this case; maybe we would not blame him for Mrs Baldwin's death. However, we might perhaps think that his own feelings of blame and guilt are justified because he did not do what he thought was in Mrs Baldwin's best interests. The ethical issues here relate not just to the rights and interests of the service user and the duties of professionals to promote the welfare of service users, but to the summoning of the courage and confidence to implement the right action. While it may not be the social worker's role to question the diagnosis and treatment prescribed by a psychiatrist, the wellbeing of the service user should be the joint concern of the various health and social care professionals involved. This case illustrates the need for social workers to assert themselves in multiprofessional contexts and be clear that they can and should voice professional opinions on all aspects of service users' welfare.

The third stage of this case, when the question of what to say to the relatives arose, is probably less problematic. Given that the social worker had signed the papers for the renewal of the detention in hospital and had not challenged the consultant then or later, he no doubt felt that it was not fair to mention his views about the drugs to Mrs Baldwin's family. The situation might have been different if the social worker had believed the psychiatrist to be incompetent and likely to put other patients at risk.

Worker did not feel guilty about a bad outcome because she stuck to a deeply held principle

The following example was given to me by a youth worker. It related to her previous experience as an unqualified worker in a voluntary sector youth club about 25 years ago. She felt the case presented an ethical dilemma and she had made a judgement about what was right based on her belief in confidentiality and service user self-determination as absolute ethical principles. Although the outcome of the situation was bad, she still felt the action she decided to take was morally right.

Practice focus

Case example 7.9: Confidentiality and service user self-determination versus the service user's interests

The youth worker was working in a busy youth club on a normal youth club evening. She was approached in the coffee bar by a 15-year-old girl, Jan, who was obviously in a state of distress. The youth worker took her into a quiet room. From that initial contact,

Jan swore the worker to secrecy. Jan revealed to the worker over several weeks that during the past year she had been raped four times by her father and was now pregnant by him. She had also decided to commit suicide as a way out of the situation. The youth worker talked through the issues with Jan, suggesting various options for help and that suicide was not the best way out. However, Jan continued to refuse to consider any professional help and insisted that the worker should not tell anyone. The youth worker respected her request for confidentiality. Jan did commit suicide.

This case relates to a youth worker, not a social worker, and to past practice in the voluntary sector. If the worker had been working for a British social work agency, or the majority of youth club settings at the present time, agency policy would require the worker to report any cases of suspected child abuse and would advise workers not to promise absolute confidentiality. The case would have been analogous to the one given earlier about the volunteer who promised confidentiality. However, in this case, it seems there was no agency policy and the worker stuck to the principle of confidentiality because she personally believed it was an important one (this could be described as a Kantian approach). She did not feel she had any overriding duties to her agency, nor that she should adopt a different set of principles as a youth worker than she should in her everyday life; we might suggest that she was working within the committed practitioner model. She felt that Jan, at 15 years old, was capable of making her own decisions and should not be treated in a parentalist way. In spite of Jan's suicide, the youth worker felt she had acted in accordance with her moral principles and that her decision not to break the confidence was right.

This is a complex case to explore. For the majority of social workers and contemporary youth workers placed in such a situation, the judgement about whether it was right to break a confidence may hardly present a dilemma at all. It would be an ethical problem, where the solution was clear and would entail breaching Jan's request for confidentiality. Given that the confidential information was about the sexual abuse of a 15-year-old and there is even a slight risk of self-inflicted harm, a line manager or the statutory child protection services would be informed immediately.

This would cover the worker from feeling guilt if Jan did commit suicide and could be argued to be in Jan's best interests (utilitarian considerations). Other practitioners might see it as a dilemma, involving weighing up the importance of respecting Jan's right to confidentiality and to make her own decisions about her life against the likelihood of Jan committing suicide. An assessment of Jan's capacity to make 'life and death' decisions might also be required.

I am less concerned to consider what would have been the 'right' action in this case and more interested in the fact that this is a situation where a worker apparently did not feel guilty or responsible for a bad outcome. This type of worker is relatively rare in social work, partly because most social workers would not wish to be burdened with the responsibility of someone's death and they adopt a much more utilitarian approach to making ethical judgements and decisions by weighing up the possible outcomes of actions and being more prepared to take a parentalist view of what is in a service user's best interests. It is also partly because social work agencies (and many youth work agencies) have rules and procedures designed to ensure that an individual worker does not carry the total responsibility for the outcome of an intervention. Some people may feel that the youth worker should have acted differently and was at least partly to blame for Jan's death. The youth worker was in a position of responsibility in relation to the young people in the club and had a duty to promote their welfare. To adhere rigidly to a personally held principle of confidentiality was not appropriate in this context. Although the youth worker may have seen her relationship with Jan in the context of a voluntary non-directive counselling role, given that Jan was only 15 years old, was no doubt distressed and had confided in the youth worker, the worker should have taken immediate action. Although this example has been framed in terms of a conflict of principles (self-determination versus the interests or welfare of the service user), it might be helpful to view it in terms of character and relationships. If Jan regarded the youth worker as trustworthy, this might entail Jan not just relying on the worker not to break her confidence, but also to work alongside her during a difficult phase of her life. If we focus on the relationship between Jan and the young person as a caring relationship, then this would entail attentiveness to Jan's situation as a whole, rather than just her request for confidentiality.

Worker felt guilty about compromising an ethical principle

The manager of a day centre for people with learning disabilities described a situation when he felt he had acted 'immorally'. The reason he described his action in this way was because he had made a decision that was contrary to one of the key principles that he believed was important for social work, namely, service user self-determination.

Practice focus

Case example 7.10: Service user self-determination versus the interests of the service user and others

John, a 26-year-old man with learning disabilities who had been attending the day centre for some time, asked if he could walk to the centre on his own, rather than use the minibus provided by the social services department. Staff at the centre judged that he was capable of doing so and they thought this would help him develop his life skills, self-confidence and independence. However, John's parents were extremely worried at this suggestion, feeling that John would not be able to cope. They stated categorically that they would not allow John to attend the centre if he had to make his own way there. The centre manager reluctantly agreed that John should continue to use the bus.

When the social worker who had been the centre manager was asked why he came to this decision, it became obvious that it was not that he lacked either the moral courage to take a risk or the integrity to hold onto his deeply held professional values, but rather that he was taking into account the views and feelings of John's parents, as well as what he thought would promote greater self-determination for John. He had taken account of the context of family relationships in which the decision had to be made and weighed up the consequences for John and his parents of insisting that John should walk to the day centre. Given that John relied on his parents for care, they had a right to have their views heard. Also, it would not be in John's long-term interests if he stopped coming to the day centre or if his parents were excessively anxious. So this social worker had in effect gone through a process of weighing up the outcomes of the proposed change against the status quo and made the judgement that the least harm would be done if the status quo was maintained. By deciding to act on this judgement, the social worker did not act 'unethically', he actually exhibited moral sensitivity to the complexities of the situation and went through a serious process of moral reasoning to come to this decision.

What this social worker's judgement and decision show is that the principle of service user self-determination is not the only ethical principle or even the paramount ethical principle for social work practice. Other principles such as promoting the good of the service user (which involves factors other than self-determination) and promoting the general good (which involves people other than just the service user) are also important. If we accept utilitarianism as a theory of ethics, then these are ethical principles. If we continue to analyse this case in terms of principles, then this social worker could be described as facing an ethical dilemma involving a conflict between the principles of service user self-determination and the promotion of the greatest good for the greatest number of people. In order to resolve the dilemma, he had to make a choice; and whichever choice he made would go against one of the principles. So it was not surprising that he was left feeling dissatisfied with the outcome. However, should he feel guilty that John was not allowed to exercise his freedom to walk to the day centre? Surely he should not, provided he felt he had done all he could to persuade and encourage the parents to allow a trial run. He may feel *regret* that John has not been allowed to walk to the centre, but not guilt. By reflecting on this and discussing it, will this worker feel any less guilty in the future? It is hard to say, but if he accepts that service user self-determination is not an absolute moral principle and therefore it can be morally right to go against that principle, it might make it easier for him to understand the nature of the decisions he has to make.

Worker did not feel guilty because she clearly prioritized her values

This case is about the ethical difficulties experienced by a black practitioner working in a voluntary sector Asian women's project in a British city. The project offered groupwork, educational opportunities and individual support to women who mainly came from various parts of India, Pakistan and Bangladesh. The worker herself was of Punjabi origin.

> **Practice focus**
>
> **Case example 7.11: The needs of black children versus the 'betrayal' of the black community**
>
> A woman of Punjabi origin moved from another part of the country into the area where the Asian women's project was based. She was on her own, with five children under six years old, having fled a violent husband. She felt isolated as a newcomer, was given little support from the statutory services and found it hard to cope with the children. Her husband followed her and began harassing her. Some black professionals were providing her with limited support. In the course of her work, the worker at the Asian women's project discovered that the woman was locking up her children in her house and going out, either to seek help or just for a break. The worker discussed this with her, explaining why it was not an appropriate thing to do and that the children were being put at risk. However, the woman continued to leave her children locked in the house. The worker had to warn the woman that, if she continued to leave her children unattended at home, she would have to report the woman to the statutory social work agencies and the implications of this might be that the children could be taken into care.
>
> Finally, the worker decided that she must inform the statutory social work agency because of the potential danger to the children. The worker found this a tough decision to make because she felt that in the past the social work agency had treated black women very badly and had been insensitive to the complexities of cultural and gender issues. She said: 'It was a betrayal of the black community in a sense. In the past I had campaigned about the insensitivity of social services. But on this occasion I felt I had to do it because of the risk to the children.' The worker in this case said she did not feel guilty about what she had done. She felt it was the right course of action. Having explained to the woman on several occasions that she should not leave the children on their own and having worked with her to try to sort out her domestic and financial problems, she had given the woman due warning.

This case highlights some of the tensions felt by black workers in a professional position. In an interview, this worker explained how a large part of her job was trying to explain British laws to Asian women, and the powers and roles of the various authorities and services. The women often found it hard to comprehend that neglect of and violence towards children were illegal. The statutory social work and other agencies generally were insensitive to the needs of the Asian women and were unwilling, or unable, to take into account the whole picture of a woman's life, including her religion and cultural background. The workers at the Asian women's project were in a sense mediating between western and Asian cultures and values. Often their role was resented by members of the Asian community, particularly the men. The workers in the Asian women's project were concerned not just about balancing the needs and interests of different sections of the black community, but also about trying to adopt a committed/radical approach to practice and to work from a black feminist perspective. This particular worker commented that it was important for her to be clear about her own values and about her professional commitments. While she had a strong commitment to help the Asian community, she was not prepared to cover up or ignore cases of family violence or neglect where women or children were at risk of harm. She said that she rarely felt guilt or self-blame about the actions she had taken, since she was clear where she stood. She commented that some black workers who were more ambivalent about their professional roles, particularly statutory social workers, seemed to have a tougher time.

This worker is clearly very aware of her position as a black woman and has a sense of solidarity with black women service users in their experience of racism and cultural insensitivity. Her practice can be understood within the framework of a political ethics of care or situated ethics of social justice, as discussed in Chapter 3. She has clearly demonstrated attentiveness to the woman's situation and a sense of responsibility in relation to her plight. Her position is one of empathy and solidarity in a context of oppressive power relations. But she also had to take the children's needs and interests into account.

Courage and commitment in multiprofessional working: a team manager's case

All the above cases relate to whether or not social workers should have felt blame or guilt about the outcomes of their judgements, decisions and actions. I have argued that it is important that social workers come to considered ethical judgements and decisions. At the beginning of this chapter, it was suggested that making an ethical judgement in a professional context should be regarded as an essentially rational process that can be justified by the social worker. In justifying judgements and decisions, it is often useful to make appeal to general and impartial principles, as demonstrated in relation to the case examples in the previous section. Yet part of the process of decision-making will also involve taking account of the particularities of the situation faced and the relationships with the people involved. What judgements and decisions are made and whether they are implemented will also depend on the strength of commitment, integrity and determination of the professionals involved. These factors are hard to encapsulate in brief case studies where the details of people's lives and relationships and the feelings and views of the social workers involved are not given.

I will now discuss just one example of a social work case that raised difficult ethical issues for the team manager and social worker involved and where some of the comments from the team manager are incorporated to contextualize the case. It highlights the problems and complexities of multiprofessional working in cases regarded as 'high risk'. The case has been summarized from an interview with a team manager ('Cynthia') in a local authority department responsible for children's services.

Practice focus

Case example 7.12: Respecting a mother's rights and ensuring a baby's safety

At the age of 19, Tracey was convicted of infanticide, having stabbed to death a baby born after a concealed pregnancy. She was given a two-year noncustodial sentence, supervised by the probation service. Cynthia, who was at that time a senior mental health social worker, worked with Tracey and her family for two years after this incident. At the age of 21, Tracey became pregnant again, to the same young man as before, with whom she was now living. She phoned, very excited, to tell Cynthia, who was now a team manager of a childcare team. According to Cynthia, 'this was a very different situation [from last time]'. Tracey's family and partner were very supportive and a childcare social worker in Cynthia's team made a positive assessment. Nevertheless, Cynthia commented that 'there were obvious risks', particularly relating to the fact that Tracey had remained amnesiac about (could not remember) the events following the birth of her first child. Cynthia also felt that 'the birth of this child might act as some kind of catalyst and we couldn't be sure what the reaction would be'.

A plan was made for Tracey to be admitted to the family unit of the local hospital for assessment following the birth. However, shortly before the birth was due, the decision was changed. A guardian ad litem was appointed to safeguard the interests of the baby. The medical staff, the probation officer and guardian decided that it was too risky to allow Tracey and the baby to be admitted to the family unit. According to Cynthia:

> At the last moment they pulled the plug and said: 'we're not prepared to have her on this ward [the family unit in the hospital]'. The whole thing gathered a momentum of its own, where they were coming to conference suggesting that Group 4 [a security firm] should be involved, because of the risk she might pose to other mothers and children on the ward. This is a young woman who had been given a two-year probation sentence, not a custodial one, being treated, I felt, very respectfully by the courts and with a great deal of understanding, and had worked incredibly well with us and had matured over that time … All sorts of incredible things happened, like a professional forensic psychiatrist saw her for an hour, and said, you know, [the] health [professionals] were right … this was a very dangerous situation.

Cynthia and the childcare social worker were left having to decide what to do at this point. She said: 'both of us felt very strongly that it would have been completely wrong to have removed that child and for her [Tracey] not to have had a chance'.

Ethical issues in this case

Some of the ethical dimensions of this case are discussed below:

1. *Rights of the service user(s):* The Kantian principle of respect for persons entails that a service user should be treated with respect and fairness and should be able to make decisions about her own life, provided she is capable of rational and self-determining action and the decision does not present a serious danger to herself or others. In this case, Tracey's ability to remain 'rational' after the birth is in question, which raises the issue of the risk to the baby once born and possibly other babies in the hospital ward. It might be argued that the unborn baby

should also be regarded as a 'service user' in this case, rather than just one of the 'others' involved. Certainly, it would be the role of the social workers, as well as the guardian ad litem, to ensure that the rights of the unborn child were taken into account.

2. *The interests and welfare of the service user(s):* What are the service users' best interests? The principle of promoting service user welfare arises here along with the question of whether the professionals involved take account of Tracey's own view of her interests and welfare or what others think is best for her (parentalism). In the case of the unborn child, then we have to rely on what others think is best.

3. *The rights, interests and welfare of others:* Who are the other parties involved (Tracey's partner, her parents, the other mothers and babies in the hospital ward, the hospital as a public institution, the professionals involved – from health, probation, social services, the guardian) and what are their rights and interests? The utilitarian principle of promoting the greatest good for the greatest number comes in here, which entails questions of distributive justice.

4. *Equality and justice:* How are pregnant young women, people with criminal convictions or psychiatric problems regarded in society generally and how are they treated by powerful professionals? Is Tracey being unfairly discriminated against because of her past criminal conviction?

5. *Moral courage and professional integrity:* Do the team manager and social worker have the moral strength to stand by their analysis of the situation and their commitment to respect the rights of the mother, in spite of strong pressures from other professionals? In a case like this where there is perceived to be a risk of harm to a child, then it is often easier to err on the side of caution.

6. *The relationship of care between professionals and service users:* The nature of the relationship between Tracey and the practitioners involved is an important feature in this case. We might wonder whether the social workers are more attentive to Tracey's needs, her moral qualities and her strengths than the healthcare staff who know her less well. What responsibilities do the various professionals feel to the various people involved? Is it easier for the social workers to feel responsibility towards a living person (Tracey) whom they know quite well than to an unborn child?

How the issues arose

These issues arose because health and social care professionals have a duty to protect children. Their concern about the risks to Tracey's unborn child and to other babies she may come in contact with in the hospital leads them to propose strategies that circumscribe the freedom of choice and movement of Tracey, her partner and her family. Because there is no clear answer regarding how likely it is that any harm will occur, this creates a climate of uncertainty and anxiety and a concern among the health professionals and guardian about taking responsibility for a bad outcome. As Parton (1998, p. 21) suggests: 'where the key concern is risk, the focus becomes, not making the *right* decision, but making a *defensible* decision'. The context in which this decision is being made can be understood in relation to the discussion in Chapter 6 of the increasing concern with risk assessment and risk management in the role of welfare professionals.

Lines of argument

There are a number of lines of argument that might be pursued by the social workers in making their ethical judgement (that 'it would have been completely wrong to have removed that child'), coming to a decision and justifying their judgement and decision:

1. *Does Tracey have a right to look after her baby following its birth?* In normal circumstances, the answer to this question would be 'yes'. But because she killed her first baby, this right may be overridden in the interests of the rights and welfare of the child. The extent to which this right is removed or limited will depend on the answer to the second question.
2. *Is Tracey likely to harm her baby after the birth?* This is where the different professionals involved either disagree on what the risk to the child would be, and/or disagree in terms of how much risk they are prepared to tolerate. The social workers feel they know Tracey pretty well and judge that she is ready and able to care for the baby. The team leader commented:

   > lots of things could weaken your resolve if we hadn't known the case as well as we did ... despite the fact that I'd joint worked with the psychiatrist for two years with the case, this forensic psychiatrist 'expert' from London, you know, could make this judgement.

The other professionals seem to have greater doubts, however, with the forensic psychiatrist saying that it is a 'dangerous situation'. Furthermore, the guardian ad litem and the health professionals may have a lower tolerance of risk in this case than the social workers. Even if they all agree that the risk of harm to the baby in a supervised setting would be minimal, perhaps the guardian and health professionals see the worst-case scenario (death of the baby) as so bad that they feel they cannot take responsibility for a decision that allows Tracey to be assessed in the hospital unit following the birth. The guardian certainly would be acting with the child's best interests at heart. The health professionals also seem concerned about the risk of harm to other babies. As O'Sullivan (1999, p. 145) comments in discussing risk assessment in social work: 'one person's risk taking can be another person's hazard'.

3. *What is in Tracey's best interests?* If there is a grave danger of her harming her newborn baby, this would have serious consequences for her in that, apart from the emotional upset it would cause her, she would be likely to receive a custodial sentence. The safest option, therefore, might be to remove the baby at birth. On the other hand, if she is not given the chance to care for the baby from the time of its birth, she might not be able to bond with it and if she was allowed to care for it subsequently, she might find it difficult or be more likely to fail. It seems likely to be in Tracey's best interests to be well supervised and supported during the period after the birth, so that the baby does not have to be removed, and the risks of harm are minimized.

4. *What are the rights and interests of the unborn baby?* Clearly, once the baby is born, it has a right to life, protection from harm and a safe environment. Whether this environment would best be provided by the mother and her family is the issue at stake. It could be argued that it is in the child's interests to have continuity of high-quality care, which might be best provided in the family of origin if the mother is capable of looking after the child, rather than in what might turn out to be a series of placements.

5. *What are the rights and interests of other parties involved?* Tracey's partner has some right to be involved in the decision-making process about the care of his child, although he does not seem to feature greatly in this case, apart from being described as 'supportive'. Tracey's parents are also described as 'supportive' by the team manager, but they were never assessed as potential alternative carers 'because there was a feeling that

they could have prevented it, had been somehow involved in the event [the previous infanticide]'. A similar view seems to have been taken regarding Tracey's partner. The other parties who might be affected include the other mothers and babies in the hospital ward and this seems to have been a serious concern of the medical staff. On the other hand, the social workers felt Tracey posed no risk to other people's babies. She had lived quite happily in the community for the past few years and had done babysitting for people. The health professionals involved were concerned not to have to take responsibility if anything went wrong. Their interests, which would involve protecting their own reputations, jobs, the hospital's credibility, were to minimize the risk.

6. *Is Tracey being treated fairly?* Cynthia, the team manager, said she felt at times as though there was a 're-trial' of Tracey taking place:

> I felt, strongly, that given that there'd been a court hearing, that this young woman had been convicted of her offence, that had to be our starting point. She was a Schedule 1 offender, she'd had this desperately awful incident in her past and we had to work from that premise. And we couldn't reconsider all the other possible dimensions of what might have happened on that occasion. But all the police files were got out again, the whole thing was trawled, which is not good for any pregnant young woman.

Cynthia is taking account of considerations of injustice and discrimination against Tracey because of her past record. She does not feel this is warranted and is therefore prepared to stand up for Tracey.

7. *Professional judgement, autonomy and trust.* Cynthia and the social worker both have relationships with Tracey and judge that she is capable of looking after a baby. In this sense, they could be said to trust that, when offered the chance, she will not let them down; she will not behave in a way that is damaging to herself, her family or her child. Cynthia is an experienced social worker and is offering a considered judgement based on her experience and knowledge as a professional practitioner.

The decision

Based on her ethical judgement that it would have been wrong to remove the baby at birth and deny Tracey a chance of caring for her baby, Cynthia decided to recommend that social services should supervise the young woman and child from the moment of birth 'because health wouldn't take that responsibility'. She commented that 'the social services director at the time was very unhappy that we were carrying that responsibility', adding that in this case, like many others, 'the stakes are so high'. In fact, the young woman and her partner coped very well with the child (who was three and a half years old at the time of the interview) and hence Cynthia felt vindicated. When asked what it was that made her feel so strongly that she was prepared to 'go out on a limb' in this case, she replied:

> I think it was the understanding of the individual person and the belief that she has qualities that were necessary to parent a child and indeed to protect the child, particularly with the support of her partner who'd been long term, and who absolutely knew what had happened before ... But I think mainly, if I'd looked at that case on paper, I would have thought well, no wonder people are anxious, and it was mainly knowing and having assessed myself and then the new social worker having assessed the situation that gave me the confidence to feel that no way should she lose the opportunity to parent her child. But it is difficult ... in the children and families team we have the luxury of knowing people fairly thoroughly before we have to make very far-reaching decisions.

If we look at this case in terms of ethical principles, Cynthia was obviously concerned to respect Tracey as a person, to see her as an individual with the right and capacity to make her own choices and to promote her capacity to be self-determining by offering support (Kantian principles). There is no doubt that she was also concerned about the rights and interests of the unborn baby and other mothers and babies in the assessment unit, but she judged that the risks of harm to others (utilitarian considerations) were not sufficiently great to outweigh Tracey's rights and interests. But what enabled her to prioritize and implement her principles and duties in this way was her particular relationship with Tracey, her knowledge and understanding of her situation, her professional judgement about Tracey's capabilities, her sense of fairness and justice and her determination and commitment to support this person. In other words, Cynthia's qualities or 'virtues' and her relationship of care with Tracey were important features of this situation.

Conclusions

Discussion of the case examples in this chapter shows the importance of critical reflection on social work practice and the need to understand the complexities and contradictions inherent in the role of social worker. This enables social workers to understand more clearly how and why ethical problems and dilemmas arise in practice and to be able to better defend themselves and the profession from moral attack and reduce some of the feelings of guilt, blame and anxiety in making difficult ethical decisions. Trainee social workers, in particular, experience a lot of confusion and anxiety about their roles, which can be reduced through reflection on ethical and value issues and relating them to social work practice.

The rapid changes taking place in the structure and organization of social work services mean that it is even more important for practitioners to be clear about their value positions in order to resist the trends towards authoritarianism, the dominance of standardized and bureaucratic procedures and market values. These not only threaten professional identity and the traditional values based on respect for individual persons, but make it increasingly difficult to adopt more radical and committed forms of practice, which challenge both the traditional Kantian values and the utilitarian principles of the bureaucratic and quasi-business models of social work. It is also important to re-emphasize the importance of the face-to-face relationship with service users based on empathy, care and trust, alongside a commitment to working for social justice and challenging the poverty, inequality and oppression that are an everyday feature of the lives of so many people with whom social workers come into contact in whatever parts of the world they are working.

While it is important not to be unrealistic about what social workers can achieve, it is also important not to be overpessimistic and passive. Paulo Freire (2004, pp. 34–5), in his posthumously published letter 'On the right and the duty to change the world', writes of the dangers of deproblematizing the future. By this he means holding a mechanistic understanding of history, entailing the acceptance of the 'untouchable' power of the globalized economy. He speaks of the importance of political struggle, and in response to his own question about in what name political struggle should be undertaken, he says:

> To me it should be undertaken in the name of ethics, not obviously the ethics of markets but rather the universal ethics of

human beings – in the name of the needed transformation of society that should result in overcoming dehumanizing injustice. (Freire, 2004, p. 35)

Ethics, of course, is based upon a premise of human agency and responsibility. This does not entail social workers taking full responsibility and blame as individuals for the problems faced by service users, for the inadequacies of their employing organizations or the inequalities in society. However, it does mean that social workers individually, collectively as a profession and as global citizens should take responsibility for working together to raise awareness of the inhumane treatment and unjust policies encountered in their practice and work towards tackling them in small or larger scale ways.

Putting it into practice

Reflecting on your own practice

Aims of the exercise: to encourage readers to analyse their practice in terms of the ethical issues involved.

Using the format adopted for analysing Case example 7.12:

1. Briefly describe an ethical dilemma or problem experienced in your practice. Include reference to your feelings about the situation and the nature of your relationships with the people involved.
2. What were the ethical issues involved?
3. How did they arise?
4. What line of argument would you use to justify the course of action you took?

Practice focus

Case for discussion 7: Dilemmas for a social worker based in a public welfare office in Japan

This case comes from a newly qualified young social worker in Japan, who was working in a public welfare office. In Japan, every prefecture and city has an obligation to establish a public welfare office. These offices generally provide social services (income benefits and personal social services) for those who need social welfare. The social worker was working as a welfare officer in charge of public assistance to people whose income was below the national poverty line. This is his account of a particular case involving a single-parent family.

One of my clients was a single mother whose income was below the national poverty line due to her recent divorce. She had four children. I had over 50 cases at that time and half of them were categorized as 'mother and children' (one-parent family) cases. The duty of the public welfare office is not only to satisfy clients' needs in cash, but also in kind according to their particular circumstances. In the public welfare office, the duty of welfare officers is to calculate the total income per month that is due to their clients and to visit clients' homes to interview them and offer positive advice regarding how they can improve their lives.

In this case, I calculated the total living costs due to this mother and delivered this payment personally to her every month. When I met her the first time after her application had been approved, I said to her: 'Well, this payment is based on your living costs and covers a variety of your household's needs. First, you have to spend this money not only for the costs of daily living (such as food, clothes, telephone and so on) but also for the children's needs (such as school meals, notebooks, school clothes and so on). Second, there is an amount allowed to pay rent to the landlord of your apartment. Third, you are obliged to make this public assistance money last for 30 days, because it is allocated on a monthly basis, in other words, you are expected to make a rational calculation about how to use this money. Is that OK?' She replied to me: 'Yes, it is OK, no problem!'

Two weeks later, I took a phone call from her in the office and she insisted that the money was not enough. I was surprised and I imagined that her money had been taken by someone else. I asked her how much money she had left. She said she only had about ¥80,000 left from more than ¥300,000 that I gave her two weeks ago. I asked her what happened. She answered in a small voice: 'I do not know …'

As I was not sure why it happened, I visited her home. A detailed interview with her revealed a surprising fact. I found that she did not understand basic mathematics. I asked her first daughter, who was a junior high school student, to support her mother and to check the calculations whenever her mother bought any household goods. The daughter agreed to do this. I waited for a while, expecting a good result. However, the situation did not change. This mother always called me and told me that the money was not enough. I then discovered that her daughter did not understand basic mathematics either.

I discussed with my colleagues and boss how to deal with the case. My supervisor asked me if I had any more information about her circumstances that might be helpful in enabling me to support her. I explained her situation as follows. First, as she was not able to make a budget, she always faced difficulties in making ends meet. Second, in spite of the fact that she loved her children very much, it seemed that she did not perform many of the parenting functions very well – she did not teach them how to take care of themselves (how to eat meals politely, how to brush their teeth every night, how to change clothes every day and so on). One of my colleagues suggested that she and her children might have some psychological or intellectual problems. Following a medical assessment, two of the four children were diagnosed as suffering from mild learning disabilities.

On receiving this information, I discussed the case again with colleagues. Their view was that it was only the mother who came under the jurisdiction of the public assistance law. So the public welfare office could not offer the family all the support they might need. However, if the children were removed from the mother, for example sent to foster care or a residential home, they would be protected by other welfare laws (child welfare and disability laws). I did not agree with my colleagues on this point, which was, in effect, changing the focus of my responsibilities from the family to the mother only. From a social work perspective, it was true that it was too difficult a task for her to take care of her children. Certainly, she did not understand the role of a parent very well. All the other social workers in the public welfare office did not imagine that she could provide her children with satisfactory living conditions. However, I disagreed. I felt that the mother loved her children very much and the children loved her. If they were separated, the children would be sent to other welfare institutions (such as residential care homes) and would be looked after by the agencies. But this would mean that the mother would lose her energy to live with her children.

I thought about what to do. Should I, as a social worker, look for other possibilities that would enable her to live with her lovely children, in spite of the fact that she was not able to manage her household budgets? What kind of action would I have to take to change the lives of the members of this family in a way that would satisfy both the welfare office and the mother? One of the ethical principles of social work is to work towards positive change in the lives of clients. Do social workers have the power to make a judgement to eliminate the mother's possibilities to change in the name of her children's health and wellbeing?

What happened in this case was as follows. Many colleagues in the office suggested that I had better change my approach to her and make a decision to separate the children from the mother because of her (supposed) maltreatment. In spite of this suggestion, I also in turn suggested to my colleagues that the main objective of social work is to enlarge the possibilities for clients to make changes in their lives, according to their own choices, by offering well-designed care and support. Therefore I requested that the decision to separate the family should be postponed while I tried to discover other options to support them. In the end, my supervisor accepted my proposal and I tried to encourage the mother and her children to understand and adopt a more socially acceptable lifestyle. Although I tried to take some actions to change their lives for them, the outcomes of this practice were not regarded as satisfactory.

Unfortunately, a judgement was made by the welfare office that only the mother was eligible for support under the public assistance law. The mother was persuaded to allow her children to be separated from her and sent to other welfare agencies who would offer them a 'decent' standard of living.

Questions for discussion
1. What do you think are the main ethical issues in this case?
2. What do you think might be some of the arguments for and against separating the mother and her children?
3. The young social worker clearly felt the mother should be given every opportunity to look after her children herself. Do you think he was right to persuade his supervisor to postpone the decision to separate the mother and her children?
4. This case illustrates how the way the laws and regulations relating to social welfare are framed and institutionalized often constrains the possibilities for social workers to work creatively with individuals and families. Can you think of examples from your own country where legal or institutional requirements may result in outcomes for service users that social workers judge are unsatisfactory or unethical?

Further resources

Banks, S. and Nøhr, K. (eds) (2003) *Teaching Practical Ethics for the Social Professions*, FESET, Copenhagen.
A series of chapters written by authors from different European countries containing examples of a variety of techniques and approaches for teaching professional ethics, including methods of analysing cases, using drama, video and Socratic dialogue. This can be downloaded for free from the webpage of the European Social Ethics Project on the FESET website, which also has some cases from around the world for use with students: www.feset.org/en/home/activities/thematic-groups/esep.html.

Banks, S. and Nøhr, K. (eds) (2012) *Practising Social Work Ethics Around the World: Cases and Commentaries*, London, Routledge.
Comprises longer ethics cases from different countries around the world, each accompanied by two commentaries. Topics range from sexual abuse in Palestine to disaster relief in India and China. Also contains a series of exercises based around cases for use in teaching.

Reamer, F. (1990) *Ethical Dilemmas in Social Service: A Guide for Social Workers*, 2nd edn, Columbia University Press, New York.
Contains discussions of a number of themes in social work ethics, ranging from truth-telling to whistleblowing, and uses cases to illuminate the dilemmas and issues.

References

Abbott, P. and Meerabeau, L. (1998) 'Professionals, professionalization and the caring professions', in P. Abbott and L. Meerabeau (eds) *The Sociology of the Caring Professions*, London, UCL Press, pp. 1–19.

Abrioux, E. (1998) 'Degrees of participation: a spherical model: the possibilities for girls in Kabul, Afghanistan', in V. Johnson, E. Ivan-Smith, G. Gordon et al. (eds) *Stepping Forward: Children and Young People's Participation in the Development Process*, London, Intermediate Technology Publications, pp. 25–7.

Adams, R., Dominelli, L. and Payne, M. (2002) 'Concluding comments: facilitating critical practice', in R. Adams, L. Dominelli and M. Payne (eds) *Critical Practice in Social Work*, Basingstoke, Palgrave Macmillan, pp. 304–11.

Adams, R., Dominelli, L. and Payne, M. (eds) (2005) *Social Work Futures: Crossing Boundaries, Transforming Practice*, Basingstoke, Palgrave Macmillan.

Adams, R.M. (2006) *A Theory of Virtue: Excellence in Being for the Good*, Oxford, Oxford University Press.

Ahmad, B. (1990) *Black Perspectives in Social Work*, Birmingham, Venture Press.

Akademikerförbundet SSR (1997) *Yrkesetiska Riktlinjer för Socionomer*, Stockholm, Akademikerförbundet, SSR.

Akademikerförbundet SSR (2006) *Ethics in Social Work: An Ethical Code for Social Work Professionals*, Stockholm, Akademikerförbundet SSR.

Aldridge, M. (1994) *Making Social Work News*, London, Routledge.

Allmark, P. (1995) 'Can there be an ethics of care?', *Journal of Medical Ethics*, 21, pp. 19–24.

Almond, B. (1993) 'Rights', in P. Singer (ed.) *A Companion to Ethics*, Oxford, Blackwell, pp. 259–69.

Amy, Claire, Jordan and Glen (2010) 'Service user perspectives on the "ethically good practitioner"', *Ethics and Social Welfare*, 4(1), pp. 91–7.

Ando, H. (2010) 'The Social Context of Social Policy in Social Work in Japan', paper presented at Economic and Social Research Council/ Japanese Society for the Promotion of Science Seminar on 'The Impact of New Public Management Policies and Perspectives on Professional

Social Work: A Comparison of British and Japanese Experiences', Stirling University, Scotland, 6–7 September.

Annes, A., Abedin, S. and Sardar, Z. (1992) *Christian-Muslim Relations*, London, Grey Seal.

Aotearoa New Zealand Association of Social Workers (2008) *Code of Ethics*, Christchurch, Aotearoa New Zealand Association of Social Workers.

Aristotle ([350 BCE]1954) *The Nicomachean Ethics of Aristotle*, trans. Sir David Ross, London, Oxford University Press.

Armstrong, A. (2007) *Nursing Ethics: A Virtue-based Approach*, Basingstoke, Palgrave Macmillan.

Arnstein, S. (1969) 'A ladder of community participation', *American Institute of Planners Journal*, 35, pp. 216–24.

Arrington, R. (1998) *Western Ethics: An Historical Introduction*, Oxford, Blackwell.

Askeland, G. and Fook, J. (2009) 'Critical reflection in social work', *European Journal of Social Work*, 12(3), pp. 287–92.

Asociácia Sociálnych Pracovníkov na Slovensku (Association of Social Workers in the Slovak Republic) (1997) *The Code of Ethics for Social Workers in Slovakia*, Bratislava, ASPS.

Association for the Advancement of Social Work (2007) *Code of Professional Ethics of the Social Workers in Israel*, Tel Aviv, Union of Social Workers.

Association of Social Workers in Turkey (2003) *Ethical Principles and Responsibilities of Social Workers*, Ankara, Association of Social Workers in Turkey.

Australian Association of Social Workers (2010) *Code of Ethics*, Canberra, AASW.

Baier, A. (1995) 'The need for more than justice', in V. Held (ed.) *Justice and Care: Essential Readings in Feminist Ethics*, Boulder, CO, Westview Press.

Bailey, R. and Brake, M. (eds) (1975) *Radical Social Work*, London, Edward Arnold.

Baldwin, M. (2011) 'Resisting the EasyCare model: building a more radical, community-based anti-authoritarian social work for the future', in M. Lavalette (ed.) *Radical Social Work Today: Social Work at the Crossroads*, Bristol, The Policy Press, pp. 187–204.

Banks, S. (1990) 'Doubts, dilemmas and duties: ethics and the social worker', in P. Carter, T. Jeffs and M. Smith (eds) *Social Work and Social Welfare Yearbook 2*, Buckingham, Open University Press, pp. 91–106.

Banks, S. (1995) *Ethics and Values in Social Work*, Basingstoke, Macmillan – now Palgrave Macmillan.

Banks, S. (2001a) 'Ethical dilemmas for the social professions: work in progress with social education students in Europe', *European Journal of Social Education*, 1, pp. 1–16.

Banks, S. (2001b) *Ethics and Values in Social Work*, 2nd edn, Basingstoke, Palgrave – now Palgrave Macmillan.

Banks, S. (2003) 'The use of learning journals to encourage ethical reflection during fieldwork practice', in S. Banks and K. Nøhr (eds) *Teaching Practical Ethics for the Social Professions*, Copenhagen, FESET, pp. 53–67.

Banks, S. (2004a) *Ethics, Accountability and the Social Professions*, Basingstoke, Palgrave Macmillan.

Banks, S. (2004b) 'Professional integrity, social work and the ethics of distrust', *Social Work and Social Sciences Review*, 11(2), pp. 20–35.

Banks, S. (2005) 'The ethical practitioner in formation: issues of courage, competence and commitment', *Journal of Social Work Education*, 24(7), pp. 737–53.

Banks, S. (2009a) 'From professional ethics to ethics in professional life: implications for learning, teaching and study', *Ethics and Social Welfare*, 3(1), pp. 55–63.

Banks, S. (2009b) 'Professional values and accountabilities', in R. Adams, L. Dominelli and M. Payne (eds) *Critical Practice in Social Work*, 2nd edn, Basingstoke, Palgrave Macmillan, pp. 32–42.

Banks, S. (2010) 'Integrity in professional life: issues of conduct, commitment and capacity', *British Journal of Social Work*, 40(7), pp. 2168–84.

Banks, S. (2011a) 'Ethics in an age of austerity: social work and the evolving new public management', *Journal of Social Intervention: Theory and Practice*, 20(2), pp. 5–23.

Banks, S. (2011b) 'Re-gilding the ghetto: community work and community development in 21st-century Britain', in M. Lavalette (ed.) *Radical Social Work Today: Social Work at the Crossroads*, Bristol, The Policy Press, pp. 165–85.

Banks, S. (2012) 'Global ethics for social work? A case-based approach', in S. Banks and K. Nøhr (eds) *Practising Social Work Around the World: Cases and Commentaries*, London, Routledge, pp. 1–31.

Banks, S. and Gallagher, A. (2009) *Ethics in Professional Life: Virtues for Health and Social Care*, Basingstoke, Palgrave Macmillan.

Banks, S. and Nøhr, K. (eds) (2012) *Practising Social Work Ethics Around the World: Cases and Commentaries*, London, Routledge.

Banks, S. and Nyboe, N.-E. (2003) 'Writing and using cases', in S. Banks and K. Nøhr (eds) *Teaching Practical Ethics for the Social Professions*, Copenhagen, FESET, pp. 19–39.

Banks, S. and Williams, R. (1999) 'The personal and the professional: perspectives from European social education students', *Social Work In Europe*, 6(3), pp. 52–61.

Banks, S. and Williams, R. (2006) 'Accounting for ethical difficulties in social welfare work: issues, problems and dilemmas', *British Journal of Social Work*, 35(7), pp. 1005–22.

Banks, S., Hugman, R., Healy, L. et al. (2008) 'Global ethics for social work: problems and possibilities', *Ethics and Social Welfare*, 2(3), pp. 276–90.

Barker, P. (ed.) (2011) *Mental Health Ethics: The Human Context*, Abingdon, Routledge.

Barnard, A., Horner, N. and Wild, J. (eds) (2008) *The Value Base of Social Work and Social Care: An Active Learning Handbook*, Maidenhead, Open University Press.

Barnes, M. (2011) 'Abandoning care? A critical perspective from an ethic of care', *Ethics and Social Welfare*, 5(2), pp. 153–67.

Barroco, M. (2004) *Ética y Servicio Social: Fundamentos Ontológicos*, São Paulo, Brazil, Biblioteca Latinoamericana de Servicio Social.

BASW (British Association of Social Workers) (1975) *A Code of Ethics for Social Work*, Birmingham, BASW.

BASW (British Association of Social Workers) (1980) *Clients are Fellow Citizens*, Birmingham, BASW.

BASW (British Association of Social Workers) (1989) *Rights, Responsibilities and Remedies*, Birmingham, BASW.

BASW (British Association of Social Workers) (2002) *The Code of Ethics for Social Work*, Birmingham, BASW.

Bauman, Z. (1993) *Postmodern Ethics*, Oxford, Blackwell.

Bauman, Z. (1995) *Life in Fragments: Essays in Postmodern Morality*, Oxford, Blackwell.

Bauman, Z. (1997) 'Morality begins at home, or: Can there be a Levinasian macro-ethics?', in H. Jodalen and A. Vetlesen (eds) *Closeness: An Ethics*, Oslo, Scandinavian University Press, pp. 218–44.

Bauman, Z. (2008) *Does Ethics Have a Chance in a World of Consumers?*, Cambridge, MA, Harvard University Press.

Beauchamp, T. (1996) 'The role of principles in practical ethics', in L. Sumner and J. Boyle (eds) *Philosophical Perspectives on Bioethics*, Toronto, University of Toronto Press, pp. 79–95.

Beauchamp, T. and Childress, J. (1994) *Principles of Biomedical Ethics*, 4th edn, Oxford, Oxford University Press.

Beauchamp, T. and Childress, J. (2001) *Principles of Biomedical Ethics*, 5th edn, Oxford, Oxford University Press.

Beauchamp, T. and Childress, J. (2009) *Principles of Biomedical Ethics*, 6th edn, Oxford, Oxford University Press.

Beckett, C. and Maynard, A. (2005) *Values and Ethics in Social Work: An Introduction*, Sage, London.

Beddoe, L. and Duke, J. (2009) 'Registration in New Zealand social work', *International Social Work*, 52(6), pp. 785–97.

Bennett, C. (1994) 'Islam', in J. Holm and J. Bowker (eds) *Making Moral Decisions*, London, Continuum, pp. 95–122.

Bentham, J. (1789) *An Introduction to the Principles of Morals and Legislation*, available at www.utilitarianism.com/jeremy-bentham/index.html.

Beresford, P. (2008) 'Service user values for social work and social care', in A. Barnard, N. Horner and J. Wild (eds) *The Value Base of Social Work and Social Care: An Active Learning Handbook*, Maidenhead, Open University Press, pp. 83–96.

Beresford, P. (2011) 'Radical social work and service users: a crucial connection', in M. Lavalette (ed.) *Radical Social Work Today: Social Work at the Crossroads*, Bristol, The Policy Press, pp. 95–114.

Bevan, D. and Corvellec, H. (2007) 'The impossibility of corporate ethics: for a Levinasian approach to managerial ethics', *Business Ethics: A European Review*, 16(3), pp. 208–19.

Biestek, F. (1961) *The Casework Relationship*, London, Allen & Unwin.

Blaug, R. (1995) 'Distortion of the face to face: communicative reason and social work practice', *British Journal of Social Work*, 25, pp. 423–39.

Blum, L. (1988) 'Gilligan and Kohlberg: implications for moral theory', *Ethics*, 98, pp. 472–91.

Blum, L. (1994) *Moral Perception and Particularity*, Cambridge, Cambridge University Press.

Bond, T. (2010) *Standards and Ethics for Counselling in Action*, 3rd edn, London, Sage.

Boss, J. (1998) *Ethics for Life: An Interdisciplinary and Multi-Cultural Introduction*, Mountain View, CA, Mayfield.

Bouquet, B. (1999) 'De l'éthique personelle à une éthique professionnelle', *EMPAN*, 36, pp. 27–33.

Bowden, P. (1997) *Caring: Gender-sensitive Ethics*, London, Routledge.

Bowie, N. (1999) *Business Ethics: A Kantian Perspective*, Oxford, Blackwell.

Bowles, W., Collingridge, M., Curry, S. and Valentine, B. (2006) *Ethical Practice in Social Work: An Applied Approach*, Crows Nest, New South Wales, Allen & Unwin.

Bradshaw, P. (1996) 'Yes! There is an ethics of care: an answer for Peter Allmark', *Journal of Medical Ethics*, 22, pp. 8–12.

Brake, M. and Bailey, R. (eds) (1980) *Radical Social Work and Practice*, London, Edward Arnold.

Braye, S. and Preston-Shoot, M. (2010) *Practising Social Work Law*, 3rd edn, Basingstoke, Palgrave Macmillan.

Brill, C. (1998) 'The new NASW code of ethics can be your ally: Part 1', *FOCUS Newsletter*, February, www.naswma.org/displaycommon.cfm?an=1&subarticlenbr=96, accessed July 2011.

Briskman, L. (2005) 'Pushing ethical boundaries for children and families: confidentiality, transparency and transformation', in R. Adams, L. Dominelli and M. Payne (eds) *Social Work Futures: Crossing Boundaries, Transforming Practice*, Basingstoke, Palgrave Macmillan, pp. 208–20.

Briskman, L., Latham, S. and Goddard, C. (2008) *Human Rights Overboard: Seeking Asylum in Australia*, Melbourne, Scribe Publishing.

Brock, D. (1991) 'Decision-making competence and risk', *Bioethics*, 5(2), pp. 105–12.

Brookfield, S. (1987) *Developing Critical Thinkers*, Milton Keynes, Open University Press.

Brookfield, S. (2009) 'The concept of critical reflection: promises and contradictions', *European Journal of Social Work*, 12(3), pp. 293–304.

Browning, D. (ed.) (2006) *Universalism vs. Relativism: Making Moral Judgements in a Changing, Pluralistic, and Threatening World*, Lanham, MD, Rowman & Littlefield.

Buber, M. (1937) *I and Thou*, trans. R. Gregor Smith, Edinburgh, T. & T. Clark.

Buchanan, A. and Brock, D. (1989) *Deciding for Others: The Ethics of Surrogate Decision Making*, Cambridge, Cambridge University Press.

Bulgarian Association of Social Workers (1999) *Code of Ethics*, Sofia, Bulgarian Association of Social Workers.

Burkitt, I. (1999) 'Relational moves and generative dances', in S. McNamee, K. Gergen and Associates (eds) *Relational Responsibility: Resources for Sustainable Dialogue*, Thousand Oaks, CA, Sage, pp. 71–80.

Burrage, M. and Torstendahl, R. (eds) (1990) *Professions in Theory and History: Rethinking the Study of the Professions*, London, Sage.

Butcher, H., Banks, S., Henderson, P. and Robertson, J. (2007) *Critical Community Practice*, Bristol, The Policy Press.

Butler, I. and Drakeford M. (2005) *Scandal, Social Policy and Social Welfare*, 2nd edn, Bristol, The Policy Press.

Butrym, Z. (1976) *The Nature of Social Work*, London, Macmillan.

Callinicos, A. (2003) *An Anti-Capitalist Manifesto*, Cambridge, Polity Press.

Campbell, J. and Oliver, M. (1996) *Disability Politics: Understanding our Past, Changing our Future*, London, Routledge.

Canadian Association of Social Workers (2005a) *Code of Ethics*, CASW, Ottawa.

Canadian Association of Social Workers (2005b) *Guidelines for Ethical Practice*, CASW, Ottawa.

Caputo, J. (2000) 'The end of ethics', in H. LaFollette (ed.) *The Blackwell Guide to Ethical Theory*, Oxford, Blackwell, pp. 111–28.

Carey, M. (2009) 'Critical commentary: happy shopper? The problem with service user and carer participation', *British Journal of Social Work*, 39(1), pp. 179–88.

CCETSW (Central Council for Education and Training in Social Work) (1976) *Values in Social Work*, London, CCETSW.

Chambers, T. (1997) 'What to expect from an ethics case (and what it expects from you)', in H. Nelson (ed.) *Stories and their Limits: Narrative Approaches to Bioethics*, New York, Routledge, pp. 171–84.

Chambon, A. (1994) 'Postmodernity and social work discourse(s): notes on the changing language of a profession', in A. Chambon and A. Irving (eds) *Essays on Postmodernism and Social Work*, Toronto, Canadian Scholars' Press, pp. 63–75.

Chambon, A. and Irving, A. (eds) (1994) *Essays on Postmodernism and Social Work*, Toronto, Canadian Scholars' Press.

Chambon, A., Irving, A. and Epstein, L. (eds) (1999) *Reading Foucault for Social Work*, New York, Columbia University Press.

Charleton, M. (2007) *Ethics for Social Care in Ireland: Philosophy and Practice*, Dublin, Gill & Macmillan.

Charlton, J. (1998) *Nothing About Us Without Us: Disability, Oppression and Empowerment*, California, University of California Press.

Clancy, A. and Svensson, T. (2007) '"Faced" with responsibility: Levinasian ethics and the challenges of responsibility in Norwegian public health nursing', *Nursing Philosophy*, 8(3), pp. 158–66.

Clark, C. (2000) *Social Work Ethics: Politics, Principles and Practice*, Basingstoke, Palgrave Macmillan.

Clark, C. with Asquith, S. (1985) *Social Work and Social Philosophy*, London, Routledge & Kegan Paul.

Clark, C. and McGhee, J. (eds) (2008) *Private and Confidential? Handling Personal Information in the Social and Health Service*s, Bristol, The Policy Press.

Clarke, J. (2004) *Changing Welfare Changing States: New Directions in Social Policy*, London, Sage.

Clarke, J., Newman, J., Smith, N. et al. (2007) *Creating Citizen-consumers: Changing Publics and Changing Public Services*, London, Sage.

Clifford, D. (2002) 'Resolving uncertainties? The contribution of some recent feminist ethical theory to the social professions', *European Journal of Social Work*, 5(1), pp. 31–41.

Clifford, D. and Burke, B. (2009) *Anti-Oppressive Values in Social Work*, Basingstoke, Palgrave Macmillan.

Collins, R. (1990) 'Market closure and the conflict theory of the professions', in M. Burrage and R. Torstendahl (eds) *Professions in Theory and History: Rethinking the Study of the Professions*, London, Sage, pp. 24–44.

Community Care (1999/2000) 'Comment: a new century of uncertainty', *Community Care*, 1303, 16 December 1999–12 January 2000.

Congress, E. (1999) *Social Work Values and Ethics: Identifying and Resolving Professional Dilemmas*, Chicago, Nelson-Hall.

Congress, E., Black, P. and Strom-Gottfried, K. (eds) (2009) *Teaching Social Work Ethics and Values: A Curriculum Resource*, Alexandria, VA, Council on Social Work Education.

Connolly, M. and Ward, T. (2008) *Morals, Rights and Practice in the Human Services: Effective and Fair Decision-making in Health, Social Care and Criminal Justice*, London, Jessica Kingsley.

Corrigan, P. and Leonard, P. (1978) *Social Work Practice under Capitalism: A Marxist Approach*, London, Macmillan.

Crabtree, S., Husain, F. and Spalek, B. (2008) *Islam and Social Work: Debating Values, Transforming Practice*, Bristol, The Policy Press.

Cree, V. (1995) *From Public Streets to Private Lives*, Aldershot, Avebury.

Crisp, R. (ed.) (1996) *How Should One Live? Essays on the Virtues*, Oxford, Oxford University Press.

Crisp, R. and Slote, M. (eds) (1997) *Virtue Ethics*, Oxford, Oxford University Press.

Critchley, S. (2007) *Infinitely Demanding: Ethics of Commitment, Politics of Resistance*, London, Verso.

Croatia Association of Social Workers (2004) *Etčki Kodeks Socijalnih Radnika*, Zagreb, Croatia Association of Social Workers.

Dalrymple, J. and Burke, B. (2006) *Anti-oppressive Practice: Social Care and the Law*, 2nd edn, Maidenhead, Open University Press.

Dawson, A. (1994) 'Professional codes of practice and ethical conduct', *Journal of Applied Philosophy*, 11(2), pp. 125–33.

Dawson, H. (2011) 'Better for the experience', *Professional Social Work*, May, p. 15.

Day, L. (1992) 'Women and oppression: race, class and gender', in M. Langan and L. Day (eds) *Women, Oppression and Social Work*, London, Routledge, pp. 12–31.

De Silva, P. (1993) 'Buddhist ethics', in P. Singer (ed.) *A Companion to Ethics*, Oxford, Blackwell, pp. 58–68.

Deverell, K. and Sharma, U. (2000) 'Professionalism in everyday practice: issues of trust, experience and boundaries', in N. Malin (ed.) *Professionalism, Boundaries and the Workplace*, London, Routledge, pp. 25–46.

Doel, M., Allmark, P., Conway, P. et al. (2009) *Professional Boundaries: Research Report*, Sheffield, Sheffield Hallam University, available from http://shura.shu.ac.uk/1759/.

Dolgoff, R., Loewenberg, F. and Harrington, D. (2009) *Ethical Decisions for Social Work Practice*, 8th edn, Belmont, CA, Brooks Cole.

Dominelli, L. (1996) 'Deprofessionalising social work: anti-oppressive practice, competencies and postmodernism', *British Journal of Social Work*, 26(2), pp. 153–75.

Dominelli, L. (1997) *Anti-Racist Social Work*, 2nd edn, Basingstoke, Macmillan – now Palgrave Macmillan.

Dominelli, L. (2002) *Anti Oppressive Social Work Theory and Practice*, Basingstoke, Palgrave Macmillan.

Dominelli, L. (2010) *Social Work in a Globalizing World*, Cambridge, Polity Press.

Dominelli, L. and McLeod, E. (1989) *Feminist Social Work*, Basingstoke, Macmillan.

Downie, R. (1971) *Roles and Values*, London, Methuen.

Downie, R. (1989) 'A political critique of Kantian ethics in social work: a reply to Webb and McBeath', *British Journal of Social Work*, 19, pp. 507–10.

Downie, R. and Loudfoot, E. (1978) Aim, skill and role in social work', in N. Timms and D. Watson (eds) *Philosophy in Social Work*, London, Routledge & Kegan Paul, pp. 111–26.

Downie, R. and Telfer, E. (1969) *Respect for Persons*, London, Routledge & Kegan Paul.

Downie, R. and Telfer, E. (1980) *Caring and Curing*, London, Methuen.

Doyal, L. and Gough, I. (1991) *A Theory of Human Need*, Basingstoke, Macmillan – now Palgrave Macmillan.

Driver, J. (2009) 'The history of utilitarianism', *The Stanford Encyclopedia of Philosophy*, http://plato.standford.edu/entries/utilitarianism-history/, accessed July 2011.

Du Gay, P. (2000) *In Praise of Bureaucracy: Weber, Organisation, Ethics*, London, Sage.

Dunleavy, P. and Hood, C. (1994) 'From old public administration to new public management', *Public Money and Management*, 14(3), pp. 9–16.

Dunleavy, P., Margetts, H., Bastow, S. and Tinkler, J. (2006) 'New public management is dead: long live digital-era governance', *Journal of Public Administration Research and Theory*, 16(3), pp. 467–94.

Dworkin, R. (1977) *Taking Rights Seriously*, Cambridge, MA, Harvard University Press.

Dzur, A. (2008) *Democratic Professionalism, Citizen Participation and the Reconstruction of Professional Identity, Ethics and Practice*, Philadelphia, Pennsylvania State University Press.

Eastham, M. (2002) 'Vocation and social care', in M. Nash and B. Stewart (eds) *Spirituality and Social Care*, London, Jessica Kingsley, pp. 71–92.

Edmundson, W. (2004) *An Introduction to Rights*, Cambridge, Cambridge University Press.

Edwards, P. (1998) 'The future of ethics', in O. Leaman (ed.) *The Future of Philosophy: Towards the Twenty-first Century*, London, Routledge, pp. 41–61.

Edwards, S. (1996) *Nursing Ethics: A Principle-based Approach*, Basingstoke, Macmillan – now Palgrave Macmillan.

Ejaz, F.K. (1991) 'Self-determination: lessons to be learned from social work practice in India', *British Journal of Social Work*, 21, pp. 127–42.

Etzioni, A. (1969) *The Semi-professions and their Organisation*, New York, Free Press.

Etzioni, A. (1995) *The Spirit of Community*, London, Fontana.

Etzioni, A. (1997) *The New Golden Rule: Community and Morality in a Democratic Society*, New York, Basic Books.

Exworthy, M. and Halford, S. (eds) (1999) *Professionals and the New Managerialism in the Public Sector*, Buckingham, Open University Press.

Farley, M. (1993) 'Feminism and universal morality', in G. Outka and J. Reeder (eds) *Prospects for a Common Morality*, Chichester, Princeton University Press, pp. 170–90.

Feinberg, J. (1973) *Social Philosophy*, Englewood Cliffs, NJ, Prentice Hall.

Ferguson, I. (2007) 'Increasing user choice or privatising risk? The antinomies of personalisation', *British Journal of Social Work*, 37(3), pp. 387–403.

Ferguson, I. (2008) *Reclaiming Social Work: Challenging Neo-liberalism and Promoting Social Justice*, London, Sage.

Ferguson, I. and Lavalette, M. (eds) (2009) *Social Work After Baby P: Issues, Debates and Alternative Perspectives*, Liverpool, Liverpool Hope University.

Ferguson, I. and Woodward, R. (2009) *Radical Social Work in Practice: Making a Difference*, Bristol, The Policy Press.

Ferreira, S. (2010) 'Eco-spiritual social work as a precondition for social development', *Ethics and Social Welfare*, 4(1), pp. 3–23.

Fook, J. (2002) *Social Work: Critical Theory and Practice*, London, Sage.

Foucault, M. (1984) 'On the genealogy of ethics: an overview of work in progress', in P. Rabinow (ed.) *The Foucault Reader*, Harmondsworth, Penguin, pp. 340–72.

Foucault, M. (1999) 'Social work, social control, and normalization: discussion with Michael Foucault', in A. Chambon, A. Irving and L. Epstein (eds) *Reading Foucault for Social Work*, New York, Columbia University Press, pp. 83–97.

Frankena, W. (1963) *Ethics*, Englewood Cliffs, NJ, Prentice Hall.

Franklin, B. (1989) 'Wimps and bullies: press reporting of child abuse', in P. Carter, T. Jeffs and M. Smith (eds) *Social Work and Social Welfare Yearbook 1*, Milton Keynes, Open University Press, pp. 1–14.

Freidson, E. (1994) *Professionalism Reborn: Theory, Prophecy, and Policy*, Chicago, University of Chicago Press.

Freidson, E. (2001) *Professionalism: The Third Logic*, Cambridge, Polity Press.

Freire, P. (1972) *Pedagogy of the Oppressed*, London, Penguin.

Freire, P. (2004) *Pedagogy of Indignation*, Boulder, CO, Paradigm.

Furness, S. and Gilligan, P. (2010) *Religion, Belief and Social Work: Making a Difference*, Bristol, The Policy Press.

Gallagher, A. and Sykes, N. (2008) 'A little bit of heaven for a few? A case analysis', *Ethics and Social Welfare*, 2(3), pp. 299–307.

Galper, J. (1980) *Social Work Practice: A Radical Perspective*, Englewood Cliffs, NJ, Prentice Hall.

Gbadegesin, S. (2005) 'Origins of African ethics', in W. Schweiker (ed.) *The Blackwell Companion to Religious Ethics*, Oxford, Blackwell, pp. 413–22.

Gewirth, A. (1996) *The Community of Rights*, Chicago, Chicago University Press.

Gibbs, L. and Gambrill, E. (2002) 'Evidence-based practice: counterarguments to objectors', *Research in Social Work Practice*, 12(3), pp. 452–76.

Gilligan, C. (1982) *In a Different Voice: Psychological Theory and Women's Development*, Cambridge, MA, Harvard University Press.

Goovaerts, H. (2003) 'Working with a staged plan', in S. Banks and K. Nøhr (eds) *Teaching Practical Ethics for the Social Professions*, Copenhagen, FESET, pp. 83–93.

Gould, N. and Taylor, I. (eds) (1996) *Reflective Learning for Social Work*, Aldershot, Arena.

Graham, M. (1999) 'The African-centred worldview: developing a paradigm for social work', *British Journal of Social Work*, 29, pp. 251–67.

Graham, M. (2002) *Social Work and African-centred Worldviews*, Birmingham, Venture Press.

Gray, M. and Lovat, T. (2007) 'Horse and carriage: why Habermas's discourse ethics gives virtue a praxis in social work', *Ethics and Social Welfare*, 1(3), pp. 310–28.

Gray, M. and Webb, S. (eds) (2010) *Ethics and Value Perspectives in Social Work*, Basingstoke, Palgrave Macmillan.

Greenwood, E. (1957) 'Attributes of a profession', *Social Work*, 2(3), pp. 44–55.

Groenhout, R. (2004) *Connected Lives: Human Nature and an Ethics of Care*, Lanham, MD, Rowman & Littlefield.

GSCC (General Social Care Council) (2002) *Codes of Practice for Social Care Workers and Employers*, London, GSCC.

GSCC (General Social Care Council) (2008) *Raising Standards: Social Work Conduct in England 2003-08*, London, GSCC.

Gyekye, K. (2010) 'African ethics', *Stanford Encyclopedia of Philosophy*, http://plato.stanford.edu/entries/african-ethics/, accessed December 2010.

Gyford, J. (1991) *Citizens, Consumers and Councils*, London, Macmillan.

Habermas, J. (1990) *Moral Consciousness and Communicative Action*, trans. C. Lenhardt and S. Nicholsen, Cambridge, MA, MIT Press.

Hall, C., Sarangi, S. and Slembrouck, S. (1997) 'Moral construction in social work discourse', in B.-L. Gunnarsson, P. Linell and B. Nordberg (eds) *The Construction of Professional Discourse*, London, Longman, pp. 265–91.

Hall, C., Slembrouck, S. and Sarangi, S. (2006) *Language Practices in Social Work: Categorisation and Accountability in Child Welfare*, London, Routledge.

Hall, C., Juhila, K., Parton, N. and Pösö, T. (eds) (2003) *Constructing Clienthood in Social Work and Human Services: Interaction, Identities and Practices*, London, Jessica Kingsley.

Halverson, G. and Brownlee, K. (2010) 'Managing ethical considerations around dual relationships in small rural and remote Canadian communities', *International Social Work*, 53(2), pp. 247–60.

Hand, S. (ed.) (1989) *The Levinas Reader*, Oxford, Blackwell.

Hanford, L. (1994) 'Nursing and the concept of care: an appraisal of Noddings' theory', in G. Hunt (ed.) *Ethical Issues in Nursing*, London, Routledge, pp. 181–97.

Hardcastle, D. with Powers, P. and Wencour, S. (2011) *Community Practice: Theories and Skills for Social Workers*, 3rd edn, New York, Oxford University Press.

Hare, R. (1952) *The Language of Morals*, Oxford, Clarendon Press.

Hare, R. (1963) *Freedom and Reason*, Oxford, Clarendon Press.

Hare, R. (1981) *Moral Thinking*, Oxford, Oxford University Press.

Harris, J. (2003) *The Social Work Business*, London, Routledge.

Harris, J. (2009) 'Customer-citizenship in modernised social work', in J. Harris and V. White (eds) *Modernising Social Work: Critical Considerations*, Bristol, The Policy Press, pp. 67–87.

Harris, N. (1987) 'Defensive social work', *British Journal of Social Work*, 17, pp. 61–9.

Harris, N. (1994) 'Professional codes and Kantian duties', in R. Chadwick (ed.) *Ethics and the Professions*, Aldershot, Avebury, pp. 104–15.

Harvey, D. (1990) *The Condition of Postmodernity*, Oxford, Blackwell.

Hayes, D. (2009) 'Social work with asylum seekers and others subject to immigration control', in R. Adams, L. Dominelli and M. Payne (eds) *Practising Social Work in a Complex World*, Basingstoke, Palgrave Macmillan, pp. 114–26.

Hayes, D. and Humphries, B. (eds) (2004) *Social Work, Immigration and Asylum: Debates, Dilemmas and Ethical Issues for Social Work and Social Care Practice*, London, Jessica Kingsley.

Healy, L. (2001) *International Social Work: Professional Action in an Interdependent World*, Oxford, Oxford University Press.

Healy, L. (2007) 'Universalism and cultural relativism in social work ethics', *International Social Work*, 50(1), pp. 11–26.

Hekman, S. (1995) *Moral Voices, Moral Selves: Carol Gilligan and Feminist Moral Theory*, Cambridge, Polity Press.

Held, V. (2006) *The Ethics of Care: Personal, Political, and Global*, Oxford, Oxford University Press.

Hochschild, A. (1983) *The Managed Heart: Commercialisation of Human Feeling*, Berkeley, CA, University of California Press.

Hohfeld, W. ([1919]1964) *Fundamental Legal Conceptions*, London, Greenwood Press.

Hollis, M. and Howe, D. (1990) 'Moral risks in the social work role: a response to Macdonald', *British Journal of Social Work*, 20, pp. 547–52.

Holm, J. and Bowker, J. (eds) (1994) *Making Moral Decisions*, London, Continuum.

Holmes, J. (1981) *Professionalisation: a Misleading Myth? A Study of the Careers of Youth and Community Work Courses in England and Wales from 1970 to 1978*, Leicester, National Youth Bureau.

Hong Kong Social Workers Association (1998) *Code of Practice*, Hong Kong, HKSWA.

Horne, M. (1999) *Values in Social Work*, 2nd edn, Aldershot, Wildwood House.

Houston, S. (2003) 'Establishing virtue in social work: a response to McBeath and Webb', *British Journal of Social Work*, 33, pp. 819–24.

Houston, S. (2010) 'Discourse ethics', in M. Gray and S. Webb (eds) *Ethics and Value Perspectives in Social Work*, Basingstoke, Palgrave Macmillan, pp. 95–107.

Howe, D. (1992) 'Child abuse and the bureaucratisation of social work', *The Sociological Review*, 40(3), pp. 491–508.

Hughes, G. (2001) *Aristotle on Ethics*, London, Routledge.

Hugman, R. (1991) *Power in Caring Professions*, Basingstoke, Macmillan – now Palgrave Macmillan.

Hugman, R. (1998a) *Social Welfare and Social Value*, Basingstoke, Macmillan – now Palgrave Macmillan.

Hugman, R. (1998b) 'Social work and de-professionalization', in P. Abbott and L. Meerabeau (eds) *The Sociology of Caring Professions*, 2nd edn, London, UCL Press, pp. 178–98.

Hugman, R. (2005) *New Approaches in Ethics for the Caring Professions*, Basingstoke, Palgrave Macmillan.

Hugman, R. (2008) 'Ethics in a world of difference', *Ethics and Social Welfare*, 2(2), pp. 118–32.

Hugman, R. (2010) *Understanding International Social Work: A Critical Analysis*, Basingstoke, Palgrave Macmillan.

Humphries, B. (2004) 'An unacceptable role for social work: implementing immigration policy', *British Journal of Social Work*, 34, pp. 93–107.

Hursthouse, R. (1997) 'Virtue theory and abortion', in D. Statman (ed.) *Virtue Ethics: A Critical Reader*, Edinburgh, Edinburgh University Press, pp. 227–44.

Hursthouse, R. (1999) *On Virtue Ethics*, Oxford, Oxford University Press.

Husband, C. (1995) 'The morally active practitioner and the ethics of anti-racist social work', in R. Hugman and D. Smith (eds) *Ethical Issues in Social Work*, London, Routledge, pp. 84–103.

Ife, J. (1999) 'Postmodernism, critical theory and social work', in B. Pease and J. Fook (eds) *Transforming Social Work Practice: Postmodern Critical Perspectives*, London, Routledge, pp. 211–23.

Ife, J. (2008) *Human Rights and Social Work: Towards Rights-based Practice*, rev. edn, Cambridge, Cambridge University Press.

IFSW/IASSW (International Federation of Social Workers/International Association of Schools of Social Work) (2000) *Definition of Social Work*, IFSW/IASSW, available at www.ifsw.org/f38000138.html.

IFSW/IASSW (International Federation of Social Workers/International Association of Schools of Social Work) (2004) *Ethics in Social Work, Statement of Principles*, Berne, IFSW/IASSW, available at www.ifsw.org.

Illich, I., Zola, I., McKnight, J. et al. (eds) (1977) *The Disabling Professions*, London, Marion Boyars.

Inter Faith Network for the UK (2004) *Connect: Different Faiths, Shared Values*, London, Inter Faith Network for the UK, in association with Timebank and the National Youth Agency, available at http://www.interfaith.org.uk.

Irish Association of Social Workers (2006) *Irish Association of Social Workers' Code of Ethics*, Dublin, IASW.

Irish Association of Social Workers (2009) *Code of Practice for Irish Association of Social Workers' Members*, Dublin, IASW.

Irving, A. (1994) 'From image to simulacra: the modern/postmodern divide in social work', in A. Chambon and A. Irving (eds) *Essays on Postmodernism and Social Work*, Toronto, Canadian Scholars' Press, pp. 21–32.

Ito, F. (2010) 'The Development of Professional Social Work in Japan: Its Relevance of Neo-liberalism', paper presented at Economic and Social Research Council/Japanese Society for the Promotion of Science Seminar on 'The Impact of New Public Management Policies and Perspectives on Professional Social Work: A Comparison of British and Japanese Experiences', Stirling University, Scotland, 6–7 September.

Jameson, F. (1991) *Postmodernism or, The Cultural Logic of Late Capitalism*, London, Verso.

Jameton, A. (1984) *Nursing Practice: The Ethical Issues*, Englewood Cliffs, NJ, Prentice Hall.

Jansen, T., van den Brink, G. and Kole, J. (eds) (2010) *Professional Pride: A Powerful Force*, Amsterdam, Uitgeverij Boom/Eleven International Publishing.

Japanese Association of Social Workers (JASW), Japanese Association of Social Workers in Health, Japanese Association of Certified Social Workers and Japanese Association of Psychiatric Social Workers, Joint Committee on Ethics (2004) *Code of Ethics of Social Workers*, Tokyo, JASW et al.

Jeffs, T. and Smith, M. (1994) 'Young people, youth work and a new authoritarianism', *Youth and Policy*, 53, pp. 1–14.

Johansson, H. and Hvinden, B. (2005) 'Welfare governance and the remaking of citizenship', in J. Newman (ed.) *Remaking Governance: Peoples, Politics and the Public Sphere*, Bristol, The Policy Press, pp. 101–18.

Johnson, T (1972) *Professions and Power*, London, Macmillan.

Jones, P. (1994) *Rights*, Basingstoke, Macmillan.

Jordan, B. (1975) 'Is the client a fellow citizen?', *Social Work Today*, 6(15), pp. 471–5.

Jordan, B. (1990) *Social Work in an Unjust Society*, Hemel Hempstead, Harvester.

Joseph, J. and Fernandes, G. (eds) (2006) *An Enquiry into Ethical Dilemmas in Social Work*, Mumbai, College of Social Work, Nirmala Niketan.

Kant, I. ([1785]1964) *Groundwork of the Metaphysics of Morals*, New York, Harper & Row.

Keown, D. (2005) 'Origins of Buddhist ethics', in W. Schweiker (ed.) *The Blackwell Companion to Religious Ethics*, Oxford, Blackwell, pp. 286–96.

Koehn, D. (1994) *The Ground of Professional Ethics*, London, Routledge.

Koehn, D. (1998) *Rethinking Feminist Ethics: Care, Trust and Empathy*, London, Routledge.

Kohlberg, L. (1981) *Essays on Moral Development*: vol. 1, *The Philosophy of Moral Development: Moral Stages and the Idea of Justice*, New York, Harper & Row.

Kohlberg, L. (1984) *Essays on Moral Development:* vol. 2, *The Psychology of Moral Development*, San Francisco, Harper & Row.

Koggel, C. and Orme, J. (2010) 'Care ethics: new theories and applications', *Ethics and Social Welfare*, 4(2), pp. 109–14.

Kosaka, H. (2010) 'The Dominance of Care-Management Approach for the Elderly in Japan: The Emergence of Bio-Politics under the "Long-Term Care Insurance" Act', paper presented at Economic and Social Research Council/Japanese Society for the Promotion of Science Seminar on 'The Impact of New Public Management Policies and Perspectives on Professional Social Work: A Comparison of British and Japanese Experiences', Stirling University, Scotland, 6–7 September.

Kuhse, H. (1997) *Caring: Nurses, Women and Ethics*, Oxford, Blackwell.

Kutchins, H. (1991) 'The fiduciary relationship: the legal basis for social workers' responsibilities to clients', *Social Work*, 36(2), pp. 106–13.

Langan, M. and Lee, P. (eds) (1989) *Radical Social Work Today*, London, Unwin Hyman.

Lansdown, G. (1995) 'Children's rights to participation: a critique', in C. Cloke and M. Davies (eds) *Participation and Empowerment in Child Protection*, London, Pitman, pp. 19–38.

Larson, M. (1977) *The Rise of Professionalism: A Sociological Analysis*, Berkeley, CA, University of California Press.

Lavalette, M. (ed.) (2011) *Radical Social Work Today: Social Work at the Crossroads*, Bristol, The Policy Press.

Lavalette, M. and Ferguson, I. (eds) (2007) *International Social Work and the Radical Tradition*, Birmingham, Venture Press.

LeCroy, C. (2002) *The Call to Social Work: Life Stories*, Thousand Oaks, CA, Sage.

Leeson, C. (2010) 'The emotional labour of caring about looked-after children', *Child and Family Social Work*, 15(4), pp. 483–91.

Leighton, N. (1985) 'Personal and professional values: marriage or divorce?', in D. Watson (ed.) *A Code of Ethics for Social Work: The Second Step*, London, Routledge & Kegan Paul, pp. 59–85.

Leonard, P. (1997) *Postmodern Welfare: Reconstructing an Emancipatory Project*, London, Sage.

Levinas, E. (1989) 'Ethics as first philosophy', trans. S. Hand, in S. Hand (ed.) *The Levinas Reader*, Oxford, Blackwell, pp. 75–87.

Levinas, E. (1997) 'On Buber, Marcel, and philosophy', in H. Jodalen and A. Vetlesen (eds) *Closeness: An Ethics*, Oslo, Scandinavian University Press, pp. 27–44.

Levy, C. (1976) *Social Work Ethics*, New York, Human Sciences Press.

Levy, C. (1993) *Social Work Ethics on the Line*, Binghampton, NY, Haworth Press.

Li, C. (1994) 'The Confucian concept of *jen* and the feminist ethics of care: a comparative study', *Hypatia: A Journal of Feminist Philosophy*, 9(1), pp. 70–89.

Llewelyn, J. (1995) *Emmanuel Levinas: The Genealogy of Ethics*, New York, Routledge.

Lloyd, L. (2010) 'The individual in social care: the ethics of care and the "personalisation agenda" in services for older people in England', *Ethics and Social Welfare*, 4(2), pp. 188–200.

Løgstrup, K. (1997) 'On trust', in H. Jodalen and A. Vetlesen (eds) *Closeness: An Ethics*, Oslo, Scandinavian University Press, pp. 71–89.

Long, A. and Harrison, S. (1996) 'Evidence-based decision-making', *Health Service Journal*, 106, pp. 8–11.

Lukes, S. (1987) *Marxism and Morality*, Oxford, Oxford University Press.

Lund, B. (1999) '"Ask not what your community can do for you": obligations, New Labour and welfare reform', *Critical Social Policy*, 19(4), pp. 447–62.

Lymbery, M. (2000) 'The retreat from professionalism: from social worker to care manager', in N. Malin (ed.) *Professionalism, Boundaries and the Workplace*, London, Routledge, pp. 123–38.

Lyotard, J.-F. (1984) *The Postmodern Condition: A Report on Knowledge*, trans. G. Bennington and B. Massumi, Manchester, Manchester University Press.

McAuliffe, D. and Chenoweth, L. (2007) 'Leave no stone unturned: the inclusive model of ethical decision-making', *Ethics and Social Welfare*, 2(1), pp. 38–49.

McBeath, G. and Webb, S. (2002) 'Virtue ethics and social work: being lucky, realistic, and not doing one's duty', *British Journal of Social Work*, 32, pp. 1015–36.

McDermott, F. (1975) 'Against the persuasive definition of self-determination', in F. McDermott (ed.) *Self-determination in Social Work*, London, Routledge & Kegan Paul, pp. 118–37.

McDonald, C. (2006) *Challenging Social Work: The Institutional Context of Social Work*, Basingstoke, Palgrave Macmillan.

McFarlane, S. (1994) 'Buddhism', in J. Holm and J. Bowker (eds) *Making Moral Decisions*, London, Continuum, pp. 17–40.

MacIntyre, A. (1985) *After Virtue: A Study in Moral Theory*, 2nd edn, London, Duckworth.

Mackenzie, C. and Stoljar, N. (eds) (2000) *Relational Autonomy: Feminist Perspectives on Autonomy, Agency and the Social Self*, Oxford, Oxford University Press.

McLaughlin, K. (2007) 'Regulation and risk in social work: the General Social Care Council and the Social Care Register in context', *British Journal of Social Work*, 37(7), pp. 1263–77.

McNamee, S., Gergen, K. and Associates (eds) (1999) *Relational Responsibility: Resources for Sustainable Dialogue*, Thousand Oaks, CA, Sage.

Machin, S. (1998) 'Swimming against the tide: a social worker's experience of a secure hospital', in G. Hunt (ed.) *Whistleblowing in the Social Services: Public Accountability and Professional Practice*, London, Arnold, pp. 116–30.

Macklin, R. (2003) 'Dignity is a useless concept', *British Medical Journal*, 327, pp. 1419–20.

Malin, N. (2000) 'Professionalism and boundaries of the formal sector: the example of social and community care', in N. Malin (ed.) *Professionalism, Boundaries and the Workplace*, London, Routledge, pp. 7–24.

Marshall, T. (1963) 'Citizenship and social class', in T. Marshall, *Sociology at the Crossroads and Other Essays*, London, Heinemann, pp. 67–127.

Marshall, T. (1972) 'Value problems of welfare-capitalism', *Journal of Social Policy*, 1, pp. 15–30.

Martin, M. (2000) *Meaningful Work: Rethinking Professional Ethics*, New York, Oxford University Press.

Martyn, H. (ed.) (2000) *Developing Reflective Practice: Making Sense of Social Work in a World of Change*, Bristol, The Policy Press.

Marx, K. and Engels, F. ([1848]1969) 'Manifesto of the Communist Party', in L. Feuer (ed.) *Marx and Engels: Basic Writings on Politics and Philosophy*, Glasgow, Collins/Fontana, pp. 43–82.

Mayer, J. and Timms, N. (1970) *The Client Speaks*, London, Routledge & Kegan Paul.

Mazibuko, F. and Gray, M. (2004) 'Social work professional associations in South Africa', *International Social Work*, 47(1), pp. 129–42.

Mbiti, J. (1989) *African Religions and Philosophy*, London, Heinemann.

Mendus, S. (1993) 'Different voices, still lives: problems in the ethics of care', *Journal of Applied Philosophy*, 10(1), pp. 17–27.

Mill, J. S. ([1863]1972) *Utilitarianism, On Liberty, and Considerations on Representative Government*, London, Dent.

Millerson, G. (1964) *The Qualifying Associations: A Study in Professionalisation*, London, Routledge & Kegan Paul.

Milner, J. (2001) *Women and Social Work: Narrative Approaches*, Basingstoke, Palgrave – now Palgrave Macmillan.

Moffet, J. (1968) *Concepts of Casework Treatment*, London, Routledge & Kegan Paul.

Moon, D. (1988) 'Introduction: responsibility, rights and welfare', in D. Moon (ed.) *Responsibility, Rights and Welfare: The Theory of the Welfare State*, Boulder, CO, Westview Press, pp. 1–15.

Mullaly, B. (1997) *Structural Social Work: Ideology, Theory, and Practice*, Ontario, Canada, Oxford University Press.

Mullender, A. and Ward, D. (1991) *Self-directed Groupwork: Users Take Action for Empowerment*, London, Whiting & Birch.

Munro, E. (2011) *The Munro Review of Child Protection*, Part 1: *A Systems Analysis*, London, Department for Education, www.education.gov.uk/munroreview/downloads/TheMunroReviewofChildProtection-Part%20one.pdf, accessed April 2011

Nagel, T. (1979) 'The fragmentation of value', in T. Nagel, *Mortal Questions*, Cambridge, Cambridge University Press, pp. 128–41.

NASW (National Association of Social Workers) (1996) *Code of Ethics*, Washington, DC, NASW.

NASW (National Association of Social Workers) (2008) *Code of Ethics*, Washington, DC, NASW.

National Federation of Social Workers in Romania (2004) *Ethical Code of the Profession of Social Worker*, Mamamures, National Federation of Social Workers in Romania.

Newman, J. (2005) 'Participative governance and the remaking of the public sphere', in J. Newman (ed.) *Remaking Governance: Peoples, Politics and the Public Sphere*, Bristol, The Policy Press, pp. 119–38.

Noddings, N. (1984) *Caring: A Feminine Approach to Ethics and Moral Education*, Berkeley, CA, University of California Press.

Noddings, N. (2002) *Starting at Home: Caring and Social Policy*, Berkeley, CA, University of California Press.

Nordvedt, P. and Nordhaug, M. (2008) 'The principle and problem of proximity in ethics', *Journal of Medical Ethics*, 34, pp. 156–61.

Norman, R. (1998) *The Moral Philosophers*, Oxford, Clarendon Press.

Nussbaum, M. (2000) *Women and Human Development*, Cambridge, Cambridge University Press.

Nussbaum, M. (2006) *Frontiers of Justice*, Cambridge, MA, Belnap/Harvard University Press.

Oakley, J. and Cocking, D. (2001) *Virtue Ethics and Professional Roles*, Cambridge, Cambridge University Press.

O'Connor, J. (1973) *The Fiscal Crisis of the State*, New York, St Martin's Press.

Offe, C. (1984) *Contradictions of the Welfare State*, London, Hutchinson.

Ohnishi, K., Ohgushi, Y., Nakano, M. et al. (2010) 'Moral distress experienced by psychiatric nurses in Japan', *Nursing Ethics*, 17(6), pp. 726–40.

Okin, S. (1994) 'Gender inequality and cultural difference', *Political Theory*, 22, pp. 5–24.

O'Neill, M. (2010) *Asylum, Migration and Community*, Bristol, The Policy Press.

O'Neill, O. (2002) *Autonomy and Trust in Bioethics*, Cambridge, Cambridge University Press.

Orme, J. (2002) 'Social work, gender, care and justice', *British Journal of Social Work*, 32(6), pp. 799–814.

Orme, J. and Rennie, G. (2006) 'The role of registration in ensuring ethical practice', *International Social Work*, 49(3), pp. 333–44.

Osborne, T. (1998) 'Constructionism, authority and the ethical life', in I. Velody and R. Williams (eds) *The Politics of Constructionism*, London, Sage, pp. 221–34.

O'Sullivan, T. (1999) *Decision Making in Social Work*, Basingstoke, Macmillan – now Palgrave Macmillan.

O'Sullivan, T. (2010) *Decision Making in Social Work*, 2nd edn, Basingstoke, Palgrave Macmillan.

Outka, G. and Reeder, J. (eds) (1993) *Prospects for a Common Morality*, Chichester, Princeton University Press.

Øvrelid, B. (2008) 'The cultivation of moral character: a Buddhist challenge to social workers', *Ethics and Social Welfare*, 2(3), pp. 243–61.

Øvretveit, J. (1997) 'How patient power and client participation affects relations between professions', in J. Øvretveit, P. Mathias and T. Thompson (eds) *Interprofessional Working for Health and Social Care*, Basingstoke, Macmillan – now Palgrave Macmillan, pp. 79–102.

Pardeck, J., Murphy, J. and Choi, J. (1994) 'Some implications of postmodernism for social work practice', *Social Work*, 39(4), pp. 343–6.

Parton, N. (1994) 'The nature of social work under conditions of (post) modernity', *Social Work and Social Sciences Review*, 5(2), pp. 93–112.

Parton, N. (1998) 'Risk, advanced liberalism and child welfare: the need to rediscover uncertainty and ambiguity', *British Journal of Social Work*, 28, pp. 5–27.

Parton, N. (1999) 'Reconfiguring child welfare practices: risk, advanced liberalism, and the government of freedom', in A. Chambon, A. Irving and L. Epstein (eds) *Reading Foucault for Social Work*, New York, Columbia University Press, pp. 101–30.

Parton, N. (2002) 'Postmodern and constructionist approaches to social work', in R. Adams, L. Dominelli and M. Payne (eds) *Social Work: Themes, Issues and Critical Debates*, 2nd edn, Basingstoke, Palgrave Macmillan, pp. 237–46.

Parton, N. (2003) 'Rethinking *professional* practice: the contributions of social constructionism and the feminist "ethics of care"', *British Journal of Social Work*, 33, pp. 1–16.

Parton, N. (2006) *Safeguarding Childhood: Early Intervention and Surveillance in Late Modern Society*, Basingstoke, Palgrave Macmillan.

Parton, N. and O'Byrne, P. (2000) *Constructive Social Work: Towards a New Practice*, Basingstoke, Macmillan – now Palgrave Macmillan.

Payne, M. (1989) 'Open records and shared decisions with clients', in S. Shardlow (ed.) *The Values of Change in Social Work*, London, Routledge, pp. 114–34.

Payne, M. (2005) *Modern Social Work Theory*, 3rd edn, Basingstoke, Palgrave Macmillan.

Pease, B. and Fook, J. (1999) 'Postmodern critical theory and emancipatory social work practice', in B. Pease and J. Fook (eds) *Transforming Social Work Practice: Postmodern Critical Perspectives*, London, Routledge, pp. 1–22.

Picht, W. (1914) *Toynbee Hall and the English Settlement Movement*, London, G. Bell and Sons.

Pierson, C. (2006) *Beyond the Welfare State? The New Political Economy of Welfare*, 3rd edn, Cambridge, Polity Press.

Pinker, R. (1990) *Social Work in an Enterprise Society*, London, Routledge.

Plamenatz, J. (1966) *The English Utilitarians*, Oxford, Blackwell.

Plant, R. (1970) *Social and Moral Theory in Casework*, London, Routledge & Kegan Paul.

Pollitt, C. (2010) 'Cuts and reforms: public services as we move into a new era', International Institute of Administrative Sciences, Knowledge Portal, www.pa-knowledge.org/documents/IIASPORTALPAPER.pdf, accessed April 2011, pp. 1–14.

Preston-Shoot, M. (2011) 'On administrative evil-doing within social work policy and services: law, ethics and practice', *European Journal of Social Work*, 14(2), pp. 177–94.

Pyles, L. (2009) *Progressive Community Organising: A Critical Approach for a Globalising World*, New York, Routledge.

Ragg, N. (1977) *People Not Cases*, London, Routledge & Kegan Paul.

Raphael, D. (1981) *Moral Philosophy*, Oxford, Oxford University Press.

Rauner, D. (2000) *They Still Pick Me Up When I Fall: The Role of Caring in Youth Development and Community Life*, New York, Columbia University Press.

Rawls, J. (1973) *A Theory of Justice*, Oxford, Oxford University Press.

Reamer, F. (1999) *Social Work Values and Ethics*, 2nd edn, New York, Columbia University Press.

Reamer, F. (2006) *Social Work Values and Ethics*, 3rd edn, New York, Columbia University Press.

Reamer, F. and Shardlow, S. (2009) 'Ethical codes of practice in the US and UK: one profession, two standards', *Journal of Social Work Values and*

Ethics, 6(2), www.socialworker.com/jswve/content/view/120/168/, accessed July 2011.

Rest, J. (1994) 'Background: theory and research', in J. Rest and D. Narváez (eds) *Moral Development in the Professions: Psychology and Applied Ethics*, Hillsdale, NJ, Lawrence Erlbaum, pp. 1–26.

Rhodes, M. (1986) *Ethical Dilemmas in Social Work Practice*, Boston, MA, Routledge & Kegan Paul.

Roger, J. (2000) *From a Welfare State to a Welfare Society: The Changing Context of Social Policy in a Postmodern Era*, Basingstoke, Macmillan – now Palgrave Macmillan.

Rommelspacher, B. (2010) 'Ethics in social work between secularism and re-Christianisation', in D. Zaviršek, B. Rommelspacher and S. Staub-Bernasconi (eds) *Ethical Dilemmas in Social Work: International Perspective*, Ljubljana, University of Ljubljana, pp. 65–77.

Ronnby, A. (1993) 'The Carer Society and Ethics', unpublished paper, Department of Social Work and Humanities, Mid-Sweden University, Östersund.

Rosenau, P. (1992) *Post-modernism and the Social Sciences: Insights, Inroads, and Intrusions*, Princeton, NJ, Princeton University Press.

Ross, W. (1930) *The Right and the Good*, Oxford, Clarendon Press.

Rossiter, A. (2011) 'Unsettled social work: the challenge of Levinas's ethics', *British Journal of Social Work*, 41, pp. 980–95.

Rossiter, A., Prilleltensky, I. and Walsh-Bowers, R. (2000) 'A postmodern perspective on professional ethics', in B. Fawcett, B. Featherstone, J. Fook and A. Rossiter (eds) *Practice and Research in Social Work: Postmodern Feminist Perspectives*, London, Routledge, pp. 83–103.

Ruddick, S. (1989) *Maternal Thinking: Towards a Politics of Peace*, Boston, Beacon Press.

Rummery, K. (2011) 'A comparative analysis of personalisation: balancing an ethic of care with user empowerment', *Ethics and Social Welfare*, 5(2), pp. 138–52.

Russian Union of Social Educators and Social Workers (2003) *The Ethical Guideline of Social Educator and Social Worker*, Moscow, Russian Union of Social Educators and Social Workers.

SACSSP (South African Council for Social Service Professions) (2006) *Policy Guidelines for Course of Conduct, Code of Ethics and the Rules for Social Workers*, Pretoria, SACSSP, available at www.sacssp.co.za.

Sandel, M. (1998) *Liberalism and the Limits of Justice*, 2nd edn, Cambridge, Cambridge University Press.

Sartre, J.-P. (1969) *Being and Nothingness*, trans. H. Barnes, London, Methuen.

Schön, D. (1983) *The Reflective Practitioner: How Professionals Think in Action*, New York, Basic Books.

Schön, D. (1987) *Educating the Reflective Practitioner: Towards a New Design for Teaching and Learning in the Professions*, San Francisco, Jossey-Bass.

Schweiker, W. (2005a) 'On religious ethics', in W. Schweiker (ed.) *The Blackwell Companion to Religious Ethics*, Oxford, Blackwell.

Schweiker, W. (ed.) (2005b) *The Blackwell Companion to Religious Ethics*, Oxford, Blackwell.

Scourfield, J. (2007) 'Social care and the modern citizen: client, consumer, service user, manager and entrepreneur', *British Journal of Social Work*, 37(1), pp. 107–22.

Scourfield, P. (2010) 'A critical reflection on the involvement of "experts by experience" in inspections', *British Journal of Social Work*, 40(6), pp. 1890–907.

Seedhouse, D. (1998) *Ethics: The Heart of Health Care*, Chichester, Wiley.

Sen, A. (1993) 'Capability and well-being', in M. Nussbaum and A. Sen (eds) *The Quality of Life*, Oxford, Clarendon Press, pp. 30–53.

Sevenhuijsen, S. (1998) *Citizenship and the Ethics of Care: Feminist Considerations on Justice, Morality and Politics*, London, Routledge.

Shah, N. (1989) 'It's up to you sisters: black women and radical social work', in M. Langan and P. Lee (eds) *Radical Social Work Today*, London, Unwin Hyman, pp. 178–91.

Shaw, M. and Martin, I. (2000) 'Community work, citizenship and democracy: re-making the connections', *Community Development Journal*, 35(4), pp. 401–13.

Shaw, W. (1999) *Contemporary Ethics: Taking Account of Utilitarianism*, Oxford, Blackwell.

Siegrist, H. (1994) 'The professions, state and government in theory and history', in T. Becher (ed.) *Governments and Professional Education*, Buckingham, Society for Research into Higher Education/Open University Press, pp. 3–20.

Singer, P. (ed.) (1993) *A Companion to Ethics*, Blackwell, Oxford.

Singer, P. (1994) *Rethinking Life and Death: The Collapse of our Traditional Ethics*, New York, St Martin's Press.

Singer, P. (2009) *The Life You Can Save: Acting Now to End World Poverty*, New York, Random House.

Singer, P. (2011) *Practical Ethics*, 3rd edn, Cambridge, Cambridge University Press.

Slote, M. (1992) *From Morality to Virtue*, New York, Oxford University Press.

Smart, J. and Williams, B. (1973) *Utilitarianism: For and Against*, Cambridge, Cambridge University Press.

Smith, D. (ed.) (2004) *Social Work and Evidence-based Practice*, London, Jessica Kingsley.

Smith, M.K. (1994) *Local Education: Community, Conversation, Praxis*, Buckingham, Open University Press.

Smith, M. (2011) 'Reading Bauman for social work', *Ethics and Social Welfare*, 5(1), pp. 2–17.

Social Work Task Force (2009) *Building a Safe, Confident Future: The Final Report of the Social Work Task Force*, http://publications. education.gov.uk/default.aspx?PageFunction=productdetails&PageMo de=publications&ProductId=DCSF-01114-2009.

Social Workers Registration Board (Kāhui Whakamana Tauwhiro) (2008) *Code of Conduct for Social Workers*, Wellington, New Zealand, Social Workers Registration Board.

Solomon, R. (1992) *Ethics and Excellence*, Oxford, Oxford University Press.

Solomon, R. (1997) 'Corporate roles, personal virtues: an Aristotelian approach to business ethics', in D. Statman (ed.) *Virtue Ethics: A Critical Reader*, Edinburgh, Edinburgh University Press, pp. 205–6.

Spicker, P. (1988) *Principles of Social Welfare*, London, Routledge.

Stalley, R. (1978) 'Non judgmental attitudes', in N. Timms and D. Watson (eds) *Philosophy in Social Work*, London, Routledge & Kegan Paul.

Statman, D. (1997) 'Introduction to virtue ethics', in D. Statman (ed.) *Virtue Ethics: A Critical Reader*, Edinburgh, Edinburgh University Press, pp. 3–41.

Steckley, L. and Smith, M. (2011) 'Care ethics in residential child care: a different voice', *Ethics and Social Welfare*, 5(2), pp. 181–95.

Sullivan, W. (2005) *Work and Integrity: The Crisis and Promise of Professionalism in America*, 2nd edn, San Francisco, Jossey-Bass.

Sullivan, W. and Kymlicka, W. (eds) (2007) *The Globalisation of Ethics*, Cambridge, Cambridge University Press.

SWAN (Social Work Action Network) (2009) *The Social Work Action Network (SWAN) Draft Constitution*, http://www.socialworkfuture. org/index.php/swan-organisation, accessed October 2011.

Swanton, C. (2003) *Virtue Ethics: A Pluralistic View*, Oxford, Oxford University Press.

Tascón, S. (2010) 'Ethics of responsibility', in M. Gray and S. Webb (eds) *Ethics and Value Perspectives in Social Work*, Basingstoke, Palgrave Macmillan, pp. 85–94.

Taylor, C. (1989) *Sources of the Self: The Making of Modern Identity*, Cambridge, Cambridge University Press.

Taylor, C. and White, S. (2000) *Practising Reflexivity in Health and Welfare*, Buckingham, Open University Press.

Taylor, D. (1989) 'Citizenship and social power', *Critical Social Policy*, 26, pp. 19–31.

Thompson, I., Melia, K. and Boyd, K. (2000) *Nursing Ethics*, 4th edn, Edinburgh, Churchill Livingstone.

Thompson, N. (2006) *Anti-Discriminatory Practice*, 4th edn, Basingstoke, Macmillan – now Palgrave Macmillan.

Timms, N. (1983) *Social Work Values: An Enquiry*, London, Routledge & Kegan Paul.

Toren, N. (1972) *Social Work: The Case of a Semi-Profession*, Beverley Hills, CA, Sage.

Toulmin, S. (2001) *Return to Reason*, Cambridge, MA, Harvard University Press.

Tronto, J. (1993) *Moral Boundaries: A Political Argument for an Ethic of Care*, London, Routledge.

Tronto, J. (2001) 'Does managing professionals affect professional ethics? Competence, autonomy and care', in P. DesAutels and J. Waugh (eds) *Feminists Doing Ethics*, Lanham, MD, Rowman & Littlefield, pp. 187–202.

Tronto, J. (2010) 'Creating caring institutions: politics, plurality, and purpose', *Ethics and Social Welfare*, 4(2), pp. 158–71.

UN (United Nations) (1948) *Universal Declaration of Human Rights*, www.un.org/en/documents/udhr, accessed August 2011

UN (United Nations) (1959) *Declaration of the Rights of the Child*, reprinted in P. Newell (1991) *The UN Convention and Children's Rights in the UK*, London, National Children's Bureau, pp. 182–3.

UNHCR (United Nations High Commissioner for Refugees) (2008) *UNHCR Guidelines on Determining the Best Interests of the Child*, www.unhcr.org, accessed August 2011.

Urmson, J. (ed.) (1975) *The Concise Encyclopedia of Western Philosophy and Philosophers*, London, Hutchinson.

Van Ewijk, H. (2009) 'Citizenship-based social work', *International Social Work*, 52(2), pp. 167–79.

Veatch, R. (1999) 'Abandoning informed consent', in H. Kuhse and P. Singer (eds) *Bioethics: An Anthology*, Oxford, Blackwell, pp. 523–32.

Velody, I. and Williams, R. (eds) (1998) *The Politics of Constructionism*, Sage, London.

Vetlesen, A. (1994) *Perception, Empathy and Judgment: An Inquiry into the Preconditions of Moral Performance*, Pennsylvania, Pennsylvania State University Press.

Vetlesen, A. (1997) 'Introducing an ethics of proximity', in H. Jodalen and A. Vetleson (eds) *Closeness: An Ethics*, Oslo, Scandinavian University Press, pp. 1–19.

Wallcraft, J. and Bryant, M. (2003) *Policy Paper 2: The Mental Health Service User Movement in England*, London, Sainsbury Centre for Mental Health.

Ward, N. (2011) 'Care ethics and carers with learning disabilities: a challenge to dependence and paternalism', *Ethics and Social Welfare*, 5(2), pp. 168–80.

Warnock, G. (1967) *Contemporary Moral Philosophy*, London, Macmillan.

Warnock, M. (1998) *An Intelligent Person's Guide to Ethics*, London, Duckworth.

Webb, S. (2001) 'Some considerations on the validity of evidence-based practice in social work', *British Journal of Social Work*, 31(1), pp. 57–79.

Webb, S. (2002) 'Evidence-based practice and decision-analysis in social work', *Journal of Social Work*, 2(1), pp. 45–63.

Webb, S. (2006) *Social Work in a Risk Society: Social and Political Perspectives*, Basingstoke, Palgrave Macmillan.

Webb, S. and McBeath, G. (1989) 'A political critique of Kantian ethics in social work', *British Journal of Social Work*, 19, pp. 491–506.

Webb, S. and McBeath, G. (1990) 'A political critique of Kantian ethics in social work: a reply to Prof. R. S. Downie', *British Journal of Social Work*, 20, pp. 65–71.

Webster, P. (2010) 'Codes of conduct', in M. Gray and S. Webb (eds) *Ethics and Value Perspectives in Social Work*, Basingstoke, Palgrave Macmillan, pp. 31–40.

Wenar, L. (2011) 'Rights', *Stanford Encyclopedia of Philosophy*, http://plato.stanford.edu./entries/rights/, accessed July 2011.

White, S. and Stancombe, J. (2003) *Clinical Judgement in the Health and Welfare Professions: Extending the Evidence Base*, Maidenhead, Open University Press.

White, S., Fook, J. and Gardner, F. (eds) (2006) *Critical Reflection in Health and Social Care*, Maidenhead, Open University Press.

White, S., Wastell, D., Broadhurst, K. and Hall, C. (2010) 'When policy o'erleaps itself: the "tragic tale" of the integrated children's system', *Critical Social Policy*, 30(3), pp. 405–29.

Whitley, C. (1969) 'On duties', in J. Feinberg (ed.) *Moral Concepts*, Oxford, Oxford University Press, pp. 53–9.

Wicclair, M. (1991) 'Patient decision-making capacity and risk', *Bioethics*, 5(2), pp. 91–104.

Wilding, P. (1982) *Professional Power and Social Welfare*, London, Routledge & Kegan Paul.

Yelloly, M. and Henkel, M. (eds) (1995) *Learning and Teaching in Social Work: Towards Reflective Practice*, London, Jessica Kingsley.

Yip, K.-S. (2004) 'A Chinese cultural critique of the global qualifying standards for social work education', *Social Work Education*, 23(5), pp. 597–612.

Young, I. (2008) 'Structural injustice and the politics of difference' in G. Criag, T. Burchardt and D. Gordon (eds) *Social Justice and Public Policy: Seeking Fairness in Diverse Societies*, Bristol, The Policy Press, pp. 77–104.

Younghusband, E. (1981) *The Newest Profession: A Short History of Social Work*, Sutton, IPC Business Press.

Zaviršek, D., Rommelspacher, B. and Staub-Bernasconi, S. (eds) (2010) *Ethical Dilemmas in Social Work: International Perspective*, Ljubljana, University of Ljubljana.

Index